REFLECTIONS

A TAPESTRY OF THOUGHTS

Collected Essays 2012-2015

Kingsley L. Dennis

BTB

BEAUTIFUL TRAITOR BOOKS

Published by Beautiful Traitor Books –
http://www.beautifultraitorbooks.com/

ISBN-13: 978-0-9954817-1-8 (paperback)

First published: July 2016

Cover Concept: Kingsley L. Dennis
Cover Design - Ibolya Kapta

Non-fiction – Essays - New Thought

Kingsley L Dennis, PhD, is an author and researcher. He currently lives in Andalusia, Spain.

He can be contacted at his personal website:
www.kingsleydennis.com

By the same author

The Foundation: The Enigma of a Community

The Citadel: A Mystery at the Heart of Civilization

The Phoenix Generation: A New Era of Connection, Compassion, and Consciousness

Mundus Grundy: Trouble in Grundusland

Meeting Monroe: Conversations with a Man who Came to Earth

Dawn of the Akashic Age: New Consciousness, Quantum Resonance, and the Future of the World (co-authored with Ervin Laszlo)

Breaking the Spell: An Exploration of Human Perception

New Revolutions for a Small Planet

The Struggle for Your Mind: Conscious Evolution & The Battle to Control How We Think

The New Science & Spirituality Reader (co-edited with Ervin Laszlo)

New Consciousness for a New World

After the Car (co-authored with John Urry)

Introduction: A Few Words...

There is always the danger of there being too many words. Why do we need more? And why do we need a book about someone's thinking – about their 'reflections'? I have no answer that is good enough, other than I wanted to share this with you.

These are changing times, and there is a lot going on out there in the world; as well as inside each of us – in *our world*. And the world is not something separate or distinct from us. We are intimately connected with it, in more ways we could possibly imagine. We are all in this together: a curse perhaps, but also most definitely a blessing. The world is in us, and we are in the world. And as individuals, we all share the same species heart. And so, I just wanted to reach out and share...maybe not so much the words, but the experience. Thanks for being here.

Kingsley L. Dennis
May 2016

PART ONE

PART TWO

PART THREE

APPENDIX

PART ONE

1. ENDGAME OF AN ERA

As a civilization we are in the throes of living out an 'endgame'. No, it is not the endgame of our species, or any similar dire situation, for the human evolutionary project will continue. Yet it is the endgame of an era. For many of us living in the developed nations, we are witnessing the endgame of the Second Industrial Revolution. Yet overall, this endgame concerns a way of living, a social-political model that has now come to the end of its life. Simply put, we cannot go on living as we have been doing for the past 150 years. Why 150 years? Well, this is roughly the time since oil was first discovered and utilized for fuelling our rapid social expansion. All life is a living system; as such it requires the continual inflow of energy in order not to atrophy (the law of entropy). At regular stages of growth new energy sources are required in order to 'boost' the growth and expansion of any system. And for millennia the human species has been evolving towards a planetary civilization. We are now on the cusp of this, and the reason we managed to arrive at this point so rapidly is due, as I have said, to the finding of oil as the most recent energy boost. In just 150 years many societies have gone through the most incredible development, to the point where we have sophisticated technological infrastructures that enable us to circumnavigate the globe like '*Phileas Fogg*' both physically and virtually. On top of this we have oil-fertilized our agriculture into mass food production to sustain the vastly expanding human population. Our light switches illuminate our rooms instantly; we fly to other countries as if taking a taxi; and we have access to a kaleidoscope of goods and services one could only have dreamed of previously. All this because we have had a tap onto the most precious energy source so far discovered on our planet. This has been our rocket fuel. Our current 150 years of rapid industrial acceleration has been built upon the notion of a perpetual-growth machine. This extraordinary period in our cultural evolution has now been accepted, and taught, as the norm. Yet back in the early 1970s the now infamous 'Limits to Growth' report concluded that the end of growth would probably arrive between 2010 and 2050.

Let's be realistic - from now on only relative growth is possible. Some aspects of the global economy may continue to grow, 'relative' to others, yet the overall trend is one of contraction. Those who support continued growth often forget that there are factors external to the economic system that make 'business as usual' near impossible - and that this situation is not temporary but permanent. These factors include: the depletion of important resources; the proliferation of disruptive environmental impacts; and a financial system that is no longer suited to the current crisis. However, there is another significant factor which most commentators leave out completely, perhaps because it cannot be 'physically verified' – this is the presence of human consciousness.

The modern world has witnessed a different type of consciousness emerging over the past 150 years, a post-Industrial Revolution cognitive mind. New technological innovations that helped to alter our perceptions of the dimensions of space and time in the world began to birth a psychological consciousness; a consciousness that wanted to look beyond the borders and horizons of the physical frontier. For any great epochal shift to be successful it requires a change in the parameters of human consciousness; this has always been the case. We are slowly beginning to recognize this fact and to notice a change in our psychology and consciousness. Life on planet Earth is undergoing three types of revolutions: physical, psychic and cosmological.

Our human socio-cultural cycles are very much a part of our evolutionary history, with marked eras between hunter-gatherer, agrarian, city-state, industrial and planetary. Cultural historian William Irwin Thompson has marked these cultural ecologies or cycles as:

1 Hominization: 4000000–200000BC

2 Symbolization: 200000–10000BC

3 Agriculturalization: 10000–3500BC

4 Civilization: 3500BC–1500AD

5 Industrialization: 1500–1945

6 Planetization: 1945–present

Currently, our struggles are between a system marked by the inequalities of a dysfunctional global system (marked by the 'old consciousness') and that of an integral-ecology era (represented by the 'new consciousness'). This is a transition period which is manifesting through resource wars and the ongoing struggle for control and management. At the same time there are many forecasts trying to predict the future of life on planet Earth without a comprehension of the 'bigger picture'. We are often unable to discern the uncertain, the unpredictable and the unexpected. The

Western mindset has a preoccupation, or even obsession, with a linear view of history and progress. Yet the concept of a linear development of human civilizations is erroneous and misleading. Linear development does not take into account living in ways that enable all other people to live as well; living in ways that respect the lives of others and that respect the right to the economic and cultural development of all people; to pursue personal fulfilment in harmony with the integrity of nature; and working with like-minded people to preserve or restore the essential balances of the environment.

Yet in the months and years ahead we are going to witness some sharp degrees of change as we realize that our 'accepted norms' of linearity are breaking down. This year especially will see much change occurring in our lives as we see dysfunctional systems falling apart. Yet it is not a time to be worried, negative, or stressed; rather, it is an opportunity to re-align ourselves with the way forward. We now need to make decisions over our life priorities. We need to educate ourselves, and to gain balanced and helpful information. It is time to make these steps as our old world transforms herself...

A Tale to Finish: 'Friends'

An Arabian legend tells of two friends who were travelling through the desert and at one point they fell into disagreement about the trip whereby one of the friends slaps the other across the face.

The friend who had been slapped said nothing, only wrote in the sand: 'Today my best friend slapped me in the face.'

Both friends continued on their journey and eventually arrived at an oasis where there were baths to refresh themselves. The friend who had bee slapped jumped into the large baths yet soon found himself starting to drown. The other friend immediately jumped in after him and saved him. After recovering the first man took a pen and wrote on a stone: 'Today my best friend saved my life.'

Intrigued, the friend asked: 'Why is it that after I hurt you, you wrote in the sand and now after saving you, you write on a stone?

Smiling, the other friend replied: 'When a good friend offends us, we write in the sand where the wind of forgetfulness and forgiveness will be responsible for clearing it off; on the other hand, when something great happens to us, we burn it into stone in memory of the heart where no wind in the world can erase it.'

2. WHY WE ARE IN NEED OF A WORLDSHIFT NOW

It is now apparent to even casual observers that our world is reaching a critical stage. Most of what we see in the daily news reports informs us of dramatic Earth changes as a result of climatic disruptions: earthquakes, floods, hurricanes, volcanic eruptions, etc. We are also witnessing a surge in people protest as decades of corrupt or inefficient social systems are taking their toll. Yet within this outward surge of turmoil and disruption there are other shifts occurring, such as the transition from the industrial-globalization model of the last two centuries into a more ecological-cosmological worldview. We can perhaps say that our current struggles are between the present model marked by the inequalities of dysfunctional global systems, and that part of humanity which is realizing that a new model needs to be manifested and put into place. Thus, the revolution(s) we are currently witnessing are not only of the physical kind, with civil disobedience, rioting, and unrest. There are also revolutions occurring now in our perceptions and worldviews — a revolution in our collective psyche.

Why we are in need of a worldshift is that the old model is attempting to maintain its grip on power, resulting in resource wars, loss of civil liberties, and the on-going struggle for control and management. At the same time there are many forecasts trying to predict the outcome of the present geopolitical turmoil based upon what has gone before; there is a lack of ability to discern the uncertain, the unpredictable, and the unexpected. The western mindset has a preoccupation, or even obsession, with a linear view of history and progress. Yet the concept of a linear development of human civilizations is erroneous and misleading. Many ancient teachings, both spiritual and secular, and many indigenous cultures, have long known about and taught the concept of cyclic processes that repeat themselves over long periods of historical time. These expansions in social cycles also coincide, or are co-existent with, changes in perception and worldviews. In other words, major social revolutions are accompanied by great shifts in human consciousness. Why a positive worldshift is so timely is that these decades are ripe for a new consciousness to enter into our social systems and push for change at exactly the time when such systems are at their weakest point.

The spiral of cultural history involves a complex interplay of various cycles and systems; of social systems, energy systems, and communication revolutions — all co-dependent and integral. The 21st century has been reached through a growing series of critical thresholds — ecological, biological, social, and technological — moving towards current global, social, and environmental limits. However, at such thresholds new arrangements can be catalyzed into being. The 'modern mind' that has exerted itself upon the present world and which largely developed through a trajectory of western history and industrialization, finally arriving at the technological age, exhibits a great deal of short-sightedness. It is a narrow mental framework that either doesn't quite seem to understand past patterns of historical change, or doesn't want to. It seems to posses a great amount of guilt (myth of the Fall?); a large amount of blindness (the myth of progress?); and little historical remembrance (ignorance is bliss?). It is little wonder then that a majority of people living today, especially in the developed nations, are surprised, bemused, and somewhat dazed to find themselves staring into a melting pot of uncertainty.

It is our responsibility to recognize that we are living through an extraordinary passage of change, whereby what we do for the next twenty years, from now to 2030, will create the template for the future. And what happens between now and 2050 will be a crucial period for establishing these patterns of change and getting them in place to serve for the long run.

Our current global systems, now more complex and pervasive than ever, form an intricate and entangled web of interconnections, dependencies, and dubious alliances. We are, quite literally, struggling with the older energies of black goo, sulfuric slime, and the dangerous blackened coal pits where humans dig like slaves. Yet we need to recognize, and quickly, that *there's no infinity in a finite world.* Despite some of the optimistic claims from the energy industry, planet Earth is a finite resource. The world we are moving into requires new myths, whereby we are not constrained by the powers of corporate greed, political tyranny, and the suppression of human creative vision. It would certainly help if we could break away from the culture of cultivating uselessness. As if bored with our experiences, we create a whole array of artless gadgets to amuse us and infantile our hours. We live in distracting times, racing towards the cliff edge like a convoy of excited, pharma-fuelled lemmings. Instead we should be using both our physical and our psychical energies into moving through this shift and preparing for a re-arrangement of life circumstances. Rather than hoping to maintain the cracking, crumbling, and now dysfunctional status quo we should be thinking about creating an alternative path. The industrial cultures of Modernity, which are attempting to model itself as a global culture, are an artificial device — a prosthetic artifact — that devalues our original and creative component. We may be in danger of replacing the creative capacity of the human mind with technological crutches; unless, that is, we are shocked back into our 'rightful minds'.

Yet when faced with uncertainty we might be tempted to avoid seeking out the new and to search instead where we are most secure — still within the old comfort zones/systems. The following is a classic tale that illustrates this human tendency:

Some local villagers came upon Nasrudin one night crawling around on his hands and knees under a lamppost.

'What are you looking for?' they asked him.

'I've lost the key to my house,' he replied.

They all got down to help him look, but after a fruitless time of searching, someone thought to ask him where he had lost the key in the first place.

'In the house,' Nasrudin answered.

'Then why are you looking under the lamppost?' he is asked.

'Because there is more light here,' Nasrudin replied.

There will be obstacles in the years, decades ahead, yet at the same time we should be reassured that there very definitely *is* a future awaiting us too. The degree, and quality, of the change ahead will depend very much upon the degree to which human consciousness is able to change; and to the degree that we can collectively, in our myriad of different ways, help to usher in and manifest a positive worldshift.

A Tale to Finish: 'Be Useless and Enjoy'

Lao Tse was traveling with his disciples when they came to a forest where hundreds of loggers were cutting down the trees. The whole forest had been cleared except for a single large tree with hundreds of branches. This one tree was so great that thousands of people could sit within its shade. Lao Tse asked his disciples to go and enquire why it was that this tree had not been cut down. Soon the disciples returned with the answer to their question and told the teacher:

'They say that this tree is completely useless and that nothing can be done with it - its branches are so full of knots and nothing is straight; it is no good for furniture. Also, it cannot even be used for firewood because it produces a smoke that is harmful to the eyes.'

Lao Tse nodded his head and, with a smile, said:
'Be like this tree, completely useless, and then you will grow great and thousands of people will find shade under you. Be the last yet move in the world as if you were not. Do not compete, do not try to prove yourself worthy - it is not necessary. Be useless and enjoy.

3. TOWARD A PLANETARY ERA?

Modern humanity has been living in an intervening era between the last Ice Age and the present. In the general evolutionary run of things it has been a very rapid, and short, ride. The last 15,000 years have been an evolutionary program that has taken humanity from early hunter-gatherings to a stage of social development that is on the brink of forming a new evolutionary model – that of a conscious unified species. The last two centuries especially have been an incredible wave of development and growth. The question that now confronts us is: are we soon to reach the peak of this phase in our growth just as we appear to be on the cusp of a unique planetary era?

Indeed, if we take just a brief glance at some of the features of our current globalized world we might be mistaken for thinking we already inhabit a planetary society:

·   Communications: the Internet and global communication systems; the 'always-on' flow of news and information.

·   Language: several languages are manifesting as global, such as English, Chinese, Spanish; this is encouraged by our global communication systems.

·   Economy: global economic markets; financial trade agreements; economic blocs, economics beyond nation states.

- Culture: cultural trends are dispersed globally – films, music, food, fashion, sports, etc

- Environment: threats and consequences are now global, with knock-on effects being felt worldwide.

- Travel: global mobility and tourism and now allowing for worldwide forms of contact, exposure, and experiences.

- Boundaries: a weakening of the nation state, and a blurring of frontiers; large people flows; larger international political blocs – EU (European Union); AU   (African Union); UNASUR (Union of South American Nations); AL (Arab League); and ASEAN (Association of Southeast Asian Nations.

- Work: people live & work in different regions/countries; working from home; online commerce; migrant workers.

Our great planetary web of interrelations and interconnections has been arrived at over some 13,000 years of social development, along a familiar pattern of the capture, storage, and usage of available energies. Yet contrary to standard belief systems, such developmental processes do not occur in linear trends (a gradual line of ascent) as our basic concepts of Darwinian evolution have been used to portray.

Many ancient teachings, both spiritual and secular, and many indigenous cultures, have long known about and taught the concept of cyclic processes that are repeated over long periods of historical time. There can also be cycles within cycles; smaller cycles within larger cycles whereby social phases, from less cultured states to more cosmopolitan arrangements, can manifest within one overarching cycle. These expansions in social cycles also coincide, or are coexistent with, changes in perception and worldviews. In other words, major social revolutions are accompanied by great shifts in human consciousness. Such shifts are also parallel to shifts in how the human species understands, and subsequently harnesses, varying forms of energy, upon a progression of discovering ever-finer energies in the world, and indeed the cosmos, of which we are living participants.

Our spiral of cultural history involves a complex interplay of various cycles and systems: of social systems, energy systems and communications revolutions – all co-dependent and integral. Ecological, biological, social and technological systems are now being reorganized because our world is now leaving one model and entering a new mythology, a new model for the next stage of growth. As this transition takes place there will be inevitable disturbances as both clash and *interfere* just as the interference patterns of energy. However, a new cosmology of humankind *is* emerging. As eminent historian Lewis Mumford, in his *The Transformations of Man* (1956), writes:

Every [human] transformation ... has rested on a new metaphysical and ideological base; or rather, upon deeper stirrings and intuitions whose rationalized expression takes the form of a new picture of the cosmos and the nature of man ... we stand on the brink of [such] a new age: the age of an open world and of a self capable of playing its part in that   larger sphere ... In carrying [human] ... self-transformation to this further stage, world culture may bring about a fresh release of spiritual energy that will unveil new potentialities, no more visible in the human self today than radium was in the physical world a century ago, though always present.

In this *phase shift* into 'a new picture of the cosmos and the nature of man', as Mumford writes, there may well be a 'fresh release of spiritual energy' that in-forms this development. Yet such spiritual energies do not necessarily imply religious ecstatic states, or New Age crystal cults, or any other of these stereotyped images. Such energies are most likely to be behind increased creative innovation, awareness of the world, integral-ecological understanding, new values, communications, collaboration, ethics and empathy with our fellow humans. Spiritual energy does not have to be *otherworldly*. In fact, inner growth fosters a deeper commitment and responsibility to the world of our daily lives, and not the opposite.

A planetary era does not necessarily imply that we have a globalized model for all; that we are interdependent on our shared infrastructures, or have a global currency. These are secondary manifestations and do not portray whether or not the actual species *feel themselves* to be part of a planetary era. I would suggest that the sense of being planetary involves how we invest in our collaborations, communications, and empathic consciousness. This will be the release of the 'spiritual energy' that Mumford talks of. How we manifest our consciousness in our contacts, communities, and communications will mark how the years ahead unfold.

It would be a great shame if our present cultural evolutionary project – that took humanity from foragers to the cusp of a planetary era – was to collapse just before it managed to shift into a new era of unprecedented connectivity and collaboration.

A Tale to Finish: 'A Meeting of Tools'

It is told that there was once a carpentry where all the tools held a meeting to settle their differences. At the head of this strange assembly was the hammer acting as president, but soon the other tools declared that he had to resign because he made too much noise with his blows. Hammer admitted the charge but he refused to resign from the presidency because it would mess up the organization, and if the screw took over, as he was wanting to do, this would only screw things up and make the meeting chaotic and without order. The screw and all kinds of nuts argued against this at the same time objecting against the sandpaper taking the presidency as this would create excessive friction with his usual rough sandpaper treatment. Others agreed with this also saying that the tape measure should be thrown out the meeting as he always measured others according to a fixed pattern, as if he were the only one perfect.

Finally, the carpenter arrived into the carpentry, and placing his apron upon himself set about his work. He used the hammer, sandpaper, tape measure, nuts and screws. Finally, the initial block of rough wood turned into a beautiful and useful piece of furniture. When the work was finished the carpenter silently left the room, and once again the tools' meeting was resumed. That's when the saw began to speak; he said:

'Friends, it has been shown to us that we each have our flaws, but the carpenter works with our qualities – that's what makes us valuable. Let us not think more on the negatives we see in each other; rather let us see our skills that we each contribute, and which the carpenter appreciates and uses to the best.'

The assembly then realized that the hammer was strong and gave force to the screw; sandpaper was able to polish and smooth things over; and that the tape measure was accurate and precise. Together, they were a team capable of producing high quality furniture. This made them proud of their strengths and capable of working together. And from then on everyone became the best they could and worked in harmony to create the most beautiful and functional furniture one could ever hope to find.

4. THE HYPER-REALITY OF MODERN LIVING

The Argentinean writer Jorge Luis Borges once famously wrote of a great Empire that created a map that was so detailed it was as large as the Empire itself. The actual map itself grew and decayed as the Empire itself conquered or lost territory. When the Empire finally crumbled, all that remained was the map. This 'imaginary map' finally became the only *remaining reality* of the great Empire: a simulation of the physical reality that now encompasses everyone. In some sense we can say that today's world is moving further towards existing within a simulation of reality. Our world is increasingly given meaning and order through symbols and signs, reducing the human experience to moving between artefacts that construct and maintain a perceived reality. Much of this is orchestrated through global media and the worldwide 'cultural creep' of uniform, standardizing western lifestyle patterns. Through the consumerist mass-production of objects and desirables, people's attention and focus is increasingly driven towards superficial attainments and false value systems. The global media, through movies, television, and printed material, shoulders a high responsibility for blurring the sense of meaning, values, and for deliberate distraction techniques. And, of course, for the incredible amount of propaganda and mental/emotional manipulation that lies at the heart of global media. When there is intent to flood people's consciousness with images that are often *more real than the real*, this sense of hyper-reality is in danger of eroding the presence of **meaning** and **significance**.

This shift towards propagating banal reality lies at the heart of the ever-increasing centralized control of the media. It is somewhat worrying to learn that most western media organizations are owned by only a handful of giant corporations: News Corp; Viacom; Time-Warner; Disney; Vivendi Universal, and Bertelsmann.

The mainstream media is free to offer up a kaleidoscopic view of world events like a broad canvas of fleeting colours. Each day the mosaic changes and events, tragedies, disasters, coups, and politics flash before the eyes like a glitterball. As a result the viewer rarely has the chance to focus on one issue, and thus remembers very little. Nor is there the need to remember a specific event as the next day it is likely to be replaced by the next item of news. In this way, the average viewer is granted their 'nourishment' and feeling of 'open news' whilst at the same time being denied any real 'truth' of the situation or any depth of knowledge.

The mainstream media and entertainment industry also manipulate viewers' emotions to the point whereby many of us are desensitized. The media of escapism allows us to live out our fantasies in what is considered a less harmful way. It is supposed the placate us; to make us forget the regularity of our everyday lives. It also provides us with an external platform on which to project; supplies a conversation space/talking point amongst friends and/or work colleagues; or offers a buffer zone to cover up the embarrassment of a non-communicative family. For many of us the media is now an extension of our daily lives. By being an extended part of us we are drawn in to their events, are enthralled in their dramas. They appear as an amplification of our own senses, relating, interpreting, and transcribing the world back to us.

Another more worrying possibility is that television can act as a factor in causing 'arrested development' within younger children, thus resulting in a later generation of less 'neurologically' developed adults. Child researcher Joseph Chilton Pearce has published findings that indicate how television prevents the higher brain in children from developing as television engages solely with the lower (aka. reptilian) brain.* If the higher brain is not activated sufficiently through external stimulations – which it rarely is via child institutions – then at age 11 the brain begins to destroy many of its unused neurons. This can lead to a permanent condition of arrested development. What this points to is a serious lack in proper stimulants for many children in overly institutionalized and controlled social environments. Also, our brains do not fully mature until we are around age twenty-five, which explains the early targeting of children through advertisers and conditioning institutions. The creative capacity of human imagination is being substituted for a ready-made set of imaginative programming. The corporate entertainment industry has proved to be an incredible tranquilizing abstraction and 'addiction to distraction'. We are living in 2012 A.D. = **A**ttention **D**istractor

As global mainstream media and the extension of hyper-reality creep into our daily lives we each become numb to the violations, wars, carnage, and outrages that pass off as media spectacles. Also worrying is that our younger generation is becoming ever more desensitized to extreme content as video games increasingly merge with military simulations and violent content. Children's entertainment gradually merges into 'militainment' as warfare gaming and 1st-person shooters become bestsellers and a gaming phenomenon. The simulation of violence and military machismo makes the macabre the unreal, the inconsequential and the fanciful. Immersion is permitted at the press of a button, and instant 'on-demand' gratifications satiate distraction and attention. This indeed can be a dangerous mix of painless pleasures taught to be available at the effortless touch of a button. It can become all too easy to slip into a distractive regime of escapism and pleasurable indulgence.

Over the past one and a half centuries humankind has been shifting towards the structure of a mass society; a modern project of *massification*. Our modern 'multi-tasking' environments are increasingly making the rational appear irrational, and the irrational as rational – are we not living in an upside-down, topsy-turvy world?

If we are to wake-up from the hyper-reality that manifests constantly around us we need to bring awareness to the forefront of our daily lives; to begin nurturing our own inner authority and deciding what to filter, what to internalize, and which to shut off. We need to become more active in how we engage in our world, our sense of reality, and our Earth.

* Chilton Pearce, J. *The Biology of Transcendence: A Blueprint of the Human Spirit.* Rochester, VT: Park Street Press, 2004

A Tale to Finish: 'The Apple of Understanding'

The teacher always told a parable at the end of each class, but not all the listeners would understand the meaning of it. One day one of them confronted the teacher and said:
- You tell us stories but do not explain the meaning to us.
The teacher apologized for this and then continued by saying:
- Let me recompense you by offering you a juicy apple.
- Thank you master, the disciple replied flattered.
- First, I would like to peel this apple myself, would you allow me?
- Yes, thank you very much, replied the disciple.
- Since I already have a knife in my hand, let me take advantage of this and cut the apple into pieces so it will be more comfortable for you to eat.
- Thank you teacher, I hope it is not too much trouble?
- Not at all, I just want to please you. Also, allow me to chew it before to make it easier for you to swallow.
- No teacher!, don't do that! shrieked the surprised student.

The teacher paused and said:

- If I explain the meaning of each parable .... it would be like feeding you a fruit chewed. You yourself have to find and savor its exquisite flavor.

5. MESSING WITH OUR MINDS: THE EVER FINER LINE BETWEEN NEWS AND ADVERTISING

The manufacturing of consent is endemic within modern societies. Throughout history the need to 'persuade and influence' has always been manipulated by those people in power as a means to maintain authority and legitimacy. In more recent years the overall manipulation of the mass public mind has become less about making speeches, and more about becoming a pervasive presence within the lives of each of individual.

Edward Bernays has often been called 'the father of public relations' as it was his teachings and research that spurred the post-war years of propaganda. Bernays, a nephew of Sigmund Freud, utilized psychological and psychoanalytical ideas to construct an informational system (propaganda) capable of manipulating public opinion. Bernays, apparently, considered that such a manipulative apparatus was necessary because society, in his regard, was composed of too many irrational elements (the people) which could be dangerous to the efficient mechanisms of power ('democracy'). Bernays wrote that 'The conscious and intelligent manipulation of the organized habits and opinions of the masses is an important element in democratic society'.[1] Bearing in mind that Bernays was speaking/writing in the early 1920s we can expect the mechanisms of propaganda (mass manipulation) to have progressed to a very advanced degree. Within the context of our modern mass societies propaganda has morphed into a mechanism for not only engineering public opinion but also as a means for consolidating social control.

Modern programs of social influence could not exist without the mass media. Today it exists as a combination of expertise and knowledge from technology; sociology; social behaviorism; psychology; communications; and other scientific techniques. Almost every nation needs a controlled mainstream media if it is to regulate and influence its citizenry. By way of the mainstream media a controlling authority is able to exert psychological influence upon people's perception of reality. This capacity works hand-in-hand with the more physical components, such as enforcing the legal system and national security laws (surveillance and monitoring). State control, acting as a 'psychological machine', instigates specific psychological manipulations in order to achieve desired goals within its national borders (and often beyond). Examples of these psychological manipulations include the deliberate use of specific cultural symbols and embedded signifiers that catalyze conditioned reflexes in the populace. These triggers have included 'Red' and 'Communist' during the US's 1950s McCarthyism; or 'Muslim Terrorist' during the currently constructed 'War on Terror'. Targeted reactions can thus be achieved making the populace open to further manipulation in this state. This is a process of psychic re-formation that works repeatedly to soften up the people through continued and extensive exposure to particular stimuli. These are the symbols we live by – artificial and man-made in order to construct a compliant society.

Today's media, which includes the dominant presence of advertising, extensively uses the notion of 'attractors' and 'attractor patterns' to target audience consciousness. This type of symbol-manipulation is often referred to in the business as neuro-marketing. Mainstream media corporations are using the huge growth in global communications to further shape their science of targeting human consciousness. In the case of neuro-marketing many advertisers first audience-test their commercials using brain-scanning techniques in order to know which part of a person's brain is being activated by the specific strong attractors. For example, it has been discovered that specific attractors can bypass the logical part of the brain and impacting the emotional part. In such cases as in the film industry the advertisers place an award symbol (such as an Oscar or Golden Globe) which has proven to be an effective 'strong attractor' that influences the emotional part of the brain. The philosophy here is to adjust the level of consciousness of an advertisement in relation to the measurable level of consciousness of the consumer.[2] Advertisers are aware that a person's consciousness passes on messages indirectly to the body in the form of galvanic skin response, pupil response, electrical nerve response, etc, and so every element of the screen promotion must elucidate the correct conscious reception. In order to achieve this correct set of attractor patterns all elements are deliberately worked on: the music, the visuals, the script, the voice. Interesting, symbolic strong attractors that have the most impact to persuade the audience include visuals such as smiley faces and cute animals (dogs wagging their tails and kittens purring). In terms of voice they include words such as 'honesty'; 'integrity'; 'freedom'; 'hope and change'; 'friendship', etc. For this reason it can be seen how politicians use a great deal of these attractor-patterns in their speeches and promotional material.[3]

Other methods of blatant propaganda include governing bodies use the 'reality of truth' by releasing 'seemingly accurate' statistics that tell of plausible situations. Again, this is the 'expert in the white lab-coat' tactic. For such propaganda/information to be effective it cannot be too far off the truth; in other words, it must have the appearance of reality. Trade, employment, and financial figures are an example of this. And which members of the general public have the knowledge and/or resources to check and confirm such figures? Those people that do know are usually those that have a vested interest in maintaining the illusion, such as traders and financiers. And when a nation releases its unemployment figures, are they really counting the many who are jobless but not signing on, or are dispossessed, or immigrants? As a norm, statistics of a negative connotation are usually drawn from the smallest possible pile. And once a false (or 'doctored') claim is disseminated and accepted by the public, it becomes established and hard to deconstruct or invalidate (unless persuasive anti-propaganda is just as effective).

Modern societies are set-up to accommodate both individualism and the mass collective. Yet the forms that the accepted 'individualism' takes are often a sheath to hide the workings of a mass psyche. It is the 'allowed liberty' that is provided to the modern person in pursuit of material gains as long as there exists a contribution to the overall plan of the ruling authority. Liberty then is an expression of mobility within a pre-described system: it does not denote liberty external to the system. Examples are the rock clichés that the mainstream media love to promote and adorn their front pages. Notables are the raging antics of destroying hotel rooms and throwing televisions out of the window; behaviour which later got morphed into copycat corporate rock PR. In essence, such 'rebels' are allowed, and even encouraged, because their antics sell records. Rebelliousness in these forms is thus another contribution to a consumerist society, albeit through a different lens. And today there are many forms in which individualism is allowed to manifest.

The display of diversity in the information coming from the mainstream media gives the illusion of independent reportage and news. Yet the mainstream media of any given nation(s) is owned by only a small handful of corporate entities, with high-level state relations. An individual is thus 'attracted' to a particular newspaper, for example, relative to their views, beliefs, lifestyles, etc; all of these being 'diversified patterned behaviour' within the system. The mainstream media caters for these needs by operating a variety of newspapers that support these mythical standpoints, whether they be politically left, right, left/right of centre, liberal, independent, this, that, or any other of the positions available for the 'diversity within the unity' of the mass mind. Yet the shift toward propagating banal reality lies at the heart of the ever-increasing centralized control of the media. It is somewhat worrying to learn that most western media organizations are owned by only a handful of giant corporations: News Corp; Viacom; Time-Warner; Disney; Vivendi Universal, and Bertelsmann. For example, Disney (The Walt Disney Company) is the largest entertainment and media multinational in the world. Disney owns the TV networks ABC, Disney Channel, ESPN, A&E, and the History Channel, as well as publishing, merchandising, and theatre subsidiaries. They also own Walt Disney Pictures, Touchstone Pictures, Hollywood Pictures, Miramax Film Corp., Dimension, and Buena Vista International, as well as 11 theme parks around the world. News Corp comes in next as the world's second largest media multinational with an incredible range of TV and satellite channels, magazine and newspaper holdings, record companies and publishing companies based worldwide, with a strong presence in Asian markets. Similarly, Time-Warner owns more than 50 magazines; a film studio as well as various film distributers; more than 40 music labels (including Warner Bros, Atlantic, and Elektra); and several TV networks (such as HBO, Cartoon Network, and CNN). Viacom owns TV networks CBS, MTV, VH1, Nickelodeon, Comedy Central, Paramount Pictures, and nearly 2000 cinema screens, as part of their media empire. Likewise, Vivendi Universal owns 27% of US music sales via labels such as Interscope, Geffen, A&M, Island, Def Jam, MCA, Mercury, Motown and Universal. They also own Universal Studios, Studio Canal, Polygram Films, Canal+, and numerous Internet and mobile phone companies. Then there is Bertelsmann which, as a global media corporation, runs Europe's second largest TV, radio and production company (the RTL Group) with 45 TV stations and 32 radio channels; Europe's largest printing and publishing firm (Gruner & Jahr); the world's largest English-language general trade book publisher (Random House); the world's largest book and music club group (Direct Group); and an international media and communications service provider (Arvato AG).

In our media-saturated environments people are allowed to live out their fantasies in what is considered a less harmful way; to help alleviate the so-called 'drudgery of repetitive lives'. It also provides people with a conversation space/talking point amongst friends and/or work colleagues; or offers a buffer zone to cover up the embarrassment of a non-communicative family. And if all hell breaks lose at work, at least you have True Blood or Friends waiting for you on the home screen!

In terms of mainstream news reporting it is always important to check the source when reading a news item; i.e., is it of an independent source or is it 'according to a government source', etc. The mainstream media is largely fed via global news services; the two largest being Reuters (now Thomson Reuters) and Associated Press. This again constitutes a centralization of news information, as well as the various well-established political press offices. When such sources (especially PR offices) disseminate information as 'truthful news', it is doing nothing more than was parodied in Orwell's 1984 as Newspeak. Independent media, such as is now coming of age and maturity on the Internet, has served to counter-neutralize some of the overwhelming persuasive power of the mainstream media propaganda. For this reason there are concerted efforts underway to curtail the 'wild' and 'uncensored' nature of the Internet. In other words, this means there is considerable corporate and political will to rein in the Internet under the umbrella of corporate and governmental/state control, or at least surveillance of its use.

What has changed the game-plan over the past two decades has been the rise of distributed and decentralized global communications between individuals. The Internet in particular, as well as other forms of social media, has spurned the growth of individuals seeking information between themselves which is often external to the consensus of various nation states. This has had the effect of shifting people away from conditioned patterns of propaganda and belief systems. This bottom-up intervention has seriously compromised the patterning techniques of ruling authorities. There are now efforts underway to censor those information sites critical of the state. It is therefore imperative that our independent media be protected; our social networks of free speech preserved; and our right to seek and speak the truth defended. Messing with our minds has no place in a truly democratic and egalitarian future.

[1] Bernays, E. L. (2004/1928) Propaganda. New York: Ig Publishing.

[2] This idea, as well as neuro-marketing, was given to me in personal correspondence by Darryl Howard, who sent me his research 'Advertising in the New Paradigm' (Darryl Howard & Associates).

[3] Anyone wishing to know more on this subject should investigate Neural-Linguistic Programming (NLP).

A Tale to Finish: 'Crazies'

There was once a wise and powerful king who ruled in a remote city of a far kingdom. And the king was feared for both his might and his love of wisdom. At the heart of the city was a well whose water was cool and crystalline, and all the inhabitants drank from this well, even the king and his courtiers, because there was no other well in the city. One night, while everyone was asleep, a witch entered the city and poured seven drops of a strange liquid into the well, and said:
'From now on, anyone who drinks this water will go crazy'
The next morning all the inhabitants drank the water from the well, except the king and his lord chamberlain, and very soon everyone went mad, as the witch had foretold. During that day, all people went through the narrow streets and public places whispering to each other:
'The king is mad. Our king and his lord chamberlain have lost their reason. Naturally, we can not be ruled by a mad king. We must dethrone him!'

That night, the king ordered a golden cup of water from the well to be brought to him. And when they brought the cup the king and his lord chamberlain drank heavily from it. Soon after that there was great rejoicing in that distant city of a far kingdom because the king and his lord chamberlain had regained their reason.

6. MONEY CREATION & THE ILLUSION OF WEALTH

The incumbent global financial system is in dire straits and is a behemoth waiting to implode. It is intrinsically unsustainable with its labyrinthine financial agreements and credit swaps. These include mortgage-backed securities, collateralized debt obligations, credit default swaps, predatory lending, derivatives and off-balance sheet financing, etc. The financial system has become an almost impossible marketplace to regulate as risky mortgages and debts are funded through what is known as the 'shadow banking system' and thus further obscured from external checks. The current economic myth of a 'perpetual growth' economy requires a relatively cheap and plentiful supply of resources, alongside expanding markets. With energy and resource constraints impacting the global marketplace at a critical time of great economic instability, the result is a time-bomb waiting to explode.

The global effects of the ongoing great recession are being felt through many giant financial institutions that are still carrying billions in toxic assets. This is the same for sovereign nations who are riddled with debt, especially various states within the European Union. Losses worldwide to date have been trillions (whether dollars, pounds, or Euros), and the ongoing rounds of quantitative easing and bailouts only serve to further frustrate, anger, and *pauperize* the people. For many, the phrase 'bailout fatigue' is now an all too familiar phrase which shows that the ineffective actions being taken are increasingly remote from many people's sense of reality. The years ahead are likely to bring further economic disruptions, increasing bankruptcies and bank failures; resulting in many nation states having to implement greatly unpopular austerity measures. Governments are likely to become more repressive in the face of financial instability and mounting debt. This is likely to result in a deepening restriction of freedom of expression and civil rights as social protests grow. We have to face the prospect of a future where our once cheap consumer lifestyles become not so cheap anymore. This will indeed be the case when resource and economic growth falters in such countries as China. A radical overhaul of the global economy is not only necessary, it is inevitable.

John Kenneth Galbraith, the Canadian-American economist, famously said that 'The process by which money is created is so simple that the mind is repelled.' And in fact he was right: money creation is a fantastically simple illusion of wealth. The word says it all – *money is created*. It is an artificial construct of consensus value. That is, people worldwide accept the varying rates of currency exchange and, importantly, the value of goods tied to monetary exchange. The value of money is a shared illusion that we all 'buy' into – yet it is also a very necessary one if we are to engage in our everyday lives. Money creation goes something like this:

An individual goes into a bank with $1000 and deposits the money in an account. The individual now has a $1000 asset in storage and the bank has a $1000 legal responsibility for custodianship. Now the rules on bank accountability allows each bank to loan out a proportion of the money they have on deposit which, in theory, is about 90%. Since most banks only keep a very small fraction of their actual deposits in reserve in their bank, this procedure is called 'fractional reserve banking.' Banks are now in a position to start making lucrative financial deals since they make no money from holding onto people's money (unless charging for bank services or debt interest). These financial deals operate through such activities as merchant banking and investment banking. These sectors deal with high-level business and private equities; and with underwriting and securities respectively. The other more commonly known type of banking is called commercial banking. In our example, a commercial bank can loan out 90% of the initial $1000 deposited, and thus provides $900 for another borrower. This $900 is now in circulation and may get passed on to another person, as payment, which then may be deposited back in the commercial bank. If a bank now has this $900 on deposit it can loan out 90% of it, a further $810. If the bank then receives this $810 from another person then it can lend out 90% against this which is $729. This process goes on and on until, for example, the initial $1000 has now developed into $10,000. However, only $1000 is actually held in reserve by the bank. The $10,000 it may hold in various accounts has been money created out of the original lump sum. It is still very real in terms of purchasing power, yet it represents $9000 of debt. All of the $9000 was *loaned into existence* without ever being physical created. The money was 'backed' by the initial holding yet the new 'wealth creation' does not exist as physical money. Thus, if every person went to the bank to reclaim their part of the $10,000 (called a 'bank run') then the bank would not be able to pay because they would not actually have the money on account. The bank may then be forced to pay back as much as feasibly possible before entering bankruptcy. In effect, each person has their money as long as everybody doesn't ask for it at the same time. Also, everyone's money is allegedly 'safe' as long as everybody doesn't start defaulting on their loans. On top of this there is the interest payment that has to be paid back with each loan. This again means that more money needs to be paid back than originally exists. Are we starting to get the picture?

What this tells us is that money growth is a process of debt accumulation. First, bank credit is money *loaned into existence*, and thus is a debt upon which further debt (interest) must be paid. The second type of money creation comes from the central banks which have the exclusive authority to lend money (i.e. print money) which is then exchanged for government debt. The central bank for each nation has the sole monopoly on creating currency as a legal tender. In other words, government spending and money in circulation is backed, yet again, by debt. Further, the majority of central banks in the developed world are 'independent', which means they are privately owned and thus beyond political interference. Let me repeat this important, and often overlooked point: money creation (ie. printing money), government debt and private debt, are largely under the authority of private institutions. As Mayer Amschel Rothschild (1743-1812), one of the world's most famous bankers, once said: 'Give me control over a nation's currency, and I care not who makes its laws.' Anyone wishing to know further details only has to investigate the history of the central banking system.

To continue, the creation of money is therefore a debt-creation process. All monies are backed by debt. At the everyday bank level all new money *is loaned into existence.* At the government and state level, all money is simply printed 'out of thin air' and then exchanged for government debt. Both types of debts are also accompanied by interest payments on the debt. We can thus say that money is backed by debt and this debt must pay interest. So here comes another question: if interest is accumulated on top of the debts, then where is the money to cover these extra interest payments? Answer – it doesn't exist *unless extra money is loaned into existence to cover the interest payments on outstanding debt.* At the same time the amount of debt each year is expanding by x %, because of interest growth. As debt expands upon previous percentage growth it becomes an exponential system. What this means is that the amount of debt circulating will always be more than the amount of available money. It also implies that the global banking system not only is *perpetually expanding* but also that it must do so in accordance with its own institutional processes.

What has also added to this expanding currency bubble is the fact that liquid currencies are no longer backed by the gold standard. Where once bank notes could be converted at the banks for gold coins (a procedure often suspended during times of war), this gave paper money a well-trusted unit of value. Global currencies – especially the reserve currency of the US dollar – were backed by the unit value of gold. However, the end of the gold standard was heralded in 1971 when the dollar was stripped of its gold backing allowing it to peg its own value. This also meant that money could be printed at greater rates since it was not tied to any fixed gold price. The amount of *created money* now in 'circulation' is shocking. Trillions of dollars/sterling pounds/Euros are affectively in existence today – that is, as digits on a computer screen - supplying debt-relief and credit. Only that they are not in *actual* existence. It is nothing more than *an illusion of artificial debt.* Yet the illusion for most people is very real and very painful.

The illusion of wealth (i.e. debt) creation is hurting many of us because our socio-economic systems have tied almost all individuals into this *counterfeit cage* where they are not so much physically enclosed but rather entangled within a digital prison of credit and debt. Our so-called 'credit systems' (i.e. debt) makes people work for the banksters whilst for many the debt can never be repaid. In other words, money and credit is itself a form of debt, masquerading as false wealth. Credit is a socially-constructed form of slavery - an assault upon the human spirit - whilst the world is built on a debt that can never be repaid. Credit cards too are extensions of this symbolic debt environment and form part of the armory of *silent weapons* that wage a *quiet war* against the people. As a further insult to injury, many of these global institutions – international banks and multi-national corporations – now exist beyond (and often above) the power of nation states.

Modern societies have shifted by stealth from paper money to digital money. Our financial institutions, and hence our 'credit rating' (what an inhuman word!) values a person's 'worth' by binary digits on a screen. Personal independence is being undermined by our systems (that were supposed to work *for* us) stripping people of their physical assets, as was evident during the 2008 financial crash and the ongoing instability of liquid currency markets. The economic system is a farce, yet a highly dangerous one.

What this means for the average person is that we need to establish for ourselves a way of life that takes us away from dependency on the banks, and to get rid of our addiction to credit. That is: only spend what we need to; take our cash out of the bank (place it in a safe or somewhere safe); look for local currency schemes; establish or join barter networks; shift to a more self-sustaining lifestyle (growing your own food, etc). And for goodness sake, we each must learn to live within our means. The alternative is to live within *their* means. And that, at least for me, is not a prospect I favor.

A Tale to Finish: 'Two Men'

Two men who were unjustly imprisoned for a long time shared a cell together where they received all sorts of abuse and humiliation at the hands of the prison guards. Finally they were both freed and, after many years, ran into each other one day in the street. One of them asked the other: 'Do you ever remember the guards and how they treated us?'

'No, thank God, I've forgotten everything', said the other. 'What about you?'

'I've continued hating them with all my strength' he replied. His friend looked at him a moment, then said:

'I feel for you. If so, it means you are still imprisoned.'

7. DEMOCRATIC UNFREEDOM - SOCIAL TECHNIQUE & THE MANUFACTURE OF CONTROL

A comfortable, smooth, reasonable, democratic unfreedom prevails in advanced industrial civilization, a token of technical progress

Herbert Marcuse

As Noam Chomsky pointed out, in both 'old' and 'new' world orders the central goal has pivoted around the issue of control: 'Control of the population is the major task of any state that is dominated by particular sectors of the domestic society and therefore functions primarily in their interest…'[1] Such 'particular sectors' as referred to are the minority elite who pursue controlling strategies to 'engineer' nation and international affairs in line with their aims. And these aims are for the most part based on greed and power; and the need to keep the masses contented and docile.

The construction of what Marcuse refers to as *democratic unfreedom* is often implemented through scientific rationalism. The pattern often adopted is in parading rational thinking as the vehicle in which to present specific agendas most suitable to hierarchical power structures. And it is through the rationalism of the elite technocratic establishment that global governance has found its most articulate expression. One of these forms is through corporatism, and the rise of the conglomerates. A particular example of corporatism and social control can be found within how global food systems are monopolized and managed.

The control and management of global food supplies has been a corporate and political priority for decades, with US-based conglomerates leading the charge. As elite establishment political figure Henry Kissinger once remarked in 1970 'Control oil and you control nations; control food and you control the people'. Recent research places multinational corporations behind the push towards controlling global food supplies.

The 1974 UN World Food Conference in Rome outlined the necessity of maintaining sufficient world grain reserves, especially since the price of world grain had shot up dramatically by the huge increase in oil price during the early 1970s oil crisis (at one point world oil prices had risen by 400 per cent). At this time the US export strategy in the 1970s was to further control food trade supplies. This led to moves to consolidate power as 95 per cent of all grain reserves in the world were under the control of 6 multinational agribusiness corporations – Cargill Grain Company; Continental Grain Company; Cook Industries, Inc; Dreyfus; Bunge Company; and Archer Daniels Midland – all of which were US-based companies. The US long-term strategy was to dominate the global market in grain and agriculture commodities, as outlined in the early 1970s by Richard Nixon. This policy coincided with taking the dollar off the gold exchange standard in August 1971 to make US grain exports competitive in the rest of the world. However, in order for the US to become the world's most competitive agribusiness producer it had to replace the traditional American family-based farm with the now widespread huge 'factory-farm' production. In other words, traditional agriculture was systematically replaced with agribusiness production through changes in domestic policy. For example, domestic farm programs that had previously protected smaller farm incomes were phased out during Nixon's term in office. This policy was then exported to developing countries in a bid to make US agribusiness more competitive and to get a foothold into foreign markets:

> The Nixon Administration began the process of destroying the domestic food production of developing countries as the opening shot in an undeclared war to create a vast new global market in 'efficient' American food exports. Nixon also used the post-war trade regime known as the General Agreement on Tariffs and Trade (GATT) to advance this new global agribusiness export agenda.[2]

In Henry Kissinger's 1974 report 'National Security Study Memorandum 200' (NSSM 200) he directly targeted overseas food aid as an 'instrument of national power'.[3] The policy shifts during the 1970s were towards increased deregulation, which meant increased private regulation by the large and powerful global corporations. This led to an increase in corporate mergers and the rise of transnational corporations (which today often have larger GDPs than many nation states).[4]

As large corporate agribusinesses were creating their food production, storage and distribution monopoly, smaller domestic farms were going bankrupt and closing. (Although this trend was predominantly occurring within the US, it later spread to other developed nations who were forced to 'modernize' their agricultural industry to compete with global trade.) For example, between 1979 and 1998 the number of US farmers dropped by 300,000 as by the end of the 1990s the agriculture market (in the US at least) was dominated by large commercial agribusiness interests. The US also operated a foreign policy of offering financial assistance 'to developing countries via the World Bank in return for these countries to open their markets up to cheap US food imports and hybridized seeds'.[5]

By the beginning of the 21st century world supplies of cereal were under the control of a few US-based monopolies. Four large agrochemical/seed companies – Monsanto, Novartis, Dow Chemical and DuPont – controlled more than 75 per cent of the US's seed corn sales and 60 per cent of soybean seed sales. By the merging of giant agrochemical and seed companies, livestock could be fed on a huge diet of drugs in order to stimulate increased growth. It has been estimated that in recent years the largest users of antibiotics and similar pharmaceutical products are not humans but animals, which consumed 70 per cent of all pharmaceutical antibiotics. Statistics show, quite shockingly, that the use of antibiotics by US agribusiness increased from 500,000 pounds to 40 million pounds (an 80-fold increase by weight) from 1954 to 2005. As a consequence, the Center for Disease Control in the US has reported an 'epidemic' rise in food-related diseases in humans as a result of eating meat containing large quantities of antibiotics. One Harvard University researcher, Ray Goldberg, who set up a research group to examine the revolution in agribusiness (including genetically modified organisms) reported that: 'the genetic revolution is leading to an industrial convergence of food, health, medicine, fiber and energy business'.[6]

Corporatism and the rise of the conglomerates is just one example in the centralization of social institutions that then play out their agendas within our societies. Global food supplies are only one aspect of a range of covert structures, operating both within and between nation states that serve to bring a *democratic unfreedom* into our lives. Other structures include, but are not limited to, financial institutions and central banking; energy cartels; pharmaceutical monopolies; communication and media empires; and data-collection centers. Our increasingly restricted social environments are now managed by a highly organized form of social *technique*.

Modern techno-societies are progressively more orchestrated around the central issue of power and control. This policy entails that technology (the consequences of social *technique*) is required to further regulate and manipulate the free expression of human activity. Historically social discipline was instilled within the masses by public executions and very overt physical threats. Nowadays this has shifted to more covert forms of control and influence. The ultimate dystopian future, for example, could be described as:

> It will not be a universal concentration camp, for it will be guilty of no atrocity. It will not seem insane, for everything will be ordered, and the stains of human passion will be lost amid the chromium gleam. We shall have nothing more to lose, and nothing to win. Our deepest instincts and our most secret passions will be analyzed, published, and exploited. We shall be rewarded with everything our hearts ever desired. And the supreme luxury of the society of technical necessity will be to grant the bonus of useless revolt and of an acquiescent smile. [7]

We should be careful, therefore, to note that the illusion of liberty can be used as a powerful form of control and domination. Such as the 'democratic right' to 'free and fair elections', as the 'free election of masters does not abolish the masters or the slaves'.[8] Joseph Goebbels (Nazi Germany's propaganda minister) was acutely aware of this potential when he stated: 'You are at liberty to seek your salvation as you understand it, provided you do nothing to change the social order'. This amounts to nothing more than running around within our own playpen. The extreme of this is a society where a revolutionary/reactionary potential ceases to exist. With many new laws coming into effect (in the US and elsewhere) that restrict public gatherings and the right to protest, this may not be far from our current social reality.

As suggested by a prior discussion on media, there is a great emphasis upon who has access to what information. Information is crucial to the manageability of a social control matrix. Many countries are so sensitive about this that they prioritize the control, availability, and flow of information. This applies not only to overtly restrictive regimes such as China ('The Great Firewall')[i], but also to so-called democratic nations such as the United States, Australia, and European states. The recent attempts to regulate Internet activity such as ACTA[ii] and SOPA[iii] are examples of this very dangerous creeping institutionalization of the free-flow of information. Despite the rapid growth in independent and alternative news sites (thanks mainly to the Internet), the sad truth is that the majority of people are still living within a highly managed *information embargo*.

Control over the flow and content of information is a feature of social *technique* and characterizes any society that is moving toward increasing digitization. To a large degree the manufacture of social control is about the management of information. That's why, in subtle and ingenious ways, modern societies are racing to establish ever more efficient structures of *information embargo*. Such institutional behavior is not restricted to developed societies but also appears in developing societies:

> Technology serves to institute new, more effective and more
> pleasant forms of social control and social cohesion. The

---

[i] http://en.wikipedia.org/wiki/Internet_censorship_in_the_People%27s_Republic_of_China
[ii] http://en.wikipedia.org/wiki/Anti-Counterfeiting_Trade_Agreement
[iii] http://en.wikipedia.org/wiki/SOPA

totalitarian tendency of these controls seems to assert itself in still
another sense - by spreading to the less developed and even to
the preindustrial areas of the world. [9]

The critical role of technology for social control of the masses was laid out
very clearly by the one-time US National Security Advisor Zbigniew
Brzezinski. Brzezinsski discussed how the information society would have
to provide an 'amusement focus' such as 'spectator spectacles' like mass
sports and mainstream media in order to provide 'an opiate for increasingly
purposeless masses'. He went on to say that 'New forms of social control
may be needed to limit the indiscriminate exercise by the individual of their
new powers'. [10] Brzezinski, as a high-ranking expert on political affairs,
was aware of the rise in the consciousness of the people and how this would
affect the capacity of power structures to maintain the mask of democracy.
Brzezinski wrote that a 'global human conscience is for the first time
beginning to manifest itself' but that 'the new global consciousness,
however, is only beginning to become an influential force. It still lacks
identity, cohesion, and focus'. [11]

The aim of open information and the free-flow of thought should therefore
be to establish a true and genuine civil society that manifests identity,
cohesion, and focus. Not to do so would be playing directly into the hands
of social *technique* that plans our pacification, purposelessness, and
disempowerment. I should hope that our agenda is not to play ball, and to
seek the very opposite – empowerment, individual and collective integrity,
and a real sense of civic purpose. It is for this reason that our
communication channels remain open…for now…

[1] Chomsky, Noam, *World Orders, Old and New*, London: Pluto Press, 1997
[2] Engdahl, F W, *Seeds of Destruction: The Hidden Agenda of Genetic Manipulation*, Global Research, 2007
[3] Cited in Engdahl, F W, *Seeds of Destruction: The Hidden Agenda of Genetic Manipulation*, Global Research, 2007
[4] Rockerfeller and Ford Foundation funding of the Harvard University study titled 'Harvard Economic Research Project on the Structure of the American Economy' (led by Wassily Leontief) helped to identify US corporate interests and expansions.
[5] Engdahl, F W, *Seeds of Destruction: The Hidden Agenda of Genetic Manipulation*, Global Research, 2007
[6] Engdahl, F W, *Seeds of Destruction: The Hidden Agenda of Genetic Manipulation*, Global Research, 2007
[7] Ellul, Jacques, *The Technological Society*, New York: Vintage Books, 1964
[8] Marcuse, Herbert, *One-Dimensional Man: Studies in the Ideology of Advanced Industrial Society*, Oxford: Routledge, 2007/1964
[9] Marcuse, Herbert, *One-Dimensional Man: Studies in the Ideology of Advanced Industrial Society*, Oxford: Routledge, 2007/1964
[10] Brzezinski, Zbigniew, *Between Two Ages: America's Role in the Technetronic Era*, New York: Viking, 1970
[11] Brzezinski, Zbigniew, *Between Two Ages: America's Role in the Technetronic Era*, New York: Viking, 1970

A Tale to Finish: 'The Lion'

A lion was captured and imprisoned in a reserve where, to his surprise, he found other lions that had been there for many years, some even their whole life having been born in captivity. The newcomer soon became familiar with the activities of the other lions, and observed how they were arranged in different groups.

One group was dedicated to socializing, another to show business, whilst yet another group was focused on preserving the customs, culture and history from the time the lions were free. There were church groups and others that had attracted the literary or artistic talent. There were also revolutionaries who devoted themselves to plot against their captors and against other revolutionary groups. Occasionally, a riot broke out and one group was removed or killed all the camp guards and so that they had to be replaced by another set of guards. However, the newcomer also noticed the presence of a lion that always seemed to be asleep. He did not belong to any group and was oblivious to them all. This lion appeared to arouse both admiration and hostility from the others. One day the newcomer approached this solitary lion and asked him which group he belonged to.

'Do not join any group' said the lion, 'those poor ones deal with everything but the essentials.'

'And what is essential?' asked the newcomer.

'It is essential to study the nature of the fence'

8. SPIRITUALITY VS. CONSUMERISM

Ritual is important, yet often it is least beneficial to those people who are ritualistically-minded and inclined to habit. The word 'tradition' is now applied to many socially embedded religious and 'spiritual' practices that have become engrained within our cultures. Yet in many instances it is possible to replace the notion of 'tradition' with 'repetition'. Certain beliefs and practices are passed on through the generations without modification or adaptation to circumstances such as the current time and place of operation. This is little more than repetition of a fixed formula that whilst was functioning in its time, is often now without its inner kinetic energy. It can be said to be like the shell of an oyster that has long been bereft of its pearl.

An example of this can be seen in this interchange between a genuine spiritual teacher who went to an Asiatic country to address the issue of repetition. The visitor explained to the incumbent sheik that the practices he was advocating belonged to a time in the past and were limited for a specific, targeted audience. Since such conditions no longer existed, what remained was merely an outer core – a spectacle. The old Sheikh, who was the head of the order, replied that 'in a world where there is no light at all, even a false gleam is perhaps something to have', and that 'I have been here so long, and so have my ancestors, that we cannot change.' The old sheikh continued with his refusal by further adding that 'we may well be wanted, and believed to be the possessors of secrets…we are here, after seven hundred years, not because of our value or viciousness, but because people want us. They want magic…many can follow a harmless path and feel better, elevated. That, in any case, is what they imagine spirituality to be.'*

However, imagining what 'spirituality to be' is like, is similar to imagining that the air we breathe is one substance. Yet this is not so, for if we have knowledge of the correct composition of a substance we find that it is composed of many elements in specific alignment and concentration. To focus on only a part of the substance and to gain nutrition from this, such as from ritual or selected practices only, is not only inefficient yet potentially harmful. Using this analogy for the air we breath, we know from science that air is composed of 21% oxygen, 78% nitrogen, and 1% of other gases including argon and carbon dioxide. Yet if a person decided to select the nitrogen component only, and to concentrate their 'ritual' breathing on this part alone they would not find themselves breathing at all after very long.

Spiritual practices in the modern world are rife with repetition; mainly because repetition reinforces mental, emotional, and physical conditioning and patterns of behaviour. Further, repetition in such 'spiritual practices' often involve the carrying on of selected elements; that is, those elements which it has been decided upon will be most useful to pass on and highlight. In such cases we need to ask – on whose authority? If one has a headache we may take an aspirin, yet to repeat this a hundred times will have a different effect than making the headache go away...we may lose much more!

Repetition in the science of inner transformation can be damaging if it is not in correct proportion to the whole. Yet each of us has a capacity to recognize that which is genuine; only that often it is clouded beneath an array of acquired traits such as laziness, greed, etc. One way to cut through this is to be sincere with oneself - to ask oneself directly if what you are doing is truly providing the nourishment and development required. If there is a need for self-justification we might ask ourselves why?

Just as in recent years the credit bubble placed many people into a false sense of security by offering the possibility to obtain untold goodies, so too does the promise of repetitious and ritualistic forms of spirituality. Many were duped into 'repetitious consumerism' because of the offering of cheap credit ('false gold'). Likewise, many people are also attracted to the window-displays of attractive practices of inner transformation. Quotations and phrases are consumed and put on display; deeds are admired and miracles invoked. Even the extremes are commercialized: ritual suffering; automatic obedience; reward and punishment, etc. Yet all are low-level emotional stimulus. As one contemporary teacher commented: 'The would-be learner, instead of realizing that there is an objective, becomes a bemused consumer of wonders and stimuli'. Such offerings may be 'consumable', yet are they part of a disciplined science that forms a unified, complete teaching of aligned development in recognition of specific contexts? As the saying goes – 'False gold exists only because real gold exists'.

The inner evolutionary imperative is not a shopping list, or the random acquisition of abilities, nor the gaining of emotional satisfaction. It is a genuine inner need that, if acted upon sincerely and with genuine intention, can be of immense benefit to the individual and to the planet.

Falsely spiritual people are easily seen through, because they think, like materialists, in transactionalist terms. They want to get something in exchange for something else' – I.S.

* John Grant, 'Travels in the Unknown East', Octagon Press, 1992

A Tale to Finish: 'The Caliph'

Based on the reports that he had been given, the Caliph appointed Nasrudin as Senior Court Advisor; and since his authority did not come from his own jurisdiction but the patronage of the Caliph, Nasrudin became a danger to all those who came for consultation - as shown by the following case:

- 'Nasrudin, you who are a man of experience', a courtier said. 'Do you know any remedy for sore eyes? I'm asking because mine hurt tremendously'.
- 'Let me share with you my experience', Nasrudin said. 'At one point I had a toothache, and found no relief until I took them out'.

9. SPIRITUALITY VS. FETISHISM

Much of what contemporary societies take to be 'spirituality' - rituals, talismans, practices, etc – have either been imported from elsewhere, appropriated from earlier forms, or become atrophied, frozen into symbol and peddled as emotional stimuli. Does this sound harsh?

Well, what is often the case is that many once-legitimate spiritual practices have lost their functionality as they have been removed from their original context. When such precise tools are used in a haphazard way they are in danger of becoming incantations at best, or worse as conditioners. When such symbols of 'higher learning' become atrophied – meaning they are no longer adapted to the culture, the time, and the people – they often incite a 'Pavlovian' dog response from the part of the practioners. It is a situation of emotional stimuli creating a wishful and often gratifying automatic reply. Such tools that perhaps once had a very precise function within a specific time and context are easily transferred into fetish totems.

People with a genuine wish to find a path of inner development can find themselves vulnerable to such unconscious, or deliberate, mechanisms. When under deliberate manipulation these emotional icons can lead people into feelings of contentment, maybe even ego-based satisfaction, yet they are not the basis for any real learning.

Spirituality involves the correct employment of precise procedures at specific stages. It is not about excitement; rather, it involves having the right knowledge and information to know what is needed. It is not a road of wishes, but a path of needs and capacity.

Often what we see as cultural forms of 'spirituality' are little other than conditioning techniques. It may be a case that the original impulse has outlived its context and usefulness; or applies to another culture in which it was projected; or that the representatives of it have chosen to 'mix-n-match' various techniques to form something which is appealing and 'holistic'. In all these ways, the real inner function of the teaching has been lost.

Spirituality has become its own marketplace in the modern world; much like the Pardoners of old would sell forgiveness of sins for a price. The responsibility rests with the individual to have a focused and attentive interior filtering mechanism. Are we searching for emotional stimuli and satisfaction? Are we unconsciously wanting to find a community to replace a lack in our social lives? Or do we truly need a precise, functioning process of inner development?

The blind imitation of practices that are often sold to us as spiritual techniques may seem harmless. Yet the misdirection of our needs, and the denial or proper nourishment, can leave a person not only vulnerable to exploitation but also starving of correct nourishment. As it is said:

'The bird which knows not of sweet water has his beak in salt water all the year'

We are living in times where there is both a great deal of empowering energy and awareness exploding, stimulating people to re-evaluate their purpose, direction, and sense of self. At the same time, for many of us, we are living in social environments that are eclectic, consumerist, commercial, and offering exorbitant choice in the belief that more is good. This encourages some people to take, experiment, taste, and dabble with a rag-bag bunch of spiritual goodies in the hope that the resulting fusion will 'do some good'. This, it seems, is a rather complex way for something which begins simply – with the self.

Society offers the entire stimulus we need; there is no need for us to seek out more. Likewise, it is not necessary that we retreat to a cave in order to escape this sensory overload. Any true spiritual endeavour has to be in harmony with one's life. If there is friction, and incompatibility with a normal, balanced life, then we must ask serious questions about the 'spirituality' we are following. There should not be an 'either/or' issue surrounding one's inner development. To work on oneself entails that we also work in life. This is the only way to form a balanced, harmonious, integrated self.

There is a story which tells of a spiritual seeker who after some time comes upon a spiritual master that she feels is genuine and whom she wishes to learn from. The seeker asks the master if he will accept her as a pupil.
'Why do you seek a spiritual path?' asks the teacher.
'Because I wish to be a generous and virtuous person; I wish to be balanced, mindful, caring, and to be in service for humanity. This is my goal' said the seeker.
'Well', replied the teacher, 'these are not goals on the spiritual path; these are the very basics of being human which we need before we even begin to learn'.

Modern society is an 'on-demand' life where we are used to receiving that which we request – a demand-supply conditioning. Because of this we are often at the mercy of the conveyor belt of spiritual-supply. Yet the first steps should begin with a person having a dialogue with themselves. We *sense* a lot of the answers; we have very refined filters within us that can, if we activate them, filter out much of the rubbish that comes our way. Then we need information. What is an active, correct projection of inner transformation in *my culture at this current time?* We don't need to learn Sanskrit to make contact with an active path of development. We only need to lose our conditioning for emotional stimulation, attachment to archaic yet appealing rituals, and our fetishism for talismans and exotic objects. Obsessive tendencies for the garb of 'something higher' are little other than fixation of greed and a form of lower-level indoctrination.

We would do well to consider that the 'spiritual', as we have come to call it, is none other than necessary human nutrition, a daily requirement for living. Yet like eating and breathing, it has to be correctly integrated into our lives without making a song and dance about it. And, of course, not forgetting that,

'If you insist on buying poor food, you must be prepared to dislike it at the serving'

A Tale to Finish: 'The Servant'

A man of spotless reputation had a servant with an ugly face and a character that was impossible. The servant could not receive an order without erupting into a fury; he behaved rudely at the table, and served so poorly, even pushing the guests and letting his employer go unattended. All reprimands to his behaviour left him indifferent and did nothing but aggravate further his negligent attitude and service. At night the house echoed with the sound of the servant's steps and often his breakages. He was even known to throw chickens down the wells, and to place obstacles on the paths where his employer often passed. You could not count on him for anything. Some friends of the employer advised him to get rid of the annoying servant and to employ another in his place.

'But why?' protested the employer smiling. 'I am very grateful to my servant for he has made me a better person. Indeed, I have been taught patience, and with each passing day he is still teaching me. And this gift makes me bear the other difficulties of life.

10. CLIPPED & TRIMMED: THE CONFORMITY OF HUMAN PERCEPTIONS

There is a famous 13th Century Persian poem that tells the story of an old woman whom upon encountering an eagle on her window sill captures it for she has never seen an eagle before. The old woman looks at the strange bird and finally says 'what a funny-looking pigeon'! She then proceeds to clip its wings, straighten the beak, and trim its claws in order to change the appearance to suit her own ideas of what a bird should look like. In this Persian poem we have a mirror of the social conditioning of human thought: altering the unfamiliar or the 'other' to make it acceptable and to fit with present perceptions. In other words, clipped and trimmed in order to fit a 'basic model'.

Throughout our lives we are subjected to indoctrination by a systemic structure of processes and institutions. Within this conditioning environment beliefs almost 'grow' into us. And once they are a part of our socially-constructed self then they are sustained, reinforced, and protected, often unconsciously, by psychological processes of perception. With few rare exceptions all people are brought up within specific culturally-defined environments. A person's dominating social milieu then attempts to offer a variety of accepted socio-cultural norms of thought and behaviour. These may operate through various forms, such as personal faith; religion; science; language and emotions; denial and doubt; happiness and fear; safety and security (identity and belonging); well-being and materialism. Once ingrained, a person is liable to perpetuate such traits believing them to have been obtained through 'free thought'. In the end, we reinforce beliefs that have grown into us, accepting and defending them as our own. So when we say 'I don't believe', what we often in fact mean to say is 'I automatically reject everything my brain is not wired to receive'. The end result is that for most of us we only 'believe' those things that we want to believe, or that fit within our perceptual paradigms and/or experiences. And because we have committed ourselves to such beliefs we then feel it imperative that we support the investment we have made. After all, who likes to be proved wrong?

Not only do we often strive to support our own cherished beliefs but we also end up agreeing with anyone, or anything, that appears to be in agreement with us. For example, notice how we often 'vote' for positive online reviews of things we like, such as a book or a film, yet will ignore, or be unlikely to vote as 'helpful', for the disagreeable reviews. By nature people seek to affirm their structures of beliefs and identity by promoting those activities and experiences that serve to reinforce and validate their own conditioned sets. People rarely seek out those experiences that will actively challenge their perceptions and thus create uncertainty and/or doubt. How many far-right conservatives would spend time reading the latest socialist newsletter? Yet the fixed idea is the enemy of free-thinking.

It is often the case that in order to get along successfully in life it is important to 'fit in' with the crowd; to avoid being a social misfit or an alienated individual. We have to learn how to get along with everyone else. We are, after all, social animals. To attempt to live according to other than the 'norm' of accepted social behaviour and thought has usually led to difficulties and certain degrees of estrangement. It can be said, especially in these current times, that leadership increasingly belongs to the mediocre. And whereas the famous edict of the temple of Delphi stated 'Know

Thyself', such ideals have been eroded, or at least diminished, in successive generations. Such ancient temples have been replaced by the edifices of education, religion, law, and politics. Various individual traits and capacities have become 'authorized' by a select few cultural and/or religious iconic institutions.

Many people may not be fully aware of these processes operating in their lives for the impacts are often gradual rather than sudden. And the process begins early on in a person's life. Through the combined effects of early childhood indoctrination, parental socialization, and educational impacts, we are often successfully conditioned to a specific 'cognitive and perceptual reality'. Once established, these belief sets then form a kind of dependency.

Collective society further serves to reinforce and modify most physical, mental, and emotional behaviour. Thus, the person who becomes deemed most socially valuable is often that person who has demonstrated their ability to adopt (and adapt to) consensual social behaviour and patterns. And when such individual beliefs are never, or rarely, called into question by the social milieu it is easier for a person to forget why they hold them. It should be remembered that beliefs are not facts: a belief is a 'belief' because it is neither knowledge, nor truth. It is a conviction of faith – a thought-form backed by emotional attachment. When examined many beliefs are found to result from indoctrination through various processes, such as emotional language and heavily-laden associations. Examples here include love of country (patriotism; nationalism); love of god; love of family and tribe; love of principles and a sense of moral self. For many of these beliefs a whole group of people – even a nation – may sacrifice much in defence of shared emotional investment. And if a majority of people share the same belief(s) then it is unlikely they will be called into question. To do so could result in a person exhibiting 'abnormal' behaviour.

It can be said that society 'clips and trims' the human mind – our daily consciousness and perceptions – in order to form a general consensus in thinking. This way, a collective mass becomes more manageable – the eagle becomes the pigeon.

These are processes we need to be aware of, so that we can reflect upon our behaviour, social roles, and our attitudes. The world, and our social milieu, is undergoing rapid changes. These are times, therefore, to begin developing our awareness, and to participate fully in the consciousness expansion that awaits us.

A Tale to Finish: 'The Wise Man and The Scientist'

A wise man once asked a scientist – 'Which do you believe: that a primitive creature, over millions of years becomes a man; or that a frog, instantly, becomes a prince?'

The man of science was indignant: 'What kind of person do you take me for?' he asked.
'I know what kind of person you are', said the wise man, 'but I am just trying to establish your opinions on yourself'.

11. HOLDING IT ALL TOGETHER – INTEGRITY & OUR SENSE OF SELF

If you can keep your head when all about you

Are losing theirs and blaming it on you…

… Yours is the Earth and everything that's in it

(Rudyard Kipling – 'If')

The above lines – taken from Rudyard Kipling's poem *If* – serves to remind us that we have gained the Earth, our sense of self, if we are able to 'keep it together'. This loose phrase of 'keeping our head' can be interpreted in various ways. To me it suggests that in these times we need to be more mindful of our actions to stay grounded and balanced – by re-living and connecting with our integrity.

As things around us continue to go awry; plans derailed; and uncertainties magnified; we will be open to increased potentials of frustration. Our comfort zones are also likely to be tested, and we may feel the rise of emotions within us that are waiting to lash out. After all, change is coming at us paradoxically both too fast and too slow. The world around us appears to be shifting fast; yet the real change we wish to see in our lives, and the lives of our loved ones, is for many of us coming too slow. We perhaps have the sensation of being stuck in some dimensional rip-tide. It can be like the sensation of running in a dream – our mind is running, or telling us to run, whilst our legs are moving in slow motion. The sensation of change, and of passing time, is rapid; yet the physical activity of change is reduced to cloud-walking. One of the immediate responses to this is frustration – a sense of being disempowered in a world where everything is seemingly breaking-down.

Another feature of our full information-rich lives is the possibility for 'burnout'. That is, receiving too much information too quickly; trying to process it at an unnatural pace. It is important that we each find a rhythm that is right for us. Recently I heard of a restaurant in the Netherlands that was offering 'Dining in the Dark'; that is, eating your food in pitch black darkness. A person had tried this experience and had written their response – they said it was a revelatory experience. All the senses were alive – the food tasted better than they could imagine. There was no distraction from the actual experience of eating. And this is the important point – no distraction from the self.

We live in a world immersed in sensory and information pollution – and our mainstream media distracts us by design. Entertainment is entrainment – i.e., something which pulls you into its resonance. So amidst busy and rushed lives it is important that we hold everything together. We need to stay focused and ground our energies. Staying grounded is also, for me, about valuing and respecting the self. It is crucial that we do not allow ourselves to become disheartened. Listening or watching the latest mainstream news does not appear to provide us with much hope for the world. More importantly, however, it does not stimulate us into aiming for self-betterment and well-being.

So we need to take a step back, and to observe our lives, and to be at ease with who we are and what we are doing right now. A little gentle reflection should not be about beating ourselves up about perceived faults or lapses. It is about acknowledging where we could make some improvements that might add to where we wish to be with ourselves. And it is about taking back our empowerment from external forces that depress and de-vitalize us. Many external impacts in the world serve to drain us, distract us, depress and dis-empower us. We have to break away from this – and focus on that which uplifts us.

We can, and should, be representative of our ideals. Further, we should aim at normalizing our new ways of thinking and being. This means not being afraid of what 'consensus society' may say about our perceptions and perspectives. We are living through an era where we are called upon to be responsible for bringing these new models of thought, behaviour, and perception to the world. Let us begin by acknowledging our integrity, and stay true to our honour and focused balance. It is important to speak our own understanding – not only to share where we are each at, but also to validate and give strength to our sense of self. The world we exist in often seems like a topsy-turvy, upside-down reality. When we can observe this more objectively we will see that our established systems of ideas are no longer sustainable or for the betterment of humanity. We thus need to acknowledge this, yet without fear or anger. Then when we have processed these truths we can be in a position to talk about them more freely. We can live our new perceptions and perspectives with inner freedom and integrity. We can hold it all together in ourselves – after all, we have within us all the tools we need…

A Tale to Finish: 'Stories'

A reputable wise man always taught his students in the form of parables and stories, which they would listen to with real pleasure. However, the students were also sometimes frustrated because they longed for something 'deeper'. The wise man did not care at all about such objections. His answer would always be the same:

'You still have to understand that the shortest distance between man and the truth is a story.'

12. GOING THE RIGHT WAY IN THE WRONG DIRECTION – THE ART OF THINKING FOR OURSELVES

As celebrated thinker Edward de Bono notes: 'If everyone is going in the same direction, then anyone who is going in a different direction is "wrong". The other direction might be better – but it is still wrong.'

Such is the powerful pull of social conformity. People cannot be fully trusted to say and do what *they think is right* if others around them are all expressing an opposite opinion. This is because the pull towards social conformity, whether conscious or unconscious, is just too strong. The danger here is that in such environments a person is more likely to give away their personal responsibility than act upon it. A group more generally exhibits a lack of responsibility on the part of its members since each person thinks that the overall responsibility can be shared. Since there is no individual blame to be accrued, a person tends to relinquish their own personal responsibility. The result is that each person reinforces the other's inertia. Thus, non-action actually becomes the accepted norm within the group. This inertia is then reinforced and validated, often through personal rationalization, since so much has been invested in the group. To be wrong could inflict much angst upon an individual; it is therefore better to rationalize one's actions as correct. This 'fear of responsibility' is a product of socialization and renders an individual less capable of dealing fluidly with the uncertainties and complexities of a full life. The result is that there is a tendency for people to prefer to submerge themselves within 'the mass'; in other words, to be a silent part of the collective behaviour of the crowd.

And it is this exact type of behaviour which has been repeatedly seized upon by dictators and rogue 'leaders' as a way of gaining authority and legitimacy.

The obedience to authority figures[iv] is a trait that has long been conditioned within an individual. A child from a young age is exposed first to parents, then to school teachers; next to uniformed civil servants; and finally to bosses. An individual is thus trained how to operate, and respond correctly, within the established hierarchical social system. This creates the 'belief' that a person is never totally free in their behaviour; they are almost always under the authority of someone above them who influences events. Paradoxically, many people insist to themselves that they have personal freedom, yet externally they fear exhibiting 'too much' freedom. It has been found that people who conform most are likely to have the least tolerance for uncertainty and ambiguity. Social conformity has thus inculcated a feeling of safety: belonging is a safe haven from where a person is protected. Yet such emotions – of comfort and dis-comfort – are often programs socially conditioned from birth. Much of our 'human behaviour' thus stems from the influences that have shaped us. Yet what is often not realized is the degree to which these social forces are deliberately constructed in order to shape and govern a collective mass. Through a range of various social institutions specific 'knowledge systems' are established and which often serve to supply a consensual and bland array of stimuli. The 'reality' of the situation is that we are subtly coerced to enrol in systems of imitation through which we are trained to memorize information which is passed as knowledge. This information is then reinforced through authoritarian institutions (such as science and 'expertism'), thus making it appear as true.

[iv] See Stanley Milgram's famous experiments on 'Obedience to Authority'.

Various methods in use include how nation states use the 'reality of truth' by releasing *seemingly accurate statistics* that tell of plausible situations. Again, this is the 'expert in the white lab-coat' tactic. For such information to be effective it cannot be too far off the truth; in other words, it must have the appearance of reality. Trade, employment, and financial figures are an example of this. And which members of the general public have the knowledge and/or resources to check and confirm such figures? And who really cares? Those people that do know are usually those that have a vested interest in maintaining the illusion, such as traders and financiers. And once a false (or 'doctored') claim is disseminated and accepted by the public, it becomes established and hard to deconstruct or invalidate.

The 'allowed' liberty of thought within society is generally an expression of free thought within a pre-described system: it does not denote *liberty external to the system*. Examples include the endless array of rock clichés that inspire excitable rebels, such as the raging antics of smashing hotel rooms and throwing televisions out of the window. These all later get morphed into copycat corporate rock PR. In essence, such 'rebels' are allowed, and even encouraged, because their antics sell records. Rebelliousness in these forms is thus another contribution to a consumerist society, albeit through a different lens.

On the other hand, alternative systems of thought are often labelled as subversive and subject to human acts of modification and/or dismissal. In this manner specific physical, mental, and emotional patterns are engrained, reinforced, and modulated by human institutions. Standardization has been exploited as the key to an orderly society of high population. Yet this very method of consensual consciousness and controlled patterns of thought is anathema to the natural need for evolutionary conscious thinking. This step by step drive toward herding people into an increasingly controlled social environment also, by its intrinsic nature, serves to debilitate social change agents.

Social agents of change are those people in every society who are not afraid to break away from the norms of social conditioning and to learn to think for themselves – often against the pull of the masses going the wrong way in the 'right' direction. The awakened individual is now required more than ever, so that conscious thinking and conscious behaviour can co-create a way forward, through the morass that surrounds us, and to light the path toward going the right way in the 'wrong' direction.

A Tale to Finish: 'The Magician'

True oriental tale tells of a very rich magician who had many flocks of sheep. This magician was very greedy. I did not want to hire shepherds, and would not encircle the meadows where they grazed their sheep. The sheep strayed into the forest, fell from the cliffs, were lost, and above all they ran away when they approached the magician, they knew that he wanted their meat and skin. And that sheep did not like. At last the magician found a remedy. Hypnotized sheep and suggested to them first that they were immortal, and do them no harm being skinned, on the contrary this treatment was excellent and enjoyable for them, then the magician suggested to them that he was a good shepherd who dearly loved his flock, he was willing to make all kinds of sacrifices for him, and thirdly, they suggested that if anything bad could happen to them, that would not happen now, in any case, not on that day, and therefore had no need to worry about it. After the magician them into his head that in no way were sheep suggested to some that they were lions, to others that they were eagles, and others that they were men or that they were magicians. Made this the sheep did not cause more discomfort or concern. No more escaping, waiting calmly instead the instant the magician's will shear or slaughter.

13. GRABBING HOLD OF REALITY: ENGAGING ENERGETICALLY WITH OUR LIVES

These days many of us feel as if we are drowning in information. Is our world not awash in a new fabric of communications, most of it digital? Google Chairman Eric Schmidt famously said by 2010-11 the human race was generating as much information every two days than it had from the very beginning of recorded history. This is an incredible amount of information flowing through the veins of our interconnected cultures. The question is: Does this affect our sense of reality?

Yes. How and why?

For the last few centuries there has been rapid cultural development among Western and Northern nations that has simultaneously imposed a linear, logic-based way of thinking. Since our modern sciences have discovered the "split brain" phenomena this has been labeled as a left-brain perspective. A dominant left-brain perspective has helped to form a world in our minds that is separate from us — "out there" — and from this position we felt it appropriate to manipulate and control our environments. This perspective was aptly described by Francis Bacon (the so-called "father of modern science") as the ability, and need, to wrestle Nature's secrets from her. Yet this perspective, which has gained ascendency over the centuries and is now our dominant mindset, also serves to "disenchant" the world — to draw us away into a distant, detached, observer position. Our interaction with the world around us has largely become passive. Subsequently, we have suffered a lessening of the imaginative function: We immerse ourselves less into the world and position ourselves as peeking at the world from the sidelines — or worse, from atop a pedestal.

Our modern Western cultures have validated and strengthened this model so that it has now become the backbone to how most of us passively receive news, information, instructions, etc. As passive observers we are given information in media-acceptable forms and we store, file, and archive this data, yet react little to it. It has become the customary feature of our complex lives and allows us to deal with the increasing impacts, events, and obligations of our lives. However, at the same time it desensitizes us to the depth, emotional value, and profundity of these impacts. In other words, we have divorced and disenchanted ourselves from our vibrant, living environments.

In a data-rich world we are becoming increasingly meaning-poor. Many of us are plagued by a feeling that we don't adequately "touch" our lives, that we only have a sense of passing through. Whilst this has been a satisfactory coping mechanism for dealing with a complex, uncertain, and often unstable world, it does little to engage us mindfully, compassionately, or creatively within our participatory reality. We often view the world as abstract, as if we are separate and isolated from the events and "invisible threads" that bind us all inextricably together. We are starved of reality because we so infrequently experience intimacy and participation with a vibrant world (only at times through what have been termed "peak experiences"). The potential for sensing and engaging with the world has chiefly been replaced by a passive reality that delivers a particular reality set to us — the "consumers." Further, it is a reality set that comes with strict cultural parameters and consensus thinking. It is little wonder that there are people who indulge in extremes — sport, intoxication, brutality, madness — in order to gain a lost sense of vibrancy and aliveness. It is often through experiencing such "euphoric" moments in our lives that we come to realize that our lives are much more interesting and entangled than we give credit for. Unfortunately, many of these epiphanies come from shocks, such as health issues or a tragic sense of loss. The good news, however, is that a reemergence of a participatory relationship with our world may be on the rise.

The incredible amounts of information we are now producing are largely due to millions of people uploading videos to YouTube, sending messages, posting to blogs and websites, and engaging in social networks. The electrical revolution that brought us radio and television taught us how to sit comfortably and receive information passively. The digital revolution that has risen dramatically within only a couple of decades is urging us to immerse ourselves in its flow. We surf the Internet, view and send images to our friends, watch a stream of videos, make our own videos, upload our music experiments, etc. The list of ways to participate is growing each day. Rather than being at the mercy of information, as the old model would have us do, we should turn this relationship around and use the medium for creating and developing our own forms of expression, communication, and voice. We have the opportunity to participate and engage with our sense of cultural reality. We should be searching for information that empowers us, reaching out for like-minded individuals and groups, organizing ourselves and strengthening our sense of self and our values. And then, of course, going out and meeting with our new connections and community (if possible) — or at least going for walks into Nature to ponder on our new creative thoughts.

Human consciousness, our thoughts and state of mind, are entangled with our lives; we can project our conscious thinking, like a laser beam, into the world. We each have the capacity to be aware of the impacts we absorb, consider them, and feel a response rather than give an automatic reaction. By remaining passive and dulled we add nothing to our environment. Yet exciting, vibrant, determined attitudes and energy enlivens the sense of our immediate reality.

To make a lasting change in the years ahead many of us will need to awaken from our passive slumber and grab hold of reality, reaching out to our world, recognizing our creative immersion, and engaging energetically with our lives. We can join the global conversation.

A Tale to Finish: 'The Price of Discouragement'

Once the word spread that the devil was pulling out of his business and was arranging to sell-off all his tools of the trade to the highest bidder. The night of the sale all the tools were arranged for the bidders to view. What a motley crew it was! There were sinister tools of hatred, jealousy, envy, malice, treachery, plus all the other elements of evil. Yet besides these there also was an instrument that seemed harmless, a wedge-shaped instrument that appeared worn out, shabby, and yet was priced so much higher than all others. Someone asked the devil what was the name of such a poor-looking instrument.
'Discouragement' answered the Devil.
'And why is the price so high for such a non-malicious sounding instrument? asked the bidder.
'Because,' spoke the Devil, 'this instrument is more useful to me than any other. I can enter the consciousness of a human being when all other ways fail me and once inside through the discouragement of that person I can do whatever I please. The instrument is worn out because I use it almost everywhere and as very few people know about this I can continue to successfully achieve my goals.'

And as the price of discouragement was so very, very high even today it remains a tool in the property of the Devil.

14. CRISIS IS A STATE OF MIND AND A STATE OF PLACE

For many of us, 2012 has felt like it's been a continued test of endurance as aspects of our lives undergo change and challenge. Ever since the financial markets crashed in September 2008, the globalized world of international media has been telling us that we are all in crisis. The banks, we are told, are failing under incredible debt — despite the trillions of printed paper notes that were offered to float the financial world into Eden. The result is that untold numbers of people are pushed into situations of stress and financial difficulties as credit debt piles up, loans are called in, mortgages cannot be paid, jobs are lost or transferred elsewhere, etc., etc. — and all the time, the media bombards us with a perplexing array of crisis news, domestic trivia, and distracting entertainment (or should it be called "entrainment"?). Naturally, this resolves little except to create and indulge a confused state of mind.

This confusion is constructed in the world around us as our external projections — it is the wants, hopes, greed, security, possessions, etc. that we manifest in our heads to be the objects we reach out for. In other words, we have become accustomed to living in outreach rather than within reach. The consequences of this behavior, and state of mind, are that many of us increasingly live outside of our means. We then normalize this state of affairs; and if we slip away from this we then crave it more. The more we are accustomed to living amongst our external projections of possession and security, the more we are vulnerable to their absence, and their dire financial costs. Crisis is often a state of mind because we live in a world that is not in the present, or perhaps not even possible for us — so we create a world of falsity to supply the needs we either think or are persuaded to think we need.

We feel anger at the banks because they are the new robber barons* who exploited our needs and wishes for credit loans, houses, new cars, modern kitchens, etc. Then the banks were repaid with taxpayer's money when their dubious trading practices turned to mush. Yet by not living with the reality of our present — by living within the allure of our external projections — we became weak and vulnerable to these temptations and promises of betterment. Their crises are now our crises for many of us because we bought into the same game, whether we understood the rules or not. We shared a similar state of mind; and this "mind" was lulled into living in a world where we thought we could have it all at little extra cost. We forgot about paying the ferryman**, his interest at 20 percent above inflation. To continue with this metaphor, it is like being stuck on the river, dependent upon the oars of another. Globalized media loves such an image that shows our collective predicament. Only that it is not a collective crisis.

Global transition is, as it says on the tin, a global phenomenon. Yet "crisis" is about a state of place as well as a state of mind; and this state of place is not universal. Where a person lives dictates, to various influential degrees, how one lives. As a traveler I have lived and traveled through various places that, as an English-born "Westerner," I am socially unaccustomed to. Such places include Turkey, Jordan, Egypt, Morocco, and recently India. When I was driving through Morocco in late 2009 — a year on from the first financial troubles — I noticed how people did not appear to be involved in our crisis, as they had their own daily survival issues to deal with. They were living within the needs and struggles of their everyday present circumstances. Such living was focused upon another kind of world. It was still a world where crises existed, only that such challenges took forms related to their cultural context. These were immediate needs, and still very much within their means.

In my recent journey in India, and the intense experiences it offered me, I felt a similar sense of a people who lived within the present. The notion of a global banking and credit crisis just is not part of the everyday experience for many of the local Indians. And why should it be? After all, this is a context and situation that has largely been constructed and maintained by Western peoples forging a world that exists to provide for us beyond our means. This, like our insatiable exploitation of finite energy sources, is clearly unsustainable. So why are so many of us "addicted" to living in a world that projects beyond our present means? Is our mind-set — our greed for need — insatiable?

Perhaps this is one of the reasons why the world appears to becoming increasingly confusing for so many people. It is becoming a distorted fantasy — like walking through a carnival hall of mirrors where shapes and sizes are oddly and grotesquely distorted. These are the distortions and distractions of our externalized objects — our projections onto the reality-canvas around us. As the safety phrase on the side mirrors of motor vehicles so expressively warn us: Objects in mirror are closer than they appear. This is because the mirrors' convexity, whilst providing a useful field of view, also makes objects appear smaller. Similarly, the mirrors of our perception distort the immediacy of our situation. Instead of living in outreach for a world that is constructed for us seemingly farther away — i.e., beyond our means — we need to be living much more within the present, and thus within sustainable needs and wishes.

The immediacy of our world — the "reality" of our essential life — is closer to us than it appears. Perhaps the side mirrors we manoeuvre our mobile lives by should serve as signs to awaken something more in us.

* A well-known term used in the 19th century that applied to businessmen, and thus businesses, who were viewed as having used questionable practices to amass their wealth.

** A reference to Greek mythology, where Charon or Kharon is the ferryman of Hades.

A Tale to Finish: 'Light'

Song Hu, an Eastern philosopher, told his disciples the following story:

Several men had been imprisoned by mistake in a dark cave where they could see almost nothing. Time passed and one of them managed to light a small torch. But the light it gave was so scarce that even with it hardly anything could be seen. It occurred to the man, however, that he could use the light to help the others make their own torch, and thus by sharing the flame the whole cavern became lit.

One of the disciples asked Hu Song:
'What do we learn by this story?'
Hu Song replied:
'It teaches us that our light remains dark if it is not shared with others. It also tells us that by sharing our light it will not diminish, but on the contrary it will grow.'

PART TWO

15. THE WAY AHEAD: CHANGING OUR INTERNAL NARRATIVES

I have written on the topic of how the decade ahead will be a testing time as it marks the peak clash between two mythologies; or rather, two defining eras. I wrote of how the "old" system, which is still incumbent, reflects a vertical top-down structure that is heavily centralized and based upon the few controlling the "much" and thus the "many." This is not only a way of life but importantly a way of perceiving and thinking that reflects a specific narrative or mythology.

I noted how as we move into a period of increasing energy constraints, contracting economies, and rising costs of living, we will need to rely more on local resources. This model, of economic re-localization and re-distribution, is a forerunner of a new system coming into being. We are heading into a decade where we will literally have to rearrange the very way we think and do business. This is the clash of mythologies, the narratives we live by, and new mythologies rarely come into existence smoothly — new social systems that emerge as a direct contender to the current one create great head-on conflict, such as in social revolutions and the infamous "clash of civilizations."

However, the way ahead will require more profound and holistic change — that is, changing our internal narratives and thus the very way in which we view the world and humanity's place within it. Such previous shifts in mythology have occurred when humanity gradually moved from a flat to a round Earth perspective. That is why I feel the times ahead are of deep significance to us all: It represents a shift in perspective, in human consciousness that will not only influence our physical socio-cultural evolution but the conscious future of humanity. It is likely we are entering a mythological milestone in how we view the way ahead as a collective species.

We are still caught within the polarized debates of "and/or." For example, are we living in a world of scarcity or abundance? For many the answer to this question depends on our own perspective on the world, e.g., are we running out of resources, or is this a fabrication and humanity will always find innovative solutions? My own take on this is that the answer is both, and the solution will come from what emerges as our overall world narrative for the future. I say "our world narrative" not from a western colonial point of view, but from the recognition that we are now living in an inherently-interconnected world. What occurs within our systems — economic, resource, communications, etc. — will impact on a global scale. Our mythologies have now entered a global stage. If the dominating narrative is one of perpetual growth within a constrained control system, then scarcity will become a dominating ideology, which in turn will empower the call for increased loss of civil liberties. Yet if a narrative of distributed networks of empowerment, community, and integral sustainability becomes a dominant narrative, then we can see the abundance available within our human capacity to innovate as well as our environmental potential.

Diverse minds around the world connecting together have the ability to create innovative solutions: the ability to see problems and issues in a new way, often by non-specialists. Innovation is a state of mind, made exponential by our connectivity. For example, now in 2012 the population is around 7 billion, and the number of known Internet users is 23 percent of the population. By 2020 the population is expected to be 7.8 billion, and Internet users are expected to be at 66 percent — that's 3 billion new people plugging in to the global conversation. [1] It is also another 3 billion new minds and problem solvers and innovators! We have to change the global conversation from complaining about problems to solving them: We have to be a part of the growing global conversation.

The immediate future will become less about wants and more about needs. For many people this may involve insecurity and frustrations. "Will the changes affect me?" they may ask. In the short term I feel it is almost inevitable that some of the impacts will be felt on a global scale. Human society has been placed within a juggernaut of converging systems that range from being corrupt and unsustainable to illusionary and damaging. And many of us have been tempted, lulled, pacified and plenty-fied into a way of life that takes us outside of our means.

We now need to "Bring It All Back Home," as Bob Dylan would say. It is now about entering into a new conversation within ourselves. A time to look at our dependencies, tendencies, addictions, and wants, and to change our own internal narrative into one that is self-sustaining, self-nourishing, and life-giving. We need to be less stimulated by external stimulants and more catalyzed by inner choices and self-empowerment.

Part of our mythological clash is about how we choose to exercise human consciousness. There are myriad ways in which modern societies limit consciousness and keep humanity distracted from their inner lives. It would not be far wrong to say that many societies are maintained to preserve incumbent power structures and their rules. Not only do our human environments serve to distract and pacify us, but they also serve to separate us from nature and the living cosmos. However, great change is part of the stimulus to awaken us to culture's imposed limits on perception; our new mythology will need to foster a rise in collective empathy and awareness.

However, this will not occur overnight. Monumental change more often than not comes through periods of gestation. We will need to live, experience, and respond to the challenges ahead in order to bring forth the changes that have been birthed and initially nurtured within our various cultures, and within collective humanity. This could be the birthing of a new narrative for the next stage of human civilization.

[1] Diamandis, P. H. & Kotler, S. (2012) Abundance: The Future Is Better Than You Think. New York: Free Press.

A Tale to Finish: 'The Tree of Happiness'

They say that for many, many years a pilgrim after walking for endless days under the relentless sun of India desired in his heart to rest in the shade of a tree to give him shelter. And so it was that suddenly he saw in the distance a leafy lone tree in the middle of the plain. Covered in sweat and swaying on his weary feet he walked happily into the tree to realize his desire. At last I can rest, he thought, as he made his way through its bushy branches reaching to the ground. What more could you want? Extending over the ground under its shelter he tried to sleep, but the ground was hard and the more the pilgrim ignored it and tried to relax, the harder it seemed the ground became. If only I had a bed, he thought. Suddenly there appeared a stunning bed with spotless silk sheets, fit for a sultan. Luxurious fabrics of Samarkand and the softest fur covered the bed. Without knowing it, the stranger had gone and sat underneath the legendary tree of wishes. The tree was able to realize any wishes expressed under its branches. The pilgrim lay down on the soft bed, relaxing. Oh, I feel so comfortable, but what a shame about the hunger I have, he thought. And before him appeared a splendid table covered with the most delicious food - rich and varied dishes exquisitely prepared and served in the most extravagant of dishes. All these wonders took shape before his astonished eyes. Whatever he had always dreamed of in the lonely nights of his long journey was now before him. The man ate and ate with the fear that such splendour would disappear as suddenly as it had appeared . But the more he ate, the more food appeared. And each new dish was even more tasty and delicious than the last. Finally he said 'I cannot eat anymore' - and at that moment the table with all its wonders vanished into thin air. It's wonderful, he thought, a feeling of happiness filled him. I will not move from here and I will be happy forever. But suddenly, a terrible idea furrowed in his mind: 'Of course this plain is famous for its fierce tigers - what if I discovered a tiger? It would be terrible to die having found such a tree of happiness. It was the thousandth of a fraction of a second, but it was enough. Fulfilling his wish, at that time appeared from nowhere a terrible tiger that devoured the pilgrim. And so, the tree of happiness was alone again, and there it is still; awaiting the arrival of a human being completely of pure heart to reside there not in fear or distrust, but in responsibility and knowledge.

16. ADAPTING TO A WORLD IN REVOLUTION

Human life upon this planet, it seems, is about to undergo a period of transition that will test our capacity to re-adapt and re-emerge on an unprecedented scale. Perhaps it is time to ask ourselves — what type of "revolutions" are we set to face on this "small planet" of ours in the days and years to come? Is humanity collectively heading toward a "near-death experience" as part of the process of transformation and renewal?

Western civilization has created a mindset that, although termed "modern," is one that is overly rational and logical, and which seeks to regulate and control. It has also, unfortunately, succeeded in taking the enchantment away from a mystifying universe. What is clear is that humanity is in the midst of great revolution. Ecological, biological, social and technological systems are now being reorganized because of new developments in energy, communications, and consciousness. Life on planet Earth is entering a phase shift of almost ground-breaking dimensions.

The 21st century has been reached through a growing series of critical thresholds, moving toward current global, social and environmental limits. However, at such thresholds new arrangements are forced into being. Such emergent new arrangements generally occur within the context of interrelated systems, where change in one system/structure has potential to affect many other structures both directly and indirectly. We can say that the revolutions set to occur on this planet will have profound physical — structural, environmental, sociocultural — as well as deep psychological effects.

The media report dramatic changes due to climatic disruption: earthquakes, floods, hurricanes, and volcanic eruptions. We are also witnessing a surge in popular protest, as decades of corrupt or inefficient social systems face their nemesis. Yet within this outward turmoil, more subtle shifts are occurring, such as the transition of the "modern" mind from the industrial-globalisation model toward a life-sustaining, ecological-integral world-view. Western thinking, with its linear notion of history and progress, has robbed us of much enchantment and promise. Many ancient teachings (both spiritual and secular) and many indigenous cultures speak to us of cyclic processes over long periods of historical time, such as the Yuga cycles. These cycles also coincide, or are coexistent with, changes in perception and worldviews. In other words, major social revolutions are accompanied by great shifts in human consciousness. Such shifts also correspond to changes in how the human species understands, and subsequently harnesses, varying forms of energy, upon a progression of discovering ever-finer and less dense/corrosive forms of energy. It is my view that in the years to come, humanity will find itself part of a world "in revolution" in adapting to utilize and make good on new developments in energy, communications, and consciousness.

With the understanding of how finer, more subtle energies work, we may develop a relationship with technology that catalyzes a "re-wiring" of the human psyche. We are already seeing this emerge with the rise of a globally connected empathic mind. This empathic mind, which is born out of increased physical and emotional connectivity, may then be the forerunner to new generations being born with heightened intuitive minds. We might refer to them as "supramental" minds, where intuitive rationality, or heightened common sense, becomes the predominant state of mind. In other words, it is recognizing mindfulness beyond our physical mind, and which encapsulates our growing awareness of our place within a grand, creatively dynamic cosmological order. We can say that it is a mindfulness that is simultaneously vertical (transpersonal) as well as horizontal (integral). Within this transpersonal-integral mindfulness, we can tell ourselves a new story — a story of a living cosmos that is dynamic, creative and which is a continuous flow-through of energy. Within a living universe the whole underlying energetic order is recreated and sustained at each moment, rather than being a lifeless, random mass. Such a shift in perception of the meaning of our cosmos holds profound implications for our understanding and significance of human life. In the coming years, humanity may advance not only in its scientific discoveries of "finer energies," but also in the species development of innate capacities and organs of intuition, empathy and new patterns of thinking. In stepping further along its evolutionary journey, humanity will see that the cosmos not only continuously sustains us but that we are all intimately related to everything that exists. After nearly 4.5 billion years of evolution upon Earth, humans may finally regard themselves as agents of participation within an active, creative cosmos.

In the years to come, humanity will find itself needing to adapt to a world in revolution — in energy, communications, and mind — as our lives are catalyzed into new arrangements and possibilities. We need to be prepared to adapt to new worlds and new world-views, and to perceive our opportunities for a creative future.

A Tale to Finish: 'The Symptoms'

Someone asked a wise man, 'I have heard that humanity is suffering from an ailment which prevents men and women from seeing truth, from knowing themselves. What is the main symptom?

The wise man answered: 'The first symptom is to believe that one is *not* suffering from this illness at all. But when it *really* starts to take hold, the patient may *agree* that he is ill, but now insists that the disease is anything other than actually it is'

17. ALL CHANGE!

Sincerity – with others and with oneself – is one of the few tools we have for gaining our personal freedom.

The value of sincerity is of great importance, now more than ever, as we are surrounded by tales, stories, and gossip, selling us such things as immediate ascension, new 'light bodies', cataclysmic futures, and so on. The reality (or the 'greater truth') of this is more subtle and yet more powerful – it is the ongoing development of human society and the evolution of human consciousness. And it *is* an ongoing work in progress – and it is as simple and as difficult as that...

So we need to be sincere with ourselves; for if we are unable to be, then who can do it for us? This sincerity means acknowledging that no matter how the world *appears* to be, external to us, the real work begins *within* us. And the real work does not arrive with a megaphone announcement; with sign-up fee-paying courses; or with emotionally stimulating/gratifying commercial events. Often, such subtlety of work begins with a silence; a quietness of acknowledgement, attention, concentration, aspiration, and intention.

There will be no great 'end of days' cataclysm at the end of December 2012 – the proof of this is that you are reading these very words *after* December 21st, and no doubt relaxing as you do so. You are still here, aren't you? If the 'greatest event' of the last 26,000 years couldn't shake you off the planet – or out of your skin – then what can? So, I would say we can safely acknowledge that the human species is here to stay. That's the good news.

The passing of 2012 heralds the passing of an important signifier. It signifies that we are entering a period of human history where ignorance can no longer be used as an excuse for inactivity. If anything, the 'Cult of 2012' woke many of us up to the realization that global humanity, and our planetary civilization, is going through a period of transition – and all may not be well at this point. Transition signifies a *re-organization*: a shifting of energies as well as physical systems; world views, perceptions, and lifestyles. And in the midst of such 'spring cleaning', we need to be prepared to be adaptive, flexible, and open for positive developmental change. Why should this be so difficult a concept to grasp? After all, we wouldn't spring clean the house without first taking out or re-arranging the furniture. So why should it be so different for us? We need to re-arrange the furniture of our thinking, beliefs, models, etc, in order to welcome in the new spring arrangements. After this, we can learn to appreciate that things can – and will – get better. First, we just have to deal with the discomfort – and the responsibility – of grand planetary change.

With the responsibility of change comes work – mental, emotional, physical, and spiritual. Since being 'human' means that we are not one 'simple unit' but an integrated, and inter-related, being of many 'bodies', it is crucial that we exist and operate in harmony. For example, we are in dis-harmony if our physical body is in good shape yet our thoughts are erratic and disturbed; or when we think we have balanced thoughts yet our emotional selves are distressed. So the real and true stability is within ourselves: from here real change emerges.

Change upon planet Earth will come through us, the people, and the attitudes, awareness, compassion, sincerity, etc, that we embody and manifest. This is the real stability that can be passed on to those around us: our family, friends, communities, social networks, and so on. As centred, subtle, uplifting energies manifest through more and more people, change will then emerge also within our physical environments. It will not appear overnight. There will be no post-2012 5th-Dimensional paradise. Yet the energies are moving in the right direction, and there are millions of people already feeling this joy of change. We must therefore maintain this intention of great opportunity within change, and not become disheartened. As the infamous phrase puts it: *Illegitimi non carborundum* ("Don't let the bastards grind you down"). Why should we any more put up with 'people-potential-bashing'? Yes, we *do* have the potential to bring forth the unprecedented potential of human energy, creativity, and vision. We therefore need to align ourselves with this potential.

Working in life, as part of life, with infectious energy, motivation, and focused intention will allow us to ride the waves of change rather than be engulfed by them. If you are reading these words now, it is because you are ready for this change and responsibility – and have the capacity to participate. Generational change is just that – it takes place over generations. Sounds like a long time? Well, in evolutionary terms we are zipping along; we are witnessing exponential change that would awe our ancestors, and make our descendents proud. No time to stop now…

The future is right here where you are standing….and as the train conductor used to shout as the train arrived at the end of one line – 'ALL CHANGE!'

Welcome to now, and beyond….the future is going to last a long time…

Society offers the entire stimulus we need; there is no need for us to seek out more.
Likewise, it is not necessary that we retreat to a cave in order to escape this sensory
overload. Any true spiritual endeavour has to be in harmony with one's life.

A Tale to Finish: 'A Different Kind of Disciple'

There was once a Teacher who dressed his disciples in robes of wool, had them carry begging bowls made of sea-coconuts, taught them to whirl in a mystic dance, and intone passages from certain classics.

A philosopher asked him: 'What would you do, as a teacher, if you went to a country where there were no sheep for the wool, where sea-coconuts were unknown, where dancing was considered immoral, and where you were not allowed to teach classics?'

The Teacher immediately answered: 'I would find, in such a place, a quite different kind of disciple'

18. A TIME FOR RE-CALIBRATION

'It is no longer the time to be better, it is the time to be otherwise'
Satprem

For thousands of years humanity has been conquerors. We never thought about opening our borders to entire nations; sharing resources; and grouping together as larger bodies of nations. We built fortresses, great walls, and opened our doors only a crack to let the caravans of exchange slither through to bring luxury goods. And now the whole planet depends on the global exchange of basic necessities and goods. Now the nations of the world are negotiating how we can next shift toward a planetary society. Yet still the old minds prevail; wishing to control this transition by controlling the resources and the consequences. Such old ways, and models, are hoping that the planet can be held in the greedy hands of the few, as it has been until now. Yet this is *not* how things are going to manifest – there are other forces now emerging that wish to assist in this coming together as a planetary society. And these 'other forces' are manifesting through the hearts and minds of the people of the planet. A collective force is arising through humanity that knows – *instinctively feels* – that other ways are now needed if we wish to transition to a new era within sustainable and harmonious limits.

This has never happened before because this point was never reached before. And why humanity never reached this point before is simply because it was not ready. In terms of new ideas and innovative thinking, it's a case of 'we don't yet know the things we don't know!' New ideas come when we are ready to make use of them – it's a process of activating access to information, rather than of significant discovery by accident! This process is difficult to frame in a 'rational' manner; especially since humans like to think of themselves as the central agents of free thought and discovery. That's why we have the syndrome of simultaneous invention/discovery, when suddenly multiple persons happen to have breakthroughs almost at the same time – history is full of such examples. Coincidence? No, it's called re-calibration…

New ideas are simply things we've never thought of…until they arrive. And they will arrive - increasingly so as we move into a time where a different frequency/energy of consciousness is manifesting. And with this will arrive solutions to some of our most pressing problems – especially around energy and resources. The solutions are already there: we are just waiting for the 'Aha' moment! You don't have to believe me; just wait and see. There are those people now who are working hard on the problems; and many young minds are soon going to join the laboratory of human problem solving. Connecting, collaborating, sharing ideas and thoughts – the planetary membrane of consciousness is an active crucible of change and vision.

At each moment of need the human mind accesses solutions to overcome the current pressing problems. Once there were predictions that the world would run out of wood to burn…then we discovered coal. Then came oil and electricity; and once again we are standing on the collective problematic precipice of need – will we leap into the abyss of chaos and breakdown? Or will humankind somehow breakthrough yet again? In times of need, new solutions come into existence. We need to prepare for the structural changes that will accommodate these new developments. Instead of lingering in the stagnant swamps of static thought, we should be acquiring an evolutionary perspective. And this is a perspective of sudden and innovative breakthroughs (what evolutionary biologists refer to as 'punctuated equilibrium')* Just as in our human fossil record, so too in our patterns of human consciousness: long periods of stasis followed by sudden leaps of progress and change. Often in those periods of stasis the seeds of developmental change are planted. The farmer knows that planted seeds do not sprout overnight. Philosophers, artists, creative change agents, amongst others, all work to plant the seeds of evolutionary potential. Then when the right temperature arrives (when the 'cosmic wind blows'), the crops will gain their moment of optimum nutrition and push rapidly through the topsoil to partake of the sun's rays – rapid growth will thus occur.

Our seeds have been planted – and continue to be planted – and the new sun is radiating upon the Earth. These seeds of radical and necessary change are poking through our planetary topsoil, and will be the harvest for the generations to come. We need to start getting excited about this – rather than lingering too long in the despondent waiting rooms of old energy. The cotton (your*self*) needs to get closer to the flame – if you wish to be set alight!

This next phase in human evolution will be focused on internal development – which means forming greater contact with one's self. Of course, there will be impressive technological changes emerging too, yet a balance will need to be found where our technologies work in conjunction with our *real* needs, rather than as crutches to conquer the world 'out there'. It is likely that technologies will become less abrasive and more subtle, even blending into the background of our everyday lives. This is already occurring, as we have shifted from the telegraph cable, to optic fiber, and now to wifi – and this transition into the ethereal will continue**. Yet the real question will concern how we, as individuals within the collective, learn to access our own truths. This will be the essence of the re-calibration needed upon this small yet beautiful planet of ours – and will be the heart of the genuine revolution set to occur.

* http://en.wikipedia.org/wiki/Punctuated_equilibrium
** See my book 'New Revolutions For A Small Planet' for more discussion on this subject.

A Tale to Finish: 'Leaving Holes Behind'

There was a boy with a bad temper. One day his father gave him a bag of nails and told him that every time he loses his cool he should drive a nail into the fence behind their home. The first day the boy drove 37 nails into the fence. Little by little he became calmer because he discovered it was much easier to control his temper than to drive nails into the fence. Finally the day came when the boy did not lose his cool at all and told his father this. The father then suggested that for every day that the boy controlled his temper he should take out a nail from the fence.

The days passed and the boy was finally able to tell his father that he had removed all the nails from the fence. Then the father took his son to the fence.

- 'Look son, you did well but look at all the holes in the fence. When you say or do something with anger you leave a scar, like this hole, and no matter how often you ask for forgiveness, the hurt is there, and physical injury is as serious as a verbal one.
Friends are real gems who should be appreciated; they will smile and encourage you to improve; they listen to you; share a word of encouragement; and always have their hearts open to receive you. Happiness does not always consist of doing what you want, if you do not always want what you do.

19. THE AKASHIC AGE: A NEW DAWN RISING

Our species – *homo sapiens sapiens* - has been on a historically long evolutionary journey prior to arriving at the point where we now find ourselves. We have finally arrived at a world that is complex and interdependent; thus, making the right type of choices is hard but entirely critical. Whereas previously we perhaps had the 'luxury' of making choices that affected only our immediate well-being and intimate locale, we must now think and act in a global context and with a long time-horizon. To be clear on this matter - we are approaching a crucial epoch that will serve as a cusp in our species development. We are leaving behind one age and entering the next. The epoch we are leaving behind is the modern age. The epoch we are about to shift into has been given many names – digital, new age, etc – yet has so far suffered from lack of true and genuine foresight. Partly to blame is the human inclination to think in linear trends, and thus to imagine the future as a logical extension of the past. But Nature – and evolution – doesn't work that way, and never has. Rather, there are long periods of static where there is relatively little change; then the onset of a *tipping point* where a crucial – and critical – leap occurs. What is on the other side of this 'leap' is often unexpected, because it does not conform to the older patterns of thinking, perception, and behavior. These periods of criticality are moments of opportunity, when catalysts for change exert a greater than normal influence on the outcome of events. It is a transition period where the anomalies begin to manifest at the periphery and witness the implosion of the incumbent status quo. At these points ideas, institutions, and beliefs tend to outlive their usefulness.

Yet there are guiding principles that can help us, if not to predict the future, then at least to foresee alternative models of the future. For example, the systems sciences can enable us to do just that – to view underlying trends that flow through the veins of biological as well as socio-cultural evolution. To put it simply, the systems that arise and evolve– corporeal, environmental, social systems – veer toward ever increasing size and complexity. We are embedded within systems that seek growth through increasingly high complexity and numerous levels of organization, greater dynamism, and closer interaction and more delicate balance with the environment. Therefore, we can foresee a future that is highly connected and integrated; more decentralized; technologically advanced; more sustainably balanced; and non-locally interconnected. By 'non-locally' interconnected it is meant that physical objects/bodies – as well as human consciousness – maintain effective forms of relationships at a distance. The term 'non-locality' comes from the quantum sciences, which are central to offering the world a new paradigm of inclusive, intrinsic, and immediate oneness. It is a paradigm that helps to explain our inherent energetic connectivity, which forms a basis for the continued physical proximity and connectivity that develops in the world. This emerging new paradigm is the key in understanding what I refer to as the Akashic Age.

Is this still far-fetched? Well, we may find that it is entirely within the domain of science and scientific validity. The new sciences, based on the physics of the quantum, show us that this wonderful world of ours is a gigantic macro-level quantum system where all things, and not only super-small quantum things, are 'entangled' - instantly interconnected. This realization has the potential to change our values and aspirations, and the very way we think and act in the world. It may hold the key to our own well-being, and the survival of the whole of the human community. Indeed, a sustainable global civilization *could* come about, and if it did, its advent would be in tune with the overall trend in the evolution of complex systems. Thus, it is entirely possible that a positive unfolding of the socio-cultural evolutionary trend could occur. However, bringing it about depends on us: on what we do today, and in the years ahead.

We are at the 'dawn' of the Akashic Age because there remain a number of dilemmas and critical thresholds that we face, and which will unfold over the next decade(s). Yet it is imperative to see these as potential opportunities as well as potential disruptors. To a large degree, these opportunities/disruptors will be based on issues of energy, communications, and consciousness. That is, energy in how we utilize our resources; communications in how we connect and collaborate; and consciousness in our patterns of thinking and inner coherence.

The path to an Akashic Age is a time of transition where our crises become our catalysts; and our disruptions become our driving force. In such times when there are major fluctuations in worldviews, values, and beliefs; we are compelled to re-organize how we think and do things. Such moments are ripe for new models to emerge. These new models are likely to first emerge on the periphery – as 'anomalies' – before creeping toward the centre to overwhelm and out-do the centralized and self-centered old systems. These new models also display a marked difference in that they operate through de-centralized and distributed channels, as horizontal networks of connection and collaboration; rather than as the vertical, top-down hierarchical systems of control in the old systems. Whereas previous models of civilization continued to grow through increasing centralization and hierarchy, they have now entered history with a death-cry and the onset of final collapse.

For our planet to have any future that is not only sustainable but also fosters human developmental growth and well-being, we need an Akashic Age that promotes the natural integrated flow of living systems. Such an age would encourage social as well as self-actualization, and plants the seeds of a new culture that respects and honors the Earth and her diverse peoples. The Akashic Age represents a new stage in human consciousness, a stage that allows humanity to rise and overcome all challenges it confronts. It is up to us to allow the possibility that such an Age may be more than just a possible future. It can be OUR future, if we truly want it to be.

A Tale to Finish: 'The Problem'

A great teacher and his guardian divided the administration of a grand monastery. One day, the guard was killed and the teacher was left with the dilemma of replacing him. The grand master then gathered all the disciples together in order to choose who would have the honor of working directly with him.

'I will present a problem', said the teacher, 'and whoever resolves it first shall be my new guardian of the temple.

After finishing his short speech, he placed a stool in the center of the room. Above the stool he placed a vase of fine porcelain of great value, with a beautiful red rose inside.

'This is the problem', said the teacher.

The disciples looked perplexed and entranced by what they saw: the sophisticated designs and rare porcelain; the freshness and elegance of the flower, its beauty and scent. But ... What did it all represent? What to do? What was the riddle? And the solution? After a few minutes, one of the disciples got up, looked at the teacher, looked at his colleagues and, walking up the vase, threw it to the ground smashing it.

'You are the new guard', said the teacher.

After the student returned to his place, the great teacher explained:

'I was very clear, I said that you were in front of a problem - and a problem is a problem. Even if it takes the form of a very expensive porcelain vase; a beautiful love that has no meaning; or a road that needs to be abandoned – we must insist on overcoming a problem because it is a necessary thing to do. No matter how beautiful or fascinating the problem appears to be, there is only one way to deal with problems – by attacking them head on.

20. A REVOLUTION IN HUMAN CONSCIOUSNESS

Recent decades have seen a great rise in ecological awareness and the perspective of living systems. Many of us are now relating on a personal and conscious level to the interconnectedness and interaction between humans, nature, and environment. However, this new paradigm of thought should not be restricted only to a material level of connectivity but also needs to embrace the nonmaterial levels of the human psyche and consciousness. The world of the inner self is increasingly opening up and being explored through transpersonal sciences, self-realization, and individual self-actualization. Through our various cultures we are developing the language, the skills, and the perceptions to sense and articulate our personal, revelatory experiences. The once shamanic realm of extra-sensory contact is becoming more normalized as we deal with a physical reality more accustomed to shifting perceptual paradigms. For example, our new scientific discoveries are explaining and validating nonlocal realities of connection and energetic entanglement. We are now learning that extended fields of conscious information and communication exist between individuals and groups as a medium of coherence that may further entangle humanity into a collective 'grand family'.

From infancy, to adolescence, and to adulthood, the distinction between inside and outside, objective and subjective, has always been a transient, undefined boundary. Our cultural parameters – our social conditioning - has sought to crystallize these fluctuating borders. However, today there are increasing numbers of people who are beginning to perceive the presence of subtle energy fields, whether around their bodies, around the bodies of others, or in the environment. The interest in metaphysical subjects these days has exploded, with a new language and mind-set emerging to deal with these increasingly common phenomena. It is now becoming acceptable to speak in terms of reiki, chi, pranic energy, and even in terms of quantum energy. Not only are many cultures and societies learning to deal with a new wave of technological social networks – with Facebook, Twitter and YouTube – but also with an increase in energetic awareness of human connections and an extended mind.

In a sense, humanity is learning how to be a more interactive collective family. Never before in our known history of the species have we come to a point where we are sailing in the same ship, afflicted by the same concerns, and affected similarly by a range of global impacts. When a poor harvest affects the growing areas in China, Australia and the US, for example, the world food distribution networks reverberate across all nations. When a virus pandemic spreads out from a crowded poultry market somewhere in South Asia, it affects all nations without reserve, grinding transport hubs to a slow crawl. This realization is now dawning on the peoples of the world: that we are already a part of the field fabric of a collective family.

This realization is being keenly felt, too, by the younger generations: generations that are growing up accustomed to having a network of hundreds, perhaps thousands, of virtual friends across the globe; sharing intimacy and empathy with an international social group of like-minded people. This younger generation is manifesting, whether conscious of it or not, non-local (i.e., field effect) relationships. These types of relationships support the individual whilst at the same time strengthening networks that form part of a unified – yet diversified - whole. It is a form that mimics the quantum state of the particle and the wave: each person is clearly isolated from another by physical space, yet at the same time is entangled in a conscious space of connectivity and communication. In other words, each is participating in a field-view of reality; a reality that creates an extended set of responsibilities as one's thoughts and actions can reverberate much further afield.

The human individual has the capacity to be consciously aware of the effect of thoughts and actions upon others: to consider their reactions, to reflect upon their thoughts, and to decide whether to behave differently. In other words, each person has the ability to develop consciously, and with awareness, from each interaction with both external and internal impacts and experiences. Sociologists have, up until now, been mainly focused on human identity as characterized by individualization. This is especially so in 'modern/postmodern' society, where each person is categorized as acting with autonomy; with a self-promoting 'service-to-self' attitude. Yet this is a myopic vision on two counts: on one hand it neglects that humans are social animals and instinctively seek groupings and attachments; and on the other it fails to recognize that the nature of human consciousness also undergoes change along with socio-cultural revolutions. It may be very likely that a form of consciousness will emerge, at first on the periphery, perhaps with the younger generations, that will then seep into the core of all our future societies.

Social scientist Duane Elgin considers the following to represent the shifting states of human consciousness over historical epochs:

1 Contracted consciousness (early humans)

2 Sensing consciousness (hunter-gatherers)

3 Feeling consciousness (agrarian era)

4 Thinking consciousness (scientific-industrial era)

5 Observing consciousness (communications era)

6 Compassionate consciousness (bonding era)

7 Flow consciousness (surpassing era)

Using this scale it would appear that global humanity is now shifting from the communications era (observing consciousness) into the bonding era (compassionate consciousness). We could perhaps shift the emphasis of the bonding era from 'compassionate consciousness' to 'empathic consciousness'. This transition from exhibiting an observing consciousness towards manifesting a compassionate/empathic consciousness represents the move from the 'old-mind' energies that brought us to the current state of a globalized world, toward the 'new-mind' energies that will bond our diverse world together in coherence and balance.

Likewise, the surpassing era could be renamed as the planetary era and represent not only the rise of non-local field awareness but also the scientific understanding of the subtle forces of the universe. This era of 'flow consciousness' would fit well with the next stage in the evolution of human consciousness that appears to be displaying elements of a transpersonal-integral nature.

None of these states, however, are completely separate from each other; rather, they overlap and merge as one era fades and converges into the next. Usually, the new era, or paradigm, emerges initially at the periphery until it reaches a tipping point where it becomes the new accepted paradigm. Already, flow consciousness is slowly percolating into our human perceptions as more and more people embrace and instinctively trust non-material information. The dominant materialist worldview is under increased scrutiny as more people awaken to the possibility that their intuitive glimpses – dreams, visions, premonitions, etc. – are trusted sources of information that originate from alternative senses. Through seeking practices that were once considered metaphysical (or even strange) - such as spiritual practices, yoga, meditation, psychotherapy, transpersonal therapy, bio-feedback, altered states of consciousness, and more - people are now accessing a once-hidden, or rather neglected, realm of senses and self-knowing.

As more people realize that the subtle realm of extrasensory information is not a figment of fantasy or delusion, but in fact has a scientific foundation, these states of consciousness will become more widely accepted, credible, and sought. Also, we may find that our orthodox social institutions will begin to incorporate them into the status quo of consensus reality and experience. Whilst the transition may not appear to unfold suddenly to us, within evolutionary terms it will be a revolution. And participating in this unfolding consciousness revolution will be both a personal growth imperative as well as a collective human responsibility.

A Tale to Finish: 'The Fox & The Lion'

A man once saw an injured fox and wondered how she would manage to be so well fed. The man decided to follow the fox to find out and after a short time he saw that the fox had settled near a place where a lion brought his prey. After eating, the lion went away, and the fox ate the remains. So the man decided to let fate serve him in the same way. He sat on the street and waited. Yet all that happened was that he became increasingly weak and hungry, and nobody was interested in him.

In the due course of time the man heard a voice, as if from nowhere, say:

'Why do you have to behave like an injured fox? Why can you not behave like a lion so that others can benefit from what you leave?'

21. TOWARD UNITY CONSCIOUSNESS

As humanity enters a time of social and cultural change, of altered perceptions and challenges to our worldview, we are almost certainly going to be coerced into altered modes of consciousness. In other words, in order to readapt and to survive the breakdowns of the old mind/old energy our collective worldview will need to shift to an ecological and more intuitive mode. This is likely to also involve a shift towards a more direct mode of perception (a form of *gnosis*).

Whilst these two modes of the cognitive and the intuitive may operate simultaneously, and have been known as the objective and subjective modes of knowledge, our modern societies have largely prioritized the objective interpretation and dismissed the subjective as the imaginative realm. This 'imaginative' realm of subjective experience is most active when we are children, although quickly diminishes as our social institutions and peer conditioning intervene to install a consensus social reality. Yet the direct-intuitive mode of perception is an evolutionary trait that is still with us, and which may be beginning to manifest in the new generations of intuitive children.

It is possible that the non-linear connections over space and time (e.g., global communications) between our species will be one of the aspects that will become more dominant in the years ahead. The Internet gives us a physical representation of these new spatial and temporal relations. The direct-intuitive mode will surely be a more effective means of comprehension and understanding as it bypasses the sensory organs that usually filter information. Also, the direct-intuitive mode operates outside of linguistic barriers, and allows access to a collective, shared participatory consciousness.

The 'participatory consciousness' view of reality reflects an intuitive mode of perception that relates with the new energies of connection, communication, collaboration, and compassion. This understanding is now being validated by the latest findings in the quantum sciences, notably quantum mechanics and biophysics. Our 'everyday consciousness' of the local view of the universe is largely unprepared for the realms of non-ordinary reality. In our present era, and in Western civilization especially, the direct-intuitive mode of perception (subjective experience) has not been encouraged, or even recognized, and so has atrophied and become the province of the esoteric sciences. It may be because the 'rational objective' view of reality allows for an increased sense of individualism, favored by the ego, and as such is the sphere of power, money, competition and greed. The direct-intuitive mode of reality, however, embraces cooperation, connection, correspondence and compassion. And it seems that we are already witnessing the emergence of this new feature of human consciousness.

The notion of the direct-intuitive perception of reality could be a step toward the next stage in human evolution – the evolutionary development of what may be termed *quantum consciousness* that is the basis for the collective mind of the human species. Various mystics and consciousness researchers have alluded to this by a variety of names; they range from cosmic consciousness, super-consciousness, transpersonal consciousness, integral consciousness, and more. All these descriptions share a common theme; namely, the rise of intuition, empathy, greater connectivity to the world and to people, and a sense of 'knowing' about what each given situation demands.

The emergence of a form of direct-intuitive consciousness would likely instil within each person a sense of the greater cosmic whole; the realization that humanity exists and evolves within a universe of intelligence and meaning - a living universe. This would serve to impart within humanity a more profound, and acknowledged, spiritual impulse. This could then lead to increased intuitive faculties and extrasensory phenomena not only becoming an implicate part of our lives but also opening up access to greater creativity and inventive capacities for participating and designing our way ahead in the world. The rise of these attributes within a small percentage of people, initially, could eventually lead to a critical mass that would tip human consciousness into a new perceptual paradigm and worldview.

Forms and intimations of these new consciousness patterns are already emerging in the world, but as yet they have not become a part of mainstream research. Such evolutionary 'mutational' agents include visionaries, mystics, artists, psychics, intuitives, spiritual teachers, and what have been termed the new 'Indigo Children'. As Dr Richard Bucke stated in his classic work on the subject, *Cosmic Consciousness* (1901), the early signs of this new evolutionary development have been appearing within humankind for some time.

This suggests that there have been attempts to help prepare the 'mental soil' for a new consciousness to slowly seed and grow. On the whole, social/cultural/material forces are slow to react to the need for an evolving paradigm of human consciousness. Yet this is nothing new, as throughout recorded history many individuals who have felt an awareness of the need to seed an evolutionary impulse into social life have been caught up in revolutionary events or been involved in social-cultural upheavals.

Perhaps it can be speculated here that in order for continued cultural and species growth there are particular periods of human history wherein humanity becomes ready, or in need of, the activation of particular faculties or evolutionary traits. It may be that during this transition period humanity will adapt, or be forced to develop, new creative and inspired aspects of consciousness. However, as in all paradigm shifts, old energies inevitably must give way to the new, and it may only be a matter of time before new generations move into evolving consciousness and its physical expressions. It is thus critical that an understanding of spiritual matters begins to permeate our everyday lives as a counterbalance to our social materialism.

We are in need of unity, not uniformity

We are not looking for 'awesome' consciousness – such as Nietzsche's super-man. Rather, it is a *different* consciousness, and thus a different type of human, that is likely to emerge. That is, not 'more of the same' - only more of those who are manifesting the new consciousness. As in the words of Satprem: *'It is no longer the time to be better, it is the time to be otherwise.'*

The human mind is like a large pot that can contain the same water for all – a unified sharing. The road to unity – with diversity – begins with the need for harmony. With the energy of harmony we can make the water still and calm. Through harmony we can celebrate our differences with tolerance, respect, patience; without judgment, gossip, or ill-feeling towards others. With harmony we can begin to come together; to work together and collaborate – to build trust and vision. First we need to smooth out the energies of disturbance that exist in the world. This begins with harmony at home – within oneself, family, partners, friends, acquaintances and contacts. From here the energy that is harmonized can reach out, seep out, into the world and resonate with others.

In these years ahead it will be to our benefit if we try to develop a consciousness that is both open to spiritual impulses whilst simultaneously aware and attentive to the needs of our communities and cultures. It is essential that we revitalize our collective sense of well-being and connectedness – our togetherness and empathy – as part of our shared human journey. It is possible that emerging glimpses of a shared participatory consciousness will allow humanity access to an unimaginable creative cosmos of information and inspiration. This would then open up new vistas of creative intelligence that could be the forerunners to the next stage along our human evolutionary journey.

A Tale to Finish: 'The Flower'

One day a grand Sultan received the visit of a dervish, who was said to have no rival in wisdom. So the Sultan decided to propose an enigma for the dervish. He took the dervish to a room in his palace where the Sultan's most gifted artisans had filled the room with so many wondrous artificial flowers. The room appeared to be like a miraculous meadow, where the many multitudes of flowers gave off their specially crafted aromas and seemed to gently sway under the influence of an unknown breeze.

- Here is my enigma - said the Sultan - one of these flowers, only one, is a real flower. Can you show me which one it is?

The dervish attentively looked around with a face showing the most delicate lines of concentration. Finally the dervish answered calmly:
- I cannot point to the real flower. However, since it is hot in here would one of your servants kindly open a window?

The Sultan ordered that a window be opened.

- This is the true flower - the dervish said a moment later. As soon as he had spoken a bee entered through the window and landed on the only real flower.

It is said that it is always difficult to be a dervish - this story tells us it is even more difficult to be a bee. However, the most difficult, at all times, is to be the flower.

22. RE-CALIBRATION: A TIME FOR WELL-BEING

We are no longer in the 'waiting room' period, wondering when things are going to start changing. Every part of our lives is already in flux, and always has been. It is erroneous to think of human life as being static – it never has been. Life often appears more static at times when there is relative social stability and, importantly, stability in cultural ideas and mass consciousness. However, all these aspects – social structures/institutions, cultural norms, thinking patterns – have entered a period of profound change and re-calibration. For the past few years many people have been feeling and sensing this re-organization ('coming apart-coming together'); yet for the most part have been observers to these shifts. Many of us were waiting for the grand 'tipping points' or explosive moments to occur – and they never arrived. This is because the change we are going to see will infiltrate our lives in order to affect transformation from within…and over time. If everything collapsed in one moment it would be catastrophic for human life on this planet. Rather than exploding like a time-bomb, we are expected to re-adjust to new contexts on this planet like a chameleon changes its skin color to blend into a new environment. Yet such a re-calibration needs to be done consciously, and in harmony with everyday life. That is why the 'waiting room' period is over – it is time for Work.

The period we are experiencing now may also prove to be disruptive in terms of health, as there are many chaotic elements surrounding life that are impacting us. These 'disruptive frequencies' are likely to cause dis-ease and illness within many people on the planet around this time. Although this is a general statement to make, I feel that many of us here now will have experiences of people around us that are taken ill. For some, these illnesses will be more serious than others. Yet the sense is that we are now compelled to de-toxify ourselves, and to be re-aligned with an energy that is moving forward and impels change upon us. A new energy is coming into the planet which is *moving* differently – it is an energy that manifests a different *gravitas*.

The new energy is more fluid and adaptable; is lighter and more rapid. As a result we need to be more responsive as the energy is moving like a web of light – it manifests through relationships and networks, and is more subtle yet distinctly active in our daily lives. It is an energy that needs to be *lived* and *handled*. As such, we will need to re-calibrate our physical and emotional well-being so that we can resonate in harmony with this fluid, interpenetrating living energy that is ever rising to the surface of human and planetary affairs.

It will be increasingly important that we seek out those aspects in our lives that promote and nurture our well-being. We live in a culture that promotes sickness and illness as a normal state. In fact, businesses and corporations build illness into their business plans. Most businesses calculate that their employees will take $x\%$ of sick leave days per year, which in turn affects $y\%$ of profit yields. So this difference is often calculated into yearly profit plans. People are expected to get ill various times throughout the year; and if we miss a few days from work with an 'illness excuse' nobody thinks anything of it. Sometimes we are expected to be ill in order to be a healthy person! And then there is the global pharmaceutical industry which really should be renamed as the 'Illness Industry' with the motto 'To cure you we must first kill you'. This expectation and 'normalization' of illness is a mis-alignment and focuses our attention in the wrong direction. Our daily life should, as far as is possible, be part of the human 'Wellness Industry' that centers on harmony with oneself in order to have harmony with others and daily life. True harmony is about coherence and fitting in with all aspects of our daily life.

No person can escape what they think, say, do, or feel – it becomes woven into the tapestry that regulates our sense of self and our well-being. It thus makes sense that we are mindful over how we manifest our expressions of though-action-feeling. Everything is woven out of the threads of human consciousness. In time new awareness, new consciousness and thinking paradigms and new models will align themselves into co-creating a new way of living and being that will replace our older models and ways. It is a wonderfully cohesive and organic process. In fact, it is only human stubbornness that makes it a prickly and sometimes uncomfortable experience! We are often our own barriers to self-development in that we are already calibrated with a vast array of conditioning. We carry around with us a weighty mix of opinions, beliefs, judgments and criticisms – like a poor donkey with a heavy load! When was the last time we asked ourselves the question: "Do our thinking patterns (belief systems) bring us emotional, physical, spiritual imbalance and dis-ease?"

Part of the re-calibration toward human well-being is the necessary work we must undertake so that we can be better aligned with a new world and a new energy that is penetrating our reality now and in the years to come. Re-calibration is about knowing when to say 'NO' to those things that no longer nurture our well-being and sense of self; and to resonate, and consciously attract, those elements in life that are beneficial and will support our mental, physical, emotional, and spiritual well-being. It's time to get on track: to know what is best for us, and to gravitate toward those things in life that nourish our well-being. Our re-calibration now takes place in the marketplace of life.

'Tell me: if the hidden treasure is now on display at the bazaar, shouldn't the Gnostic leave his cell and wander forth?" **Gharib Nawaz**

A Tale to Finish: 'The Calf's Path'

One day, a calf had to cross a virgin forest to return to its pasture. Being an irrational animal it created a winding path that curved up and down the hills.

The next day, a dog that was passing by the same trail used the same path to navigate the forest. Next came a sheep which seeing the open space started also along the path, upon which many other sheep followed, as was their sheep nature.

Later, men arrived and began to use this very same path as it weaved in and out, right and left, up and down - complaining and cursing as they went. Yet they did nothing to create a new alternative.

After much use, the trail eventually became a broader way where the poor tired animals under heavy loads were forced to travel the distance in three hours that could have been done in thirty minutes if they had not followed the path originally created by the irrational calf. Many years passed and the road became the main street of a town and, finally, the main street of a city. Yet everyone complained of the traffic as it was the worst possible way.

Meanwhile, the old and wise forest laughed, seeing that men acted blindly in following a path that is already open without ever wondering if that's the best choice.

23. THE LIVING WORK ~ RE-CONNECTING WITH THE FEMININE ENERGY

For a number of years many of us have been talking about the new consciousness emerging – or rather unfolding – over these years. However, the focus so far has been largely upon the consequences of this new 'energy consciousness' rather than on the qualities of the incoming energy itself. For example, I have discussed how this unfolding energy is shifting human social systems – *how we do things* – from a vertical to a horizontal pattern. That is, from hierarchical structures to networks and connectivity. Recently though I have been turning my focus upon the shift from the older values of **Competition ~ Conflict ~ Control ~ Censorship –** to the new values of **Connection ~ Communication ~ Consciousness ~ Compassion.** So what does this tell us about the new energy unfolding upon the Earth and permeating through humankind?

It tells us that the new energy is relational, not mechanical nor isolated. That is, it does not thrive upon self-sufficiency but upon contact and receptivity through others. It flows and works through organic, non-hierarchical systems: through networks and webs – through the threads that weave the wholeness of life together. This energy no longer thrives through top-down power structures; it no longer seeks one-to-one encounters – it flows like life itself.

Realizing this reminds me of how during the 16th-18th centuries Europe witnessed the witch hunts that put to death tens of thousands of women accused of being witches. The executioners were predominantly men who represented the church hierarchy. This was a masculine energy that for millennia had been parading and swinging its heavy paternal axe of hierarchical power. And the witches were yet another manifestation of female power that the ecclesiastical authorities could not tolerate. Many of these so-called 'witches' were women who knew about herbs; how to heal and nurture people; and how to listen to nature (others were purely innocent victims of gossip!). Yet one of the things they were accused of, amongst many, was of gathering and conspiring together. How did they gather? They gathered in witches' *circles*... Here we have the energy of hierarchical power against the energy of circular, relational flow. It was the fear of a 'magical presence' within the female that fuelled a deep repression over the centuries that has become a pattern – the denial of the subtle, the integral, the nurturing.

Our modern educational systems and institutions have also been in great denial of this integral energy and thus geared for the masculine mind. Our school curriculums were initially created by men so that young minds could be shaped to think in masculine ways; in other words, conditioned to manifest a masculine energy and consciousness. The feminine relational understanding was pushed aside to be replaced with the linear thinking patterns of the masculine mind. For some it was like trying to fit square shapes through a round hole – or through a circle where water should flow. Yet the insistence upon the masculine mind has intimidated the feminine consciousness. It has pushed it into retreat, undermining the true expression of this much needed energy. The over-bearing masculine mind has insisted that women mimic its attributes, play its games, and thus suppress its own presence.

The masculine consciousness is also behind the image of a divinity that belongs to the heavens. From 'up there', the dominance of a masculine god has made it permissible to develop a science that would 'torture

Nature's secrets from her[v] and thus take control over our environment. In this way humanity has succeeded in largely divorcing itself from the sacred interdependence of creation. Our current commercialized material 'modern' cultures reflect this sense of alienation and individualism represented by the separateness of a masculine god. Humanity no longer understands – or remembers? – that it is an essential integral part of the great wholeness of life. As a species and as a civilization we have arrived at the point where this dominant masculine consciousness can proceed no further alone...if we are to have a viable long-term future upon this planet. It is at this critical stage that there are signs that the energy is now turning; or rather, it is shifting as new permutations are emerging in the world. It is the feminine energy that seeks the flow, the networks, the connectivity...and it is coming around again.

Traditionally feminine consciousness has honoured all life as sacred; as such it manifests a reciprocity that reflects the inter-connectedness of life. Relationships with others become more important than the isolation of the self. The value of the community stands above the pursuit of individual achievement. The process of *being* takes precedence over the need to achieve through *doing*. And multi-tasking is more appropriate than being fixated upon a single end goal. Now which aspects sound more suitable for a globally inter-connected world that communicates through multiple networks simultaneously? So let us ask: which energy and consciousness may be more aligned with the way the world is re-structuring and re-calibrating itself?

---

[v] A reference to Sir Francis Bacon whose scientific method became the foundations for modern empirical science.

Welcome to the 21st century where global communications have opened up the world to the masses. The Internet, and how it operates, can be seen to represent aspects of the feminine energy and consciousness. The Internet connects people into multiple relations; it is responsible for nurturing rising empathy across the world; and shares stories, needs, and reaches out to many people and communities. Sure, it has its negative aspects too – yet that is the nature of a world of duality. Focusing on the constructive changes we see how individuals, communities, businesses, systems, etc, are re-calibrating across the world to be aligned with the new interconnectivity that symbolizes the world we are moving into. The current manifestation of feminine energy needs new pathways in order to enter and permeate our material world. Our physical structures are responding to this call by shifting from top-down structures to distributed and decentralized networks. Yet we also need to assist this re-calibration by changing the ways we think as altering the ways we *do* things will not gain permanence until human consciousness changes. In order to allow the new incoming consciousness to flow into the world we need to allow it to flow *through us*. That is, to manifest the qualities, attitudes, and our presence *in the world* that will most effectively receive, hold, and transmit this consciousness. This responsibility is our living work now.

The days of working in seclusion are over – the new energy does not support monasticism. The flow must connect between inner and outer events and states. The new living work is not a monastic endeavour but must exist within the active folds, avenues, and marketplace of life. High castles, priestly enclaves, guru sanctuaries, etc, are edifices of the past where a different energy was contained. The new energy – which shows aspects of the feminine consciousness – is a nurturing one that comes alive *through people*. Whereas the previous masculine-orientated energy wished to stand visible and powerful like the tower on the hill; the feminine energy is more subtle, and flows through the appreciative touch, the supportive word, the reassuring glance that filters through each one of us as we wend our way through life. That which was once hidden can now be made manifest through us – this is the *living work*.

Love has no power structures or hierarchies; it is not for sale. It passes freely from heart to heart along the web of oneness that connects us all.
Llewellyn Vaughan-Lee

A Tale to Finish: 'Importance'

Nasrudin began chatting with some friends. One of them suddenly asked about his wife:
- Ah, my wife! She stays at home.
- What does she do? - Asked the other.
Nasrudin shrugged and said:
- Trifles, little things of no consequence whatsoever. She carries out household chores, takes care of our children and helps them to study, goes to the market, makes repairs when necessary, such as painting the house and fixes what is broken. She brings water from the well and waters the garden, also attends her sick mother and takes care of me, sometimes visits her sister and helps with the children…things like that, little things inconsequential.
- And what do you do? - Asked another friend.
- Oh friends, I am truly important, of course! I am investigating whether God exists.

24. THE PRESENTABLE WARRIOR

For many of us the idea of the 'bigger picture' is just a luxury we cannot afford to think about. This is often because we have enough things going on in our daily lives to occupy us – we don't have the luxury of time to sit back and wonder about the larger significance of human life. We have the *here and now* to be getting on with. The 'here and now' for many of us is not a straight, nor easy, path – and requires its own particular ways of navigation. How we travel that path is what we call 'living'. Yet it is also a question of how we 'dress' for the occasion. To clarify this, I wish to cite a brief episode from 'Meeting Monroe' when on one occasion I commented on the fact that Monroe was always dressed so elegantly:

"'Elegance is an appreciation of the self' Monroe replied. 'It is a measure of respect to be, what you would say, *presentable*. We each must choose our manner and form of negotiating with life. If we are careless and dirty with ourselves, the world appears careless and dirty to our own perceptions. It is a matter of correct perspective – of intentioned organization. We must respect ourselves, if we wish to ask the same from the world that is our reality. You yourself are smart enough. You show you have respect for yourself. You are not a lazy person – although too many people are. If you wish to engage with the world, participate with your reality, you should present yourself for it. You should be saying – "Look, here I am. I'm ready for you. I'm prepared to negotiate with reality. You can work with me – I'm committed". In this slippery world you walk through, it is important to be impeccable. Don't give reasons to your detractors. Neither be an excuse for yourself nor an excuse for others to use against you.'

'You're talking like we should be warriors' I replied.

'That's right soldier – head up, back straight!' said Monroe in a tone mocking a drill sergeant. 'Warriors of a kind' he then added, smiling. 'And why should you not be? If you are not a warrior within then you have fear. Fear is one of the most dangerous things for people. Fear pulls a person further into the trap of your reality and lessens your potential for perception. Fear is a wonderful distracter; it keeps you occupied on the mundane, and on the false.'

'And what are the other dangerous things?' I asked as we sat down at the table to eat.

'Self-doubt, of course' replied Monroe almost casually as he poured me a glass of water. In a sudden flash I realized that in all our meetings it had always been Monroe who had arranged the table, provided the food, and even who served me. Although I was the 'guest', in some loose way, I could at least have been more generous in my attitude to serve. This sudden realization flushed me, and I felt so guilty – and greedy. Monroe flicked a quick glance my way, yet said nothing.'

The final realization mentioned in the above encounter – about my lack in service – was about the small details of my behaviour. Even this can be said to be part of the 'presentable warrior'; in that we should be mindful of how we present ourselves through our small daily interactions. As Monroe rightly said – 'Fear is one of the most dangerous things.' And fear can appear in our lives in many different guises: such as chaos, disruption, uncertainty, security, need, greed, envy, jealousy, and sloth; amongst others. Perhaps the 'presentable warrior' represents a path toward social normality and balance, amidst these many destabilizing forces and influences. Also, to my mind, being 'presentable' also suggests being partly invisible and/or anonymous; or rather, to live one's life without the need for grand gestures for attention. Being 'presentable' can refer to one's elegance in appearance and action; it also suggests the state of one's being. For example, it may be difficult to call oneself 'presentable' when inside we are harbouring negative and angry thoughts against someone or something. Elegance is, after all, a thorough state that is both internal and external.

Another aspect of the 'presentable warrior' that comes to mind is the ability to absorb those experiences and impacts that we might initially label as either 'positive' or 'negative' as neither of these categories. That is, impacts which may be seen as orderly or chaotic can work other than how they appear. That is, chaotic impacts may actually serve to create order, and vice versa. I am reminded of the ancient saying: *Things seemingly in opposition may in actuality be working together.* Also, chaotic events can be learning experiences that may serve as catalysts for our own development. By categorizing something – or someone – as chaotic and/or disruptive may in fact be a way of blocking (or hiding) from the developmental capacity available. I don't know what Monroe would say about all this, yet I am sure he would consider the best approach, or response, to be an elegant one. After all, it is about having an appreciation of the self. And perhaps one of the best ways to have such an appreciation is to stop categorizing everything that crosses our daily path. Instead, we can deal with the details of our lives as learning opportunities rather than wasting our time labelling everything. Is not this more elegant, a more presentable way to warrior against life – as a flowing participant and not an orderly archivist[1]?

And maybe, just maybe, we have to re-invent ourselves sometimes to present a more elegant 'us' to the world.

None should say: 'I can trust' or 'I cannot trust' until he is a master of the option, of trusting or not trusting.

Idries Shah, *Reflections*

[1]An **archivist** is an information professional who assesses, collects, organizes, preserves, maintains control over, and provides access to records and archives determined to have long-term value. (Wikipedia) – sound familiar?

A Tale to Finish: 'Two Sides'

The colored cloaks of the dervishes, copied for teaching purposes and eventually imitated as mere decoration, were introduced in Spain in the Middle Ages, in this way: A Christian king, who liked pompous parades, also took pride in his philosophical understanding. He asked a Sufi known as el-Agarin to instruct him in knowledge.
"We will offer observation and reflection, but first you have to learn its meaning in its entirety" said Agarin.
"We have studied all the preliminary steps towards knowledge through our own tradition" replied the king.
"All right", said Agarin. "I will give His Majesty a demonstration of our teaching, during the parade tomorrow." Preparations were made and the next day the group of dervishes paraded through the narrow streets of the Andalusian city. The king and his courtiers were on either side of the path: nobles on the right and knights on the left. When the procession had ended, Agarin turned to the king and said "Majesty, please ask your knights on the left the color of the dervish robes." All knights swore on the scriptures and on his honor that the clothes had been blue. The King and the rest of the court were surprised and confused, because in no way was what they had seen.
"We all saw clearly that they were dressed in brown robes" said the king; "and among us there are men of great holiness and faith, whom are highly respected." The king ordered all his knights to be punished and degraded,

whilst those who had seen the brown color were put aside to be rewarded. The process took some time. Then the king asked the Sufi el-Agarin: "What evil have you done to bewitch my men? What are these evil acts of yours that may cause the most honorable gentlemen to deny the truth of Christianity, abandon his hopes of being redeemed and betray our trust?"

The Sufi said: "The robes were visible on one side in brown. On the other side, each robe was blue. Without preparation, your bias was because you deceived yourself and misunderstood us. How can we teach someone in these circumstances?"

25. THE NEXT 'BIG THING' IS US – THE RISE OF THE NEW MONASTICS

The past few years have left many of us waiting around for the 'Next Big Thing' – or some grand televised miracle to happen. The world has recently been filled to overflowing with doomsayers and images of breakdown, violence, and corruption. Many of us have been distracted, or sidelined, into indifference. We were told we lacked the power to make any lasting change. The early years of the 21st century were largely media-centered on insecurity; and this insecurity and fear was used by opportunistic governments to strengthen incumbent structures of authority.

Yet it is my view that 2014 will be a significant year in marking a shift in human relationships and thinking patterns. I feel we are going to see an increasing emergence of what I refer to as 'disruptive innovators'; that is, individuals acting as unexpected change agents. It will be individuals, not governments, who will show a greater potential to catalyze transformation and change in the world. This is because real change occurs when the 'anomalies' (i.e., the change agents) become too numerous to be absorbed into the present system. That is why individuals and groups 'doing their own thing' are so important right now.

All great ideas and innovations began life as 'disruptive' from the periphery; from those people just 'going it alone' and following their instinct and motivation. That is why it is my view that 2014 will be an important year on the individual level rather than needing to look to global movements or grand action for change. A new model that is set to empower the coming changes is what I have referred to as the 'new monastic' model of action whereby individuals/groups get on and create new ways of doing things, without fanfare or large billboard announcements. Such 'monastic work', so to speak, often operates below the radar and is authentic through its activity rather than seeking visibility and attention. The 'monastic worker', in seeking change, chooses a way of life that has meaning and that can bring lasting change for those involved. Often the monastic worker strives for assisting change within their own communities. They are like ink dots on the blotting paper, slowly spreading their impact by diligent yet creative work. What makes this model not only more appealing today, but also much more effective, is the rise of global communications and distributed networks. Now, the hard-working monastics can connect, share, and collaborate.

Therefore, doing things our own way, participating through our 'small-scale' contributions, can have greater impact than would normally. It is an ideal time now to look towards our own lives, our future, and start to create the change for ourselves that we wish to see. A time to examine our lifestyles – the food we eat, our securities, our dependencies, our networks, our finances, etc – and to be truly honest with ourselves.

The *new monastic* acts as a synthesis between a vibrant perception of the world and a practical way of action. That is, people who are motivated by both an inner spirit as well as practical vision. Such change catalysts can create meaning and significance in everything they do – even the small seemingly mundane things. By working with a strong inner vision we are also able to transform the world external to us. Our modern modes of connectivity and communication can bring the *new monastics* into a networked gathering of 'heart-mind-spirit' in order to work with both practicality and vision.

The challenges we face may appear to be out of our hands, yet each of us has the power to choose how we respond to them. A considerate and compassionate response can be nurtured by shifting our behaviour patterns away from materialistic self-centeredness toward a more community-centred set of values. Doris Lessing, in her book *Shikasta*, tells of how the 'broken Earth' needs to regain the energies of SOWF (*'Substance Of We Feeling'*). The keys to our collective development may very well have been planted within each of us, in our social sense of responsibility – in our innate urge to *come together*. The human species is, after all, a social species (as anthropologists keenly like to remind us!). It is easy to behave 'spiritually' when one is confined to the hermit's cave – then our only struggles are with our own ceaseless thoughts. However, sincere activity also requires that each individual understands and accepts the role of their social participation; of their presence and responsibility with friends, family, and within the community.

As a global community of individuals we are being urged toward supporting and developing a shared, empathic consciousness. Through a combination of physical changes on the social, cultural, and political levels people all over the world are beginning to awaken to the audacity of our situation. From this there may be further 'awakenings' as the ironic, incredulous, and often absurd factors of many of our lifestyles are brazenly shown in the shocking light of current times. In these upcoming years the *new monastics* will continue to emerge throughout the world, becoming agents of change within communities. They will spread their influence through social networks – both physical and virtual. In order to 'change the world' we must first become change agents within ourselves. We should also recognize that human consciousness is inherently integrated into every aspect of our lives.

Humanity is naturally integrative, and does not consciously seek to separate. Integral consciousness is an aspect of the *new monastics*, whom are conscious and aware of bringing the inner world into constructive play within everyday life. Each person can be a part of this groundswell, with strong and confident voices and deeds, and yet devoid of ego and grand announcements.

The year ahead, more than ever before, is going to be about the people on the ground. It will be about how ordinary people can make a great difference; and the changes each of us makes in our lives to be more aligned with moving forward. It will be about how resilient we are; and how we nurture a focused and positive state of mind and being. It will also be about integrating our spiritual selves with practical applications in the world. Transitional periods are not normal times – they are periods where individual action can have a much larger impact on historical developments. Now is the time for individual 'monastic' endeavour to take up the challenge – and the responsibility.

We are here to work to make a change – it is time to come together. I feel 2014 will show that the 'next big thing' is actually US. Or, as Doris Lessing would say, it is time for our *Substance Of We Feeling* (SOWF) – which is needed like wine grapes need a good soil

A Tale to Finish: 'Things Pass On'

A dervish who had taken a vow of solitude had retired to a desert. One day a Sultan with his entourage passed by. The dervish, who was in a state of contemplative meditation, did not look up nor even noticed the procession. The monarch was angry with him, though was in good spirits and said:
- Those who wear the tattered cloak, and animals, are gross and uneducated and humble.

The vizier rebuked the dervish and said:
- Oh dervish! The Sultan of all the earth has just passed by. You're not going to pay homage as you should?

The dervish replied:
- The Sultan seeks homage from those hoping to benefit from their acts of goodwill! Reflect also that Sultans were created to protect and serve their subjects, and not for subjects to serve kings.

The Sultan was impressed by the wisdom of the dervish and said:
- Ask me a wish.

The dervish replied:
- What I want from you is to not come back to bother me.

- Now give me some advice - said the Sultan.

The dervish replied:
- Now you have in your hands both power and sovereignty: remember that these pass from hand to hand.

26. IT'S OKAY TO CELEBRATE OURSELVES

I never thought I would find myself watching on television the Winter Olympic Games in Sochi, Russia. I'm not particularly a person who cares for or watches sport; winter sports even less so! Yet one weekend evening in February I switched on the television and I happened to come across the figure skaters competing at Sochi. So I thought I would watch for a few minutes before turning over to watch a film I was expecting. Those few minutes turned into a couple of hours. I was blown away by the elegance, craftsmanship, and skill in the figure skating. It was a display of finesse, dedication, focus, and beauty that I had not appreciated before. So I watched another night, and another night…and not just ice skating but freestyle skiing, ski jumping, Alpine skiing, snowboarding, speed skating, bobsleigh - the whole lot! And I'm still not a sports fan…because I realized I wasn't watching so much the 'sport' – the competing, the winning, etc - but rather something else. I was watching how the human being participates, and what is capable through concentrated effort, dedication, and commitment. These winter Olympic Games were, for me, a celebration of being human; that is, what a human being can achieve when they have the right attitude. And the results can be truly amazing.

Sure, I've read some of the criticisms over the Sochi Olympic Games, yet these have mostly been rants against President Putin, Russian politics, or committee organization, etc. For me, that's missing the point. The point is that hundreds of dedicated people, from all parts of the world, came together in a spirit of participation and achievement. Many of these participants would have been training for the last two years just for this specific event. It is an event, like other events and meetings that occur worldwide that are really a celebration of ourselves. Perhaps it's about time we not only recognized this fact but also acknowledged it in a strong positive way. Why? Because our mainstream news channels are full of negative news that show the worst sides of human nature – along with other evils of the world. Yes, these things *are happening*, and I'm one of the first to accept that. Yet my point is: by focusing on the evils of the world are we helping ourselves to develop our understanding, our tools for progress, our positive focus, and our self-confidence? Are we nurturing the best aspects of human love? If not, why not?

We may think that everything in the world is obvious and right in front of us. This is a result of a material lifestyle that is constantly pushed in our faces so much that we are overwhelmed by its presence. The immediacy of such an obvious *matter-reality* (materiality) calls for our continuous attention. However, there are other elements of life that are not so easy to discern. There are times when we have to make up our minds and make decisions based on limited external evidence. Whilst our social-cultural environment is often overwhelming, our inner human realm is underwhelming. Yet it is underwhelming in a positive and subtle way, and we have an obligation to recognize and acknowledge this too. Sometimes it is difficult to work out what is the right thing to do. The philosopher Emanuel Swedenberg urged people in their daily lives to 'do the good that we know.' Doing the right thing and the wrong thing may look very similar. That is why we need to rely on our own tools of discernment. And these tools of discernment can be more polished or rustier depending on our attitudes to our self, and whether we celebrate our self or not. Blaise Pascal, the French inventor, writer and philosopher said it this way:

"There is just enough light for those who want to believe, and just enough shadow for those who do not want to believe"

We don't have to worry about finding our self-justifications, that's the easy part – they will find us! Life can be misleading at times, but that's okay. It's whether we dwell on it and allow it to mis-direct us by distraction and design. Let's be honest, our social-cultural environments – i.e. modern living – do distract us by design – just look at the current state of what we call 'democracy.' As the social critic Herbert Marcuse wrote – "*A comfortable, smooth, reasonable, democratic unfreedom prevails in advanced industrial civilization, a token of technical progress.*" So in order to deal and engage with this 'unfreedom' (please note I didn't say *fight against* it), and to transform it into something that works for us, we need to begin by celebrating ourselves.

We need to be looking at the world through our inner lens, and discerning the world through our own inner states. This is the opposite of what seems to be occurring all too frequently; that the state of the world tries to enter us and impose itself as our inner state. We need to change this relationship so that rather than the distraction entering us and deciding what is, our celebration of self participates with the world as the primary source. The 3rd century philosopher Plotinus put it like this:

> "I am vision-loving, and I create by the vision-seeing faculty within me…I gaze within and the figures of the material world take being as they fall from my brooding."

By brooding, Plotinus meant deep internal consideration, or contemplation. He informs us that if we are in a dark place, then so too do the figures and events of the material world seem dark to us.

No-one perceives the same image of the world; that is our individual responsibility. Yet if, like Plotinus, we are vision-loving within (celebration of self), then we can transform the 'figures of the material world' by how we transform ourselves.

We should not let the present distract us away from 'vision-loving' and 'vision-seeing' a better future we wish to see for ourselves and for those to come. It's okay to celebrate the positive achievements of the human being. In fact, I would dare to say it's our response-ability to do so!

A Tale to Finish: 'Two Frogs'

Two frogs fell into a bowl of milk.
'Keep swimming,' said one frog to the other; 'we'll get out somehow.'
'It's useless,' screamed the first; 'it's too thick to swim, too soft to jump, too slippery to crawl. As we die anyway someday, better be tonight.'

So the first frog stopped swimming and drowned. Her friend kept swimming and swimming without surrender. And at dawn they found her on a block of butter that she had beaten. And there she was, smiling, eating the flies that came in flocks from all directions.

27. TOWARD SYNTHESIS

We enter a time when the new year of the natural world celebrates at what we call the spring equinox. Whichever way you look at it, many of us have now entered either the new year, or Spring. The spring equinox is the time of year, in the earth's annual cycle around the sun, where day and night are equal in length. We have emerged from the dominance of darkness during the winter days – or, as Rumi put it: 'the hand of winter reveals the secrets of spring.' We may also say that life bursts forth from death.

Throughout the world, in many traditions, the spring equinox is also a time of great confrontation between the forces of darkness and light. This is symbolized in many sacred teachings as the death and resurrection of their deities. Or, in initiatory terms, as an important stage of self-realization, where the struggle between darkness and light creates the opposition needed to catalyze development. That is, advancement through struggle and opposition. Movement and change has often been symbolized through the pulling back and forth between opposites, and so through struggle and opposition. Yet such oppositions are not only in symbolic traditions and customs – they also are reflected in our social and cultural influences and trends. One historical example is in Marxist theory whereby Karl Marx stated that the struggle/opposition between class relations (bourgeoisie and working class) would create a resolution in a humane and classless society (socialism). This notion of oppositional struggle to create a third force of resolution is known as dialectic (thesis + antithesis → synthesis). Marx's ideas on dialectic struggle were heavily influenced by the idealistic philosophy of German thinker Georg Hegel. Hegel developed the concept that mind or spirit manifested itself in a set of contradictions and oppositions that were ultimately integrated and united in synthesis. For Hegel, the synthesis (the absolute), must always pass through a stage of opposition in its journey to completion and truth. On a material level, Hegel viewed this dialectic relationship as the process by which human history unfolds. That is, history (social evolution) progresses as a struggle between two opposing forces toward a developmental state of resolution.

According to Hegel, the main characteristic of resolution-in-unity was that it evolved through contradiction and denial. These struggles, says Hegel, can be found in most social domains such as history, philosophy, art, nature, and even consciousness. It is significant to note here that Hegel's thinking was highly influenced by the lesser known writings of German Christian mystic Jacob Böhme. Böhme's inner visions led him to create a cosmology where it was necessary for humanity to return to God. These states of conflict would be a necessary stage in the further completion of the evolution of the universe. Humanity's free will in this separation, conflict, and resolution was the most important gift that God could give to us. In other words, it would be our own responsibility – and a privileged responsibility at that – to work toward our reconciliation through struggle and the opposing forces of resistance.

In a similar manner the teachings of Greek-Armenian philosopher-mystic George Gurdjieff also describe a triad relationship in his *Holy Affirming* and *Holy Denying* ➔ *Holy Reconciling*. Gurdjieff referred to this as the 'Law of Three.' In this context we can see how a coming together of contradictory impulses – such as mind and spirit – would lead to a resolution that would not only be an integration of these contradictory forces but at the same time a resolution/synthesis *greater than* the sum of its parts.

Likewise, psychologist and humanistic philosopher Erich Fromm noted that society in the mid-twentieth century industrial world was suffering from what he viewed as the contradictory struggle between *having* and *being*. The ideology of continued growth and consumption - the *having* mode - was in conflict with the human need to find meaning, well-being, and personal growth - the *being* mode. Fromm saw the resolution of this conflict as being a New Human. Fromm wrote that 'We are a society of notoriously unhappy people: lonely, anxious, depressed, destructive, dependent - people who are glad when we have killed the time we are trying so hard to save.' His conclusion was that '*the physical survival of the human race depends on a radical change of the human heart.*'

Much thinking current today is typical in that it displays a lack of appreciation for the changing nature of human consciousness. Also, it fails to take into account the role of consciousness in affecting external conditions. Moreover, there is danger in thinking that opposing influences can only lead to an 'either-or' alternative. To some degree even Erich Fromm displayed this, in thinking that we can either have a *having* or a *being* mode of existence, but not both.

For me, I would say there is still something else that has not yet been taken into account. A 'something else' that participates within the mesh of opposing forces that assists to catalyze toward synthesis/resolution. And this 'something' is immaterial, yet tangible. In an analogy that Persian poet Rumi has used, we can put together the opposing ingredients of flour, water, and yeast; yet we do not create bread from this. Something else needs to be added to the mix; and this something is heat - the fire of the oven needed to bake the bread. Heat is the immaterial yet tangible force that catalyzes the ingredients into a synthesis - in this case, bread. Gurdjieff was, in a sense, referring to this immaterial force in his 'Law of Three' with his reconciling force - a force of attention and intention.

Similarly, in physical systems a tipping point occurs when it is said that the system has reached its capacity to orderly organize the energy. The alternative is either a breakdown (collapse), or for a greater amount of energy to enter the system in order to be used to catalyze and create greater order, thus pushing the system to a further stage of development. So, why am I saying all this?

I began this short essay by mentioning how the spring equinox is symbolically a time where the struggles between opposing forces (dark and light) find a balance and resolution - in this case equal hours of day and night. It also symbolizes a time of death, rebirth, and realization (initiation). I feel that the world is now going through a grander scale version of this struggle; and that a global synthesis is indeed required. As individuals each one of us also has to deal with resolving our own struggles and contradictory forces that impact from both without and within. The ultimate question in this regard must be - can we find and use that immaterial yet tangible 'reconciling' energy? And what is it?

In global affairs, art, psychology, social life - in all and everything - there is need for this 'other force' to be present. Perhaps it is present, yet in ways we do not, or cannot, perceive; and that the presence of this reconciling force is one of the mechanisms of our social and cultural evolution. And just maybe, we can also connect with and utilize this synthesizing force. What if this force was the energy of conscious and directed attention? That is, the force of conscious awareness and participation - of goal-orientated conscious intention?

Everything we do can be done differently. And not only the major things in our life - our work, our loving, etc - but also the small things: cooking, cleaning, preparing, arranging, etc. In other words, to put conscious intention into every encounter and participation - into every human act. Would this not be something? After all, would we truly wish to do harm, make mistakes, speak badly, and perform incorrectly, if we were consciously aware of these moments? Human consciousness when aware of itself can be a far greater force for resolution, synthesis, integration, and development.

We do not necessarily need to look solely toward global material forces (e.g., war) to see the potential inherent in reconciling opposing forces for betterment. These opposing and contradictory forces also operate within each one of us. Yet the first hurdle to overcome is to recognize the existence and operation of these forces. By perceiving their existence we help to bring the force of directed attention into being. With conscious awareness thus activated we can perhaps take the next step of conscious intention towards a goal-orientated outcome - resolution and harmony. *As above, so below.* As in the world, so too within us. These forces are in everything and are all around us. They are as much in our myths and stories as they are in our social systems and structures. They also exist in our sciences too.

A quick glance at quantum mechanics will tell us that packets of quanta can exist both in the state of a particle and a wave - isn't this a contradictory state of affairs, not knowing in which state to exist? It is only under observation - observer participation - that the quanta 'chooses' which state to be in and is said to *collapse* into either a particle or a wave. In other words, human directed attention collapses reality into existence. The way to reconcile the struggle in our lives, and to strive toward greater development, appears to lie with the 'heat' of our conscious awareness.[vi]

We participate in the world around us by an immaterial yet tangible force of conscious attention, directed intention, and aware participation. It is through this that we can work with opposing forces toward resolution and a higher order of synthesis and integration. It requires a form of *inner work* - we must place ourselves into all our situations and circumstances as a human crucible of change. We can be the change agent - the catalyst - by contributing conscious intention into the mix. Maybe that's why we've been hanging around so long...to be ready for this.

A Tale to Finish: 'What Affects the Mouse...'

A mouse looked through a hole in the wall is a farmer and his wife opening a package. He thought what kind of food could be there and was terrified when he discovered it was a mousetrap. He ran the farm yard to warn everyone:
- There is a mousetrap in the house, a mousetrap in the house!
The hen was clucking and scratching, I raise my head and said:
- Excuse me, I understand that is a big problem for you, but not hurt me at all, does not bother me.
The mouse turned to the lamb and said:
- There is a mousetrap in the house, a mousetrap! ...
- There's nothing I can do, if you ask for. Rest assured that you will be remembered in my prayers.
The mouse was then directed to the cow and the cow said
- But perhaps I am in danger? I think not.
So the mouse returned to the house, worried and dejected, to face the

---

[vi] For a more in-depth discussion on this we could examine the alchemical arts, and the work of Paracelsus, to further understand the role of human intention upon physical processes.

farmer's mousetrap.

That night they heard a great noise, like a mousetrap catching its prey. The farmer's wife rushed to see what was caught. In the darkness, she saw that the trap had caught the tail of a poisonous cobra. The cobra bit the woman. The farmer took her to the hospital. She returned with fever. All the world knows that to feed someone with a fever, nothing better than soup. The farmer grabbed his knife and went to get the main ingredient: chicken. As the condition of women continued, friends and neighbors came to visit.

To feed, the farmer killed the lamb. The woman did not improve and eventually died.

The farmer then sold the cow to the slaughterhouse to cover funeral expenses.

28. FREEDOM – A CONDITION OF THE HUMAN HEART

In a previous essay (*Toward Synthesis*) I noted how the humanistic philosopher Erich Fromm viewed the modern world as suffering from the contradictory struggle between *having* and *being*. The human need to find meaning, well-being, and personal growth was in conflict with a different type of world external to us. For Fromm, the resolution of this conflict was to be found in 'a radical change of the human heart.' For me, the issue of personal well-being revolves around the perception and experience of freedom. The ability to recognize, and internalize, well-being is fundamentally linked to how a person experiences their freedom.

Freedom is not simply a condition linked to battlefields, nations, and human rights. On an essential level it concerns the freedom within the self, and our battle to maintain this personal freedom within our everyday life. Erich Fromm himself wrote much on our human fear of freedom[vii]. Fromm concluded that our in-born fear of pursuing freedom against social conditioning originates in our human birth process. The helplessness of the newly born child and the need for extra long dependency upon protection continues into adulthood in our need for human security. Fromm views our susceptibility to social conditioning as thus based upon a biological predisposition. This can perhaps explain why we often reach out to an outside authority (parent, teacher, partner/lover) as a power or force to recompense us for a sense of personal isolation. Modern society has exploited this tendency by approving and supporting our dependency upon external social systems. In the same way, our cultures often disapprove of

---

[vii] See his book 'Fear of Freedom'

those individuals that show high levels of self-reliance and independence. In a world moving toward greater connectedness, collaboration, and shared compassion, the presence of personal freedom is critical. For too long we have been focused upon the play of freedom as it is exhibited outside of us – by external powers – whilst blinded to the inner restraints of personal freedom. For me, freedom is nothing if it is not a freedom of the heart.

We often talk about freedom, or hear other people talk about it, in terms of *having*. In this way it becomes a value of possession. We either have it or we don't; other people have it, or manipulate it, or control it, etc. In our modern understanding of freedom we have turned it into a commodity – a material object that we bargain with. In many situations and for many people this has been true. Also, if a person has been kidnapped, or held in prison/confinement, then freedom becomes a very real physical reality. Yet this is just one manifestation of the essence of human freedom. For my purposes I wish to discuss freedom as a *state of being*.

On an interior level freedom is not about what we have; it is more about where we are and what we do. It is about having the right attitude and perspective. In this context freedom is a process: we need freedom *from* something or freedom *to* something. We don't have or possess freedom – we **do** freedom. It is important we create a freedom to move into, otherwise where are we going? We can create our freedom from the past – and even the present – if we wish to move *toward* a different place or state of being. For example, our past should not define how we wish our present to be. We can learn from it, and develop from its experience; yet if it is no longer useful, or even detrimental, then we need to learn how to leave it behind. We all have this choice of where we want **To Be**.

If we are unable to create this freedom within ourselves then we become, in the words of Doris Lessing, the 'prisons we choose to live inside.'[viii] Let us not forget also that our interior freedom goes with us wherever we go. If we feel a lack of true freedom within then this will still travel with us whether we are in a meditation retreat in India, or in the Andes of South America. After all, we cannot escape from our very self. It is thus essential that we have the freedom to deal with the events that affect us on a daily basis. We cannot control what events happen to us, yet we do have the freedom of choice to choose how we respond to them. By progressing through our experiences, and by choosing connections and situations that are aligned with our heart, we can become an intentional traveler rather than a random one. The fundamental question to ask ourselves is: how do we want to live?

For me, how we answer this question is part of what I call the 'living work' – the work we do inside ourselves to prepare us and make us better for living in the outer world. This is where both aspects of freedom converge – at the intersection where interior and exterior worlds meet. This is where our image of the world and the physical reality of the world also merge. If we can realize that we only experience the world as 'we are', then the freedom we find in the world is but a reflection of the freedom we consciously – or unconsciously – perceive within us. In other words, our sense of freedom is as near or as far away as we make it. It may sound contradictory, yet what we need to achieve is the liberation of our own perceptions of freedom. The reason why many of us do not stop to consider this, or perhaps we don't see it as necessary, is because we do not yet have the freedom to assess the state of our own freedom! As I stated earlier, freedom is not a possession, it is a process – an <u>action</u> – and therefore something to be worked for, to be involved with. Our own freedom is a *participatory process.*

[viii] See Doris Lessing, *Prisons We Choose To Live Inside* (1987)

Perhaps this process involves the freedom to do the small things that are important for our lives; not necessarily the freedom to 'save the world' or make a grand gesture. What we need within ourselves is the freedom to make a choice; to act as we feel best; to create moments of joy that can be shared. Or it could be the freedom to begin making a change by changing one thing at a time. Our lives are part of a grand human, living tapestry. By making one small change we can influence change in many other ways through countless visible and invisible connections. Freedom is about having the choice to make these changes, and to take responsibility for our participation in the living tapestry that is life.

Personal freedom is also an expression of intelligence: not intellectual learning but rather social intelligence, spiritual intelligence, emotional intelligence, and instinctive intelligence. All this is the intelligence of personal freedom. I am reminded of Rumi who wrote of the difference between instinctive and acquired intelligence: *'There are two kinds of intelligence: One acquired/ as a child in school memorizes facts and concepts/ from books and from what the teacher says, collecting information from the traditional sciences/ ......There is another kind/ ...one already completed and preserved inside you./ A spring overflowing its spring box. A freshness/ in the center of the chest.../ This second knowing is a fountainhead/ from within you, moving out.'* This second knowing – our instinctual intelligence – is already within each one of us. As a human being we inherently have this *knowing*. For me, freedom is being able to connect with this internal knowing – and to act from it. In the end, true freedom is a condition of the human heart.

"Loving freedom, to me, means having the freedom to love yourself deeply, others deeply, and accepting the never-ending truth of change. It means having the freedom to be happy on your own and happy with others as they come in and out of our lives. It means having the freedom to connect

wonderfully with those you meet and deal successfully with those who are difficult to relate to well."
Owen Fitzpatrick

A Tale to Finish: 'The Land of Laughter'

The teacher was in a talkative mood and therefore his disciples used this opportunity to ask of the phases that he had passed through in his search for divinity.

'First', said the teacher, 'I was led by the hand to the Country of Action where I stayed for a number of years. Then I was taken to the Country of Woe and lived there until my heart was purified of all its disordered condition. That's when I was able to see the Land of Love, whose fiery flames consumed what remained of selfishness in me. After that I agreed to the Country of Silence where the mysteries of life and death were revealed before my astonished eyes.

'And was this the final stage of your search?' asked the disciples.

'No', said the teacher - the final phase was when I was taken to the hidden Temple, the heart of God himself: to the sanctuary that is the Land of Laughter.

PART THREE

29. AWAKENING TO OUR EMPATHIC MIND (PT. 1)

The tragedy of humankind is that many of us have little recognition of the powerful conscious energies inherent in our collective psyche. Our propaganda and media systems have been exploiting the mythological images, collective stereotypes, and subconscious signifiers that play on our collective vulnerabilities. Knowledge has more or less trickled down to the average person through heavily filtered channels, and most often has been doctored, amended, and/or edited. The end result has been not knowledge but consensus information, or 'allowed' information. It has served the elite power structure well that people in general have not awoken to the understanding that humanity possesses incredible capacity and inherent resources for creative expansion and evolutionary development. It is now necessary to see our future potentials, not the daily news.

For many of us we have been brought up within a social structure that demands we become a 'productive member' of our society; thus much emphasis is placed upon developing individual skills so that we can compete with each other for survival. Inherent in this is a residual fear that if we open ourselves too much to others we may lose our 'competitive edge' and defined sense of individuality. In a sense we have been partially programmed to play the role of victim or fighter, externalizing our troubles and our blame. Added to this is the fact that Western science, which has asserted itself as the dominant hegemony since the Renaissance, has been at pains to stress that matter is primary and that consciousness is a secondary by-product from our mental activity. The modern worldview which denies the primacy of consciousness is fostering forms of human alienation, both psychological and social. It is a great paradox that modern science, itself a result of human consciousness, has produced a view of the cosmos which has no room for consciousness. Yet human beings are in need of meaning and significance in their lives as much as they are in need of air to breathe and food to eat. This struggle over the conscious mind(s) of humanity, which has been going on in various forms for aeons, is coming to a crux in our present generation. The result is that we have now collectively arrived at a critical moment in our evolution of human civilization. Any society or civilization which makes the material world its sole pursuit and object of concern cannot but devolve in the long run. As Professor Needleman so aptly remarked:

> The esoteric is the heart of civilization. And should the outward forms of a human civilization become totally unable to contain and adapt the energies of great spiritual teachings, then that civilization has ceased to serve its function in the universe.[ix]

It is therefore imperative that people begin to break-away from non-developmental social conditioning and make efforts to make compassionate intent a part of our everyday experience. This includes being conscious of the type of impacts we receive, and to avoid those impacts and influences that are negative in favour of those that are positive. For example, true words encourage us and give us strength because we instinctively recognize truthfulness – our body consciousness reacts to this, even if indirectly as through the form of galvanic skin response, pupil response, or through our electrical nerve responses. In short, our body *feels* the essence of what impacts us, and negative or false information weakens us. This concept was researched scientifically through testing muscle strength. Dr. David Hawkins

---

[ix] Jacob Needleman, *New Religions* (New York: E P Dutton, 1977)

has written extensively on how muscle testing shows that various impacts create either strong or weak reactions from the body. In his work he relates how people who listened to lies proved to exhibit a weakened muscle reaction, whilst those who listened to positive words and statements showed a strong muscle response.

In his work Dr. Hawkins further notes how particular language 'attractors' such as Shame, Guilt, Apathy, Grief, Fear, Desire, Anger and Pride serve as negative, energy depleting emotions. Higher energy attractors are the positive words/emotions such as Courage, Willingness, Acceptance, Reason, Love, and Joy. According to Dr. Hawkins, over 99% of humans calibrate below the level of Joy; which is a saddening thought. What this also tells us is that our whole body functions as our mind – an extended mind. As such, our whole body can respond in empathy, and be strengthened through empathy and compassion. We need to listen more to our bodies, the information they give to us, and trust in this part of our mind – and not just the thoughts coming from our head upstairs. When the mind is receiving ambiguous impacts and news, it is the body we can often rely on to give us more accurate and truthful information.

Furthermore, during moments of cultural and social disorder/disequilibrium the human mind often works with an energy and intensity not manifested when social patterns are stable and monotone. At such dynamic periods there can be the realization that no individual is isolated; that each person is interwoven into a vibrant network and web of psychological, emotional, and spiritual interrelations. Such realizations can be heightened during periods, such as now, when it appears that human consciousness is moving through a time of critical transition.

Our self-awareness over the nature of human consciousness has been increasing greatly over the last several decades. The latest findings in the new sciences (especially quantum and neuroscience), in consciousness studies, in the popularity for inner and self-development, etc, all indicate a new awareness emerging within our collective consciousness. It is interesting to note that according to the research of Dr. David Hawkins human consciousness was dangling at below the 200 level (190)[x] for many centuries before it suddenly rose up to its present higher level some time in the mid 1980s. The overall average level of human consciousness stands at 207 (as of late 1990s). Hence, many past predictions and prophecies of doom may have been avoided because they relate to a time when human consciousness was below the 200 level. For the world to stay at levels below 200 over a prolonged period of time would, says Dr. Hawkins, cause a great imbalance that would likely lead to humanity's demise. When one's consciousness falls below 200 at any given moment a person begins to lose power and thus grow weaker and more prone to be manipulated by one's surroundings, says Hawkins. Now, however, human consciousness is on the rise; and as it rises it has the capacity to affect – or infect – other minds. As Hawkins indicates:

The power of the few individuals at the top counterbalances the weakness of the masses:

1 individual at level 300 counterbalances 90,000 individuals below level 200
1 individual at level 400 counterbalances 400,000 individuals below level 200
1 individual at level 500 counterbalances 750,000 individuals below level 200
1 individual at level 600 counterbalances 10 million individuals below level 200

---

[x] This is Dr. Hawkins scale for calibrating the level of human consciousness according to his 'Map of Consciousness'. See his work for further details

1 individual at level 700 counterbalances 70 million individuals below level 200[xi]

What this tells us is that as human consciousness rises it has an exponential capacity to affect others around, like an expanding energy wave. What this tells us is that individuals have the capacity to make change *infectious* by transmitting one's state of being amongst others. That is, energetic change will come *through our social and cultural forms*, and not by avoiding them. Developmental change on a large scale can occur by creating conscious change from within our daily lives and within our social systems, and not outside of them. By just walking on this planet, holding the focus and intention, we create incredible energy – energy that is shared. We are creating change by just being alive. That is why being without fear is so important. We need not create a black and white film in our heads when in reality we are creating colour. We can make use of the tools that are already available to us, and within us.

There is an exponentially increasing mass of us who are now awakening our empathic consciousness. Recent de-stabilizing events in our financial and political spheres have drawn people's focus to the dysfunction of many of the systems that we once gave our trust to. Even the focus on religious extremism in the media has drawn people's attention not only to the deficit of spiritual values in our major religions but also to how religion is being used as a tool for furthering social, political, and emotional control. This trance-like grip on our collective consciousness is now being stripped away as people awaken to the knowing that there is so much more to our lives than that of a materialistic and consumer-based lifestyle. Yet don't

[xi] D. Hawkins, *Power vs. Force: The Hidden Determinants of Human Behaviour* (Arizona: Veritas Publishing, 1995)

become frustrated if things don't happen tomorrow, but trust that changes and shifts are happening over time. The necessity of inner knowing, intuition, self-trust, and integrity, is now critical. And let us remember that humans are biased for compassion and empathy. The awakening of our empathic mind is our natural inheritance.

A Tale to Finish: 'The Cell'

A disciple wanted wise counsel ... he was told:
- 'Go, sit in your cell and your cell will teach you wisdom' - said the Master
- 'But if I have no cell ... If I am not a monk?' the disciple answered.
- 'Of course you have a cell. Look inside yourself'

30. AWAKENING TO OUR EMPATHIC MIND (PT. 2)

The accelerating changes occurring across our planet right now will have no alternative but to force a mind-change on a global and individual level. We are coming together as a global species like never before; despite what we have been shown and told by the mainstream media. We need to view this in both the immediate and the bigger picture. Due to our relatively short human life span we rarely reflect beyond a generation or two in front of us. We have evolved as a species that reacts to immediate concerns. This served us well in the past when we had survival needs in a restricted world of limited horizons. Yet now we need a perspective that is global at the very least – and even possibly beyond!

If we now look at the bigger picture we will see that a different type of consciousness has been emerging over the past 150 years. That is, since the dawn of the Second Industrial Revolution. The new technologies of the Second Industrial Revolution – the telephone, radar, cinema, automobile and airplane – called for a new reorientation of human perspective. A new perception of the dimensions of space and time began to birth a psychological consciousness – one that wanted to look beyond the borders and horizons of the physical frontier. The 3rd Industrial Revolution, which is now emerging, will be a convergence of digital communications combined with a young generation that is more globally aware. This has the potential to catalyze upon this planet a rising empathic, integral consciousness. Also, our global communications will encourage new relations in our extended connectivity. That is, increased multiple relations are likely to stimulate a connected, collaborative consciousness; rather than a consciousness of conflict and control. A planetary citizenry is emerging that will exhibit greater empathy, and which will create a different planetary society within perhaps two generations. Humanity already contains the seeds of these momentous potentials.

Many social changes within the upcoming years will emerge from the creative engagement and innovation of individuals and collectives worldwide - a shift catalyzed within the hearts, spirit, and minds of the people. Externally we may seem like a vast, distant, and separate collection of individuals yet in truth the human family is an intimate, closely entwined species comprised of various cultures. Many of the younger generation now are waking up to this fact. Youngsters the world over are growing up accustomed to having networks of hundreds, perhaps even thousands, of friends across the planet; sharing intimacy and empathizing easily with an international social group of like-minded souls. This younger generation is manifesting, whether conscious of it or not, a non-local level of human relationships. This expanded connectivity is impacting and affecting a change in our psychology and consciousness. We are now being impelled to live in ways that enable all other people to live as well. We are also being compelled to live in ways that respect the lives of others and that respect the right to the economic and cultural development of all people; and to pursue personal fulfilment in harmony with the integrity of nature. These traits may constitute what I refer to as an integral-ecological consciousness: a person acting and behaving as both an individual and as a part of the greater connected whole. Such multiple relations form a more varied, rich and complex life; they also provide a more diverse range of impacts and opportunities to develop the self. As well as providing challenges for developing new skills and learning, our diverse networks can form new friendships and add extra meaning to our lives.

Many young people today are comfortable in expressing themselves with strangers; they explore and express their inner thoughts, feelings, emotions and ideas with hundreds of unknown persons online, from various cultural backgrounds. More and more daily interactions are empathic as we react and share news, stories, and emotional impacts from sources around the world.

Empathy is one of the core values by which we create and sustain social life. Exposure to impacts outside of our own local and restrictive environments helps us to learn tolerance, and to live with experiences that are richer and more complex, full of ambiguities, and multiple perspectives. It is a mode of connecting that allows diverse people worldwide to construct a new form of planetary social capital. We have the resources to co-create a planetary human society where once again the focus is on social benefit rather than profit. We can see many examples of this today, such as in online collaborative tools and both local and global projects. The online global community is a model for the new paradigm that illustrates how sharing can work above the individual motive for profit. The values and ethics of communal sharing might seem odd or out-of-place to the old capitalist-consumerist mindset, yet these are the very values that will be on the rise within the coming generations.

The spectacular rise in global communication technologies (Internet and mobile phones, etc) reflects a new form of participatory consciousness, especially among younger people. This new model is a distributed one; in other words, it connects people through networks rather than through hierarchical structures. It also represents a more feminine energy that seeks relationships, to nurture and to collaborate rather than compete and conquer. It is this emerging feminine energy that underlies the rise in global empathy. Also, since people are connecting amongst themselves in multiple relations it impels them to have an active engagement. For those individuals brought-up within the older generation of communication technologies (radio, television, fixed phones), the interaction was either two-way or, for the most part, one way. In this era people were passive receivers, targeted by information they could not engage with. This has now shifted so that the receiver of the communication is both the *user* and the *producer*.

We have learnt to democratize our engagement and to activate choice through online social networks, phone messaging, video channels (e.g. You-Tube), and various other broadcast mediums. The younger generation is waking up quickly and learning how to set-up inexpensive, or free, radio sites (podcasts), home websites, newsletters, and are managing their own forms of self-expression. This new model is changing our thinking and behavior patterns. We are now getting used to dealing with multiple connections rather than single ones; and to becoming immersed in diverse relations and not just one-on-one dialogues. We are also being exposed to a myriad of viewpoints, beliefs, identities, and experiences. Within these new arrangements we are being asked to respond and engage with the outside world not in fear or with anxiety but with healthy, creative, and positive energies.

As a new generation enters a world where collaboration and connection is the new normal, we are likely to also see a different consciousness responding to such an environment. In this way, change will come through responding to new patterns and potentials. With patience, tolerance, empathy, compassion, and conscious communication we will see a different set of values catalyzing change throughout our cultures of the world.

A Tale to Finish: 'The Demon'

A demon came across another demon that was rolling on the floor, screaming and crying, as if possessed by a pain like no other.

'What's wrong with you?' asked the first demon bewildered.
'I have an angel in me and which torments me' cried out the other demon between long moans.

31. AWAKENING TO OUR EMPATHIC MIND (PT. 3)

We are going to witness a generation of young people showing a desire for human betterment that will emerge through intensified action for social, political, and ecological change. More and more young people are growing up experiencing social relations that transcend space and time, as well as cultures, national boundaries, and local ideologies. This may account for the increasing numbers of young people in developed nations becoming involved in community and social projects and NGOs; such as taking a year out to help in another culture abroad, to learn, experience, and to offer assistance. Volunteering among the young, despite what appears to be the contrary, is on the increase. Young people are even putting themselves into dangerous situations – in conflict zones – to stand up for values of peace, justice, equality, and human rights. Across the world young minds are demanding fair and equal access for all peoples to engage in open communication and free speech. And it appears that many more creative minds will be joining the global conversation as our current generation(s) increasingly 'wake up'.

In 2012 the planetary population was around 7 billion and the number of registered internet users was 33%, a rise of over 500% from the previous decade. By 2020 world population is set to be 7.8 billion and internet users worldwide is estimated to be 66% - that's a little under 3 billion new people plugging into the global conversation. In other words, nearly 3 billion new minds will be tapping in to the information flows; and that's many millions of new creative problem solvers, innovators, and visionaries. What is more, the majority of these new minds will be coming online from Asia, the Middle East, and what we refer to as the developing countries. These will be mostly young minds; and minds with necessities, with the urge for social betterment. Can we imagine the collective potential of these creative new minds; many of them thinking outside of the box, and outside of the old patterns?

It is significant that in times of relative social stability, human consciousness plays a lesser role in the behavior of society. However, when a society reaches the limits of its stability then social-cultural systems are sensitive and responsive to even the smallest fluctuations in the consciousness of its citizens. In such times, changes in values, belief sets, perceptions, etc, hold great sway over the future direction of the social situation. Human consciousness becomes a significant stimulus and catalyst for change during these times of social instability. That is why it is imperative humanity be collectively focused upon positive development and betterment rather than to be coerced, or conditioned, into a fear-based security that resists change. We should not underestimate the capacity for the human mind to adapt and evolve according to social and environmental impacts and influences.

Our modern sense of self-awareness has clearly evolved to root us in our social world: a world of extended relations and social networks. Humanity, it can be said, has been biologically hard-wired to tap into extended social connections and human communication networks. We are also hard-wired to adapt physically in response to experience - new neural processes in our brains can come into being with intentional effort, awareness, and different patterns of concentration. This capacity to create new neural connections, and thus new mental skill sets through experience, has been termed neuroplasticity. The human brain of today has to respond to the incredible amount of energy and information that is flowing through our environments and embedded in our cultural experiences. By being aware of our experiences and environmental impacts and influences we can gain a better understanding of how our brain and thinking becomes re-patterned.

Thus, how we focus our attention and awareness greatly shapes the structure of our brains. Further, the ability to grow new neural connections is available throughout our lives and not only in our young formative years. This knowledge encourages us to nurture our mindfulness, our self-awareness, and our empathic relations with others. Neuroplasticity also encourages us to be more reflective over our human networks, and to develop those social skills that underlie empathy and compassion. These new 'wired connections' are exactly what are becoming activated as individuals increasingly 'wake up' to what is happening within our communities, our societies, and upon the planet. Such distributed connections breach cultural and national borders and force us to self-reflect on our identity, values and ethics.

The opportunity is here for change and betterment like never before in our recent history. This means that the responsibility is also here; and these two factors may never be present again at exactly the right moment when they are so badly needed. What the human species may now be witnessing during these years is the rise of intuition, empathy, greater connectivity to the world and to people, and a sense of 'knowing' what changes need to be made. Furthermore, within each person is a growing sense of the greater cosmic whole: the realization that humanity exists and evolves within a universe of great intelligence and meaning. This serves to impart within humanity a more profound spiritual impulse. As a new global empathic mind emerges, people worldwide will grow up with new expressions of mindfulness that are more caring, relational, and compassionate. The 21st century is likely to be the era that births and nurtures such an evolving consciousness.

Many of the younger people across the world do not accept the social conditioning of anger, fear, and insecurity of their past generations. They want to reach out for change and betterment. Around the world there are examples of young people rejecting the conflict mentality of their elder generations. In conflict zones especially, where young minds are conditioned into unconditional hatred of fixed enemies, there is a backlash against this old programming. Younger people are reaching out across artificial borders to engage with the so-called 'enemy' and to start a new dialogue of peace and reconciliation. Such minds realize that the conflict mentality has no future, and will be left behind if it cannot accept change. Whereas many of the old programmed minds thought that a future meant putting up borders, and viewing the 'others' with suspicious eyes; many of the young minds see differently. We can see this in youth movements worldwide as there is change emerging in the mindset of young people everywhere. This is especially so in Middle Eastern territories where restrictive regimes are now encountering rising youthful demographics who are not accepting the old mentalities and old ways. All young people want what everybody wants – peace, justice, equality, freedom, etc. There is a new spring in the step of young, tech-savvy, energetic minds that are by-passing the old models. In these years ahead – at least for the next two decades – we will increasingly see the signs of the changing of the old guard (the dinosaurs!). And this time they will not be replaced by those with the same consciousness. With generational change we will see the gradual transition to an era of individuals who think differently, feel differently, connect differently, and who will want to work toward a different world.

A new narrative is emerging, one where each person is integral to the larger picture; the journey of each one of us being a part of the journey as a whole.

This new story informs us that the possibilities are open for humanity to engage in consciously creating its way forward - with harmony, balance and respect to all. This new narrative is part of humanity's evolving empathic mind and which compels us to seek greater connectivity and meaning in our lives. This most recent human story is one where *we* create the story of the future.

A Tale to Finish: 'Atoms'

Two atoms were crossing the street. One says to the other:
- Hello, how are you doing?
- Well ... I just lost an electron.
- You'll be worried? - Said the other
- No going ..! I feel completely positive.

32. THE PHOENIX GENERATION PT. 1: A NEW ERA OF CONNECTION, COMPASSION & CONSCIOUSNESS

In the years ahead we are going to see great change sweeping through our diverse human societies. Some may say we are in the midst of a 3rd Industrial Revolution. Yet rather than referring to this transition as an 'industrial' one, I consider this profound shift as a Revolution in Human Being – or rather as a *Revolution in Human Becoming.* We have entered a phase where there will be new forms, new arrangements, new structures, new perspectives, and new emerging states of *being.*

We are, quite literally, shifting from one set of C-Values – **Competition ~ Conflict ~ Control ~ Censorship –** to a new set: **Connection ~ Communication ~ Consciousness ~ Compassion**. The world is re-arranging in order to come together in countless new ways – with innovative changes in our communication, our uses of technology, through conscious awareness, through people-centered action, and more. These are the seeds coming to harvest as part of a re-awakening, re-ordering, and re-balance upon this planet. The current generation(s) will be the ones who will have to shoulder the mental and emotional responsibility of change as they are forced to let go of both external and internal systems and states that are no longer beneficial to our future development. This is why I have termed our current generation(s) the 'Bridge Generation', as we will be required to straddle both worlds. Many people in the Bridge Generation will feel the stirrings of a 'calling'; a sense to activate something – some purpose or meaning – within them. Some may be attracted to books/writings, or to events, gatherings, or other signifiers. Other ways to activate a person's calling – or *actualized* state – may come through *doing*, whilst others will be through *being*.

Change upon this planet will come through us, the people; and the attitudes, awareness, compassion, sincerity, etc, which we embody and manifest. This is the real stability that can be passed on to those around us: our family, friends, communities, social networks, and so on. As balanced, subtle, uplifting energies manifest through more and more people, change will increasingly manifest within our external environments. Again, it will not appear overnight. Already there are countless examples of how this wave of change is occurring across the planet. Such examples include how people interact with new technologies; the impacts of social media; new emerging youth groups; and the rise of a global empathic mindset. The power of energetically-connected individuals is fuelling the 'We' feeling and bringing the disenchanted together to develop their networks. Such new systems are showing that a new type of consciousness is arising, which will mark the generations to come. Those generations that come after us will be born *as change* rather than being born *into change* – this is a slight yet very significant difference.

The Phoenix Generation

The generation now being born into the world is what I refer to as the *Phoenix Generation*: those children being born now who will be young adults around 2030. I suggest that it will be this generation in particular that will assist in the transition toward forming a planetary society – a transition more radical than the shift from agrarian to urban life during the

1st Industrial Revolution. This is a revolutionary transition from national-cultural consciousness to planetary awareness and consciousness. What this entails is not only a structural shift but also a qualitative one; that is, a shift in our values, psychology, and consciousness. It is my view that those of the Phoenix Generation will be born with increased instinctive intelligence and with a greater degree of inherited wisdom.

As the Phoenix Generation grow up and integrate into and participate in their respective societies there will naturally be changes in many diverse areas of social life; such as health, politics, media, technology use, innovation, and spiritual practice. A new awareness of spirituality will emerge, where old institutional dogmas are replaced by increasing individual gnosis. We are moving toward the empowerment of the individual – of each human being – and this is frightening for the controlling authority structures. The Phoenix Generation will likely be the ones to free humanity from the dominance of erroneous ideas – ideas that forged war, created poverty and hunger, and sustained dis-ease. We are giving birth to a generation that will be successful in removing these illusions from the field of human consciousness.

Those of the Phoenix Generation will usher in a period where the feminine and masculine energies of the world will be re-balanced. Human values of love, compassion, understanding, patience, tolerance, and empathy will be more openly expressed and part of an active world – and not seen as predominantly 'female' values. The division that separates the masculine and feminine energies will gradually be replaced by a newer energy of unity – of coming together. Similarly, the artificial stigma around 'male' and 'female' roles in the world will be changed through the younger 'phoenix' men and women re-modelling role expectations. Women's participation will be more keenly appreciated, sought, and brought into collaboration in such major areas as global politics, economy, and business. An all-round intuitive energy will be the marker for the upcoming decades, and will find expression through young women of the Phoenix Generation holding key positions as change agents. We are moving toward an era of human evolution where integral energies – energies of coherence and harmony – will be established as the principle foundation.

The Phoenix Generation will actualize upon this planet in accordance with generational, evolutionary trends – giving rise to a new form of consciousness. This new wave of consciousness will then gradually seep into the core of all our future societies. Our responsibility now is to fully engage and be a part of the human *becoming* that we truly wish to see in the world. This requires that we spearhead the transition at hand and that we show, through our behaviour, the new models for change. We have the opportunity, and capacity, to do this for ourselves and, more importantly, for those to come – and this shall be our true legacy.

A Tale to Finish: 'For Fifty Years'

There once was a man who had worked all his life as a janitor at a hospital. He had worked for over fifty years and finally it was time to retire. All the doctors and nurses at the hospital arranged a farewell party for him and they all came together, including many of the patients too. When it came time for the old janitor to speak, he turned to the new janitor who was going to replace him, and said:

'Here in this hospital are all very good people and top professionals. Doctors are well trained and specialists in their fields; the nurses are also very dedicated and caring. Yet what I don't understand if that is so is why then for over fifty years everyone has been telling me over and over again "Beware of the microbes – pay attention to cleanliness and hygiene", which has been their motto all the time. Yet the truth is I've never seen one of these microbes!'

33. THE PHOENIX GENERATION PT. 2: USHERING IN AN ERA OF CHANGE

A generation of young people is arriving into a world that is more technologically assisted than in our entire history as a species. And they will be arriving with minds that see things differently than we currently do. That is, their thinking patterns will not automatically accept many of our beliefs, ideologies, or our socio-cultural systems. Especially, they will find themselves at odds with our orthodox systems of education and health, for example. In terms of education, they will require – or rather, demand – a tech-assisted educational platform the likes of which we have never seen before – because we have not yet created it. And as for health, those of the Phoenix Generation will react against the automatic acceptance of the dominant medical paradigm. They will resist being filled with old model thinking, invalid ideas, and antiquated notions. First, let us look at a new phase in education.

A New Phase in Education & Learning

The structure, content, and connectivity for this new educational platform is already emerging – and it will be a new phase in collaborative learning. In other words, the classroom is becoming global.

Our antiquated educational systems will have to adapt and go through a radical re-thinking and revision as a response to student's growing needs and attitudes. Here is what I envision:

1) Classrooms will no longer be contained within 4-walled rooms: learning spaces will be more interactive, incorporating many features of online interaction and group participation. Some of these will include interacting and working online alongside students from around the world; learning from virtual game-puzzles and online multi-media presentations; and connecting with learning environments that make use of various platforms. The student learning environment will become an open collaborative space that connects to other learning spaces across the planet – both physical and virtual. That is, MOOC – massive online open courses. This will expand the range of peer-teaching and peer-learning.

2) Not only will students have access to a varied range of teachers but they will also learn from peers around the world. That is, teaching will not be limited to the 'one person at the head of the class' model; rather, older people, retired persons, volunteers around the world, etc, will make themselves available in specially designated online platforms to offer their services for questions and learning forums. Guests from varied occupations – business leaders, scientists, creative artists, consultants, etc – will regularly join online learning forums to gladly interact with students and to pass on their own learning and knowledge.

3) Online '3-D world' platforms will also be developed as immersive learning experiences. Some teaching institutes will develop fully working virtual campuses (an extension from the online campus) where students can enroll as avatars and attend virtual classes populated by students from around the world. The learning process will shift from being a linear two-way model (teacher-student) to a multi-phase process incorporating a variety of learning possibilities with mixed-level collaborators. These mixed learning environments – no longer called classrooms – will also place students of

varying ages and abilities together. In this way older, more learned students, can also assist in the learning process of lower-level students. That is, learning environments will no longer depend upon location since many learning-teaching platforms will utilize an array of online and virtual collaborative spaces.

4) The learning process will be made more fun. It will allow for a broad range of creativity and 'free time' for brainstorming (heart-storming) ideas. The interaction between students and their varied teachers will be mutual and not one-way. Students will use an array of virtual games and online puzzle solving activities to exercise creativity. Multiple player platforms will also allow many students to work together and collaborate to solve riddles and quests – similar to video gaming yet with constructive goals and outcomes.

5) Learning modules will become more individually customized. Students will have more influence in directing their learning process according to their needs, wishes, and motivations. The old-model curriculum of preparing students for an industrial workforce will no longer apply. The world will have changed in a way that will have made many older needs obsolete. Also, the students of the Phoenix Generation will have a greater instinctual understanding of what they feel is necessary to learn for each individual. The 'one-model-fits-all' rule will no longer apply and will have been phased out. Importantly, the 'stick-carrot' reward system will also go the way of the dinosaurs. The older examination system will be replaced by a variety of comprehension/capacity feedback from both teachers and fellow peers. Understanding will be measured by one's comprehension and individualized capability – not by standardized grades. Stress and self-doubt will be replaced by enjoyment and self-confidence.

To summarize, the educational system required for the Phoenix Generation will celebrate knowledge rather than box it or narrowly categorize it. Traditional 'knowledge' subjects – mathematics, science, history, etc – will still be offered; however, they will be accompanied by a variety of modules more suited to the practical and creative needs of the new era. It will seem as if there is an endless diversity of topics for the student to connect with. The variety of creative subjects, combined with an array of collaborative online environments, will take education to a new level. Such new learning environments will allow the students to be active content-choosers, rather than passive and coerced content-consumers. Education will cease to be redundant and will assist students to become the co-creators of their world.

Now let us turn to examine, briefly, what may happen when those of the Phoenix Generation no longer accept to be a receptacle for outworn medical dogmas.

Health in the Era of the Phoenix Generation

The young people will know more on an instinctive level what will and what won't work. I foresee the following changes in the area of health during the early years of the Phoenix Generation:

1) There will be a dramatic turn away from the belief, confidence, and trust in the current health industry. The present health industry is a global trade that has commoditized human well-being into the *industrialization of illness*. The rise of 'big pharma', as it has been termed, constitutes a pharmaceutical conglomerate of global players that wield immense political influence. Theirs is an agenda that seeks to support a sickness-for-profit model at the expense

of natural, organic knowledge and well-being practices. The basic premise of the old paradigm 'illness industry' is that profits come before patients. Profits also come before transparent and objective research trials and results, according to many researchers. The pharmaceutical lobby (also known as the drug lobby) exhibits its own unhealthy influence over politics and media representation. The result of this has already seen a loss of trust in the pharmaceutical industry, especially in the arena of vaccinations.

2) The young people of the Phoenix Generation will listen more to their bodies; they will be more careful over what they ingest (food and medicine); and they will instinctively feel what their bodies need. They will recognize the innate intelligence of their bodies. As a consequence our health diagnosis will have less dependency on clinical diagnostics and more trust in one's instinct. Increased intuition over one's own health will guide people in choosing what changes they need to bring about for themselves. It will become more common for people to express the feeling, and intention, that they are in communication with their body and its needs. This will occur parallel to a loss of 'public face' and reputation of big pharma as emerging revelations make public the dishonesty of our incumbent industrialization of illness. The global corporate health industry will be one of the major old paradigm systems to suffer at the hands of (r)evolutionary change.

3) There will be increased confidence and support of what are now considered 'alternative' health practices. This will emerge as our sciences continue to validate the principles and properties of quantum energy fields. The concept of energy exchange, and vibrational medicine, in healing will become more commonplace, and increasingly sought after. This includes the use of human consciousness in non-local healing. According to medical doctor Larry Dossey, distance-healing and similar attributes of the nonlocal

mind have often been referred to as 'distant intentionality.' A major shift during the years of the Phoenix Generation will be the recognition that illness is not solely an individual matter, but is something which affects others around us. The rise and recognition of non-local healing will be central to how health is viewed and understood in the post-big pharma years. In the beginning the older doctors will have a hard time accepting this transition. However, as those of the Phoenix Generation assume the positions of doctors themselves they will usher in this new period for human health.

4) Health and illness will be viewed as transitional states – even death will be recognized as a transitional moment – and thus empathy, compassion, and love will play greater roles in the process of healing. Already we have the early signs of this change emerging in open-minded doctors and patients around the world, and in many other incidents rarely publicized. Human well-being is becoming recognized as being related to the transpersonal and nonlocal. The years ahead will usher in more education and new understanding about health, biology, and the nature of illness and disease.

5) The emergence of new scientific knowledge will help humans to live longer. Extended life will go hand in hand with surprising research findings about the nature of human DNA. We will come to realize that DNA acts to activate specific energies within us when our state/frequency is ready for this. That is, human DNA activates specific dormant functions within the human being according to evolutionary necessity. DNA will finally be accepted as an unfolding process, rather than as a static 3% protein building set of chemical reactions. This unfolding process occurs in a quantum, nonlinear way; and will be grasped in an intuitive way, helping people to have more natural insight over their well-being. The development of

personal well-being and health, with extended lives, will lead not to an increasing population but rather to a decrease. This will be because there will be a decline in the need for larger 'survival families', as is often the case in current developing nations. The instinct will shift more toward smaller families that can provide close care and nurture. Modern couples of the Phoenix Generation that live in high-population regions may even opt out themselves of raising children. Modern states are likely to begin experiencing a decline in population around 2030 rather than an increase.

In the years of the Phoenix Generation the new young minds will simply choose to do things differently – old patterns will shift. Finally, our planetary society will stabilize its population growth in line with sustainable limits. Living within sustainable limits will form part of the new understanding governing human health and well-being.

A Tale to Finish: 'Renunciation'

After reaching old age, and after a home life of many joys and sorrows, a husband and wife decided to renounce the worldly life and devote the rest of their time to meditation and pilgrimage to the most sacred shrines.

One time, en route to a Himalayan temple, the husband saw on the path in front of him a fabulous diamond. Very quickly, he placed one foot on the jewel to hide it, thinking that if his wife saw it then perhaps a sense of greed would arise in her that could contaminate her mind and delay her mystical evolution. Yet the wife, discovering the ruse of her husband, said in a fair and gentle voice:
'Dear, I would like to know how you have renounced the world if you still make a distinction between diamond and dust.'

34. THE PHOENIX GENERATION PT. 3: SHIFTS IN LIFESTYLE CHOICES

Those whom I refer to as the Phoenix Generation, coming of age over the next couple of decades, will show a marked difference in their consumption – and production – of media. They will be active *pro*sumers of media content, not only consumers. They will actively engage with information, and seek to produce content if they feel that the media they are exposed to is not representing the truth for them. Such creative engagement will also impact their lifestyle choices.

Media & Lifestyle

The following are a number of key aspects that I foresee will mark the changes in media and lifestyle choices for those of the Phoenix Generation:

- Young minds will have had enough of a fear mongering, fear-sponsoring media. As instinctual intelligence is more evident, the false facades will drop and people will be less difficult to be side-lined into controlled distraction through entertainment trivia. The old programming that dominated the mainstream media in past decades offered only a crude and brutal programming that delighted in high-tension and stressful drama: in conflicts, murder, and sexual espionage. Such programming will cease to inspire a new younger generation.

- There will be a shift in media programming toward what elevates a person rather than what closes them down. This shift will be brought about by the increasing demand from people for more informative programming. The young minds and hearts of the Phoenix Generation will increasingly reject negative news and influences, and naturally shift away from such energies. The mainstream media will be forced – through viewing figures and thus advertizing revenue – to broadcast more inspiring and uplifting programs.

- The mainstream media will be impacted greatly by the rapid rise of more community media. The larger corporations will continue to merge and consolidate as they find it difficult to exist in a consumer environment that increasingly is people-centered, and whom rejects their style of broadcast. What is now termed the 'alternative media' will become more popular as people seek local stories that inspire and interest them. So not only will community media see a revival – thanks in large part to appropriate technology – but also self-produced content will become more the norm. Those of the Phoenix Generation will themselves be content producers – producing, creating, and distributing their own inspired content-driven media. The age of top-down corporate-controlled media will no longer be the dominant force.

- Young people will become their own journalists – creating, producing, and out-sourcing their services. Individuals will not only contribute stories and news items to the mainstream media, but will also create their own media platforms. Many new voices will become recognized and verified as credible sources of information. Young media activists from around the world will be able to supply information faster than mainstream journalists. Also, they will report from areas that mainstream media either cannot, or will not, go to – such as local violent conflict zones or selective communities. Peer-to-peer programming will become more popular as people prefer to produce and share their own news, stories, and events.

- Transparency will become the new watchword as mainstream media and governments make closer ties. As online content becomes increasingly monitored by governments, and doctored by media conglomerates, transparency and integrity will become a central issue. Younger generations of people will turn their back on attempts to control and manage the flow of information. The media landscape will never be the same again as the power of the image is taken from the hands of the few into the digital fingertips of the many.

- Changes in media attitudes will also reflect changes in lifestyle choices. People will seek out those experiences and impacts that are positive, and which bring harmony to life rather than disorder. Desirable lifestyle traits sought within these years will include reconciliation, harmony, coherence, non-judgment, forgiveness, conscious communication, love, understanding, transparency, honesty, integrity, and of course humor. There will be a greater general appreciation of the role and place of meditation within peoples' lives. During these years more and more people will be shifting their priorities in life, seeking out meaning and well-being in place of career status and money. This will manifest over the years in many people leaving their traditional employment and seeking out new and alternative ways to support themselves that are more conducive to inner development and well-being.

- There will be a shift in habitation choices as young people seek for more nourishing environments to live in. This may result in many young people leaving crowded urban areas or joyless suburban neighborhoods. Alternatively, they will wish to rejuvenate their neighbourhoods into vibrant districts. This is likely to result in a revitalization of local communities, with an emphasis upon sustainability. The creative minds of the Phoenix Generation will strive to construct new models and ways of doing things that are more harmonious with environmental and ecological systems. New sustainable lifestyles will emerge rapidly as people seek well-being and personal meaning that is in balance with physical limits and resources. New communities, towns, villages, and regions will adjust to do things differently in alignment with the growing inner authority of the younger generations.

The Phoenix Generation & Emerging Technologies

The exponential rate of discovery in the coming decades of the 21st century will be extraordinary. Those of the Phoenix Generation will be born into a world where new technologies of communication and collaboration will enhance the connection with the world around them. Theirs will be a tech-assisted lifestyle like never before. They will grow up accustomed to interfacing with technology in ways we have yet to foresee. The new young minds of the Phoenix Generation will have an unprecedented relation to technology and its implications. The following gives a brief outline of the changes we are likely to see:

- Fears over privacy, data-collection, and a surveillance society will give way to technologies that enhance transparency, connection, and collaboration. The old paradigm use of technology, which played a role in neo-liberal globalization and authoritarian governance, will at first fight the rise of ungoverned social networks. These struggles may be dominant in the early stages until the new thinking is able to align technologies with models of transparency and open cooperation. Technologies will then be developed that will lay the framework for a planetary society based on an ethics of sharing and openness alongside the respect for privacy. Technologies of communication and connection will continue to foster a sense of togetherness amongst people worldwide. The open-source culture will become dominant among the younger generation as they collaborate to develop and share technological innovation and progress.

- The online 'cloud space' will become the dominant domain for the storage, transmission, and interaction of information. This will further add to the sense of moving through a 'seamless' environment where technologies will increasingly be embedded into our everyday world. This will nurture the sense of living in a 'quantum' era where instant connectivity and sharing will become second-nature to the younger minds. It will become increasingly evident that our human technologies *external* to us are only manifesting a reality that already exists *within*

- Simultaneous and instant communication across space and time will nurture within the Phoenix Generation a sense of living within a planetary society. They will feel in constant contact with like-minded people across the world. This physical connectivity will help to stimulate and catalyze collective empathy as people will feel an innate sense of being energetically connected to others. The instinctual intelligence within the younger generations especially will be shared around the world almost instantly. This fostering of collaboration will lead to an acceleration of inventions and new discoveries.

- Quantum computing will be a main driver in the development of a new generation of technologies. This will emerge alongside the new sciences providing quantifiable evidence, as well as the applied understanding, of quantum energy (that is, the scientific ability to see and measure quantum energy). This will pave the way for a re-write of human scientific knowledge. Quantum computing and quantum science will work to form the foundations of an era that at its heart will radically change the way human beings communicate and interact with their environs and the living universe. It is likely that during this time a form of *quantum communication* will be developed that will allow humanity to attempt contact with other intelligences in the galaxy. This physical technology will exist alongside our 'internal technologies' that will also be opening up to greater forms of contact (including telepathic). It will be evident during these later years of scientific discovery that humanity is not alone within the cosmos. The next evolution of quantum technologies will be the breakthrough we have been waiting for in our bid to make verifiable contact with other intelligences in the universe.

- The Phoenix Generation will also be part of a new generation of biotechnology. The old model thinking of biotechnology was focused on modifying the function and behavior of microbes and living organisms to improve performance. This ranged from enhancing the human body – recombinant gene technologies and immunology therapies – to bioengineering. The future of technology, however, will not be centered around upgrading current capacities but in their cross-convergence. The whole plethora of emerging technologies – nano/bio-technology; synthetic and quantum biology, quantum computing, etc – will increasingly merge so that the very definition of 'what is life?' will be questioned. The new era of technological innovation and progress will be the beginning of bringing technology 'alive'. As DNA becomes increasingly merged into computing and synthetic biology, we will witness the early stages of a new bio-tech creation phase that will mark the birth of a new era in *living technology*.

After this time the chief feature of modern technologies of human civilization will be the fact that they will be a part of the Earth's living eco-system

It will be difficult to underestimate the role and potential of technology in the years ahead. Not only will technological development be a central hallmark of the era of the Phoenix Generation – it will also define the future evolution of humanity.

A Tale to Finish: 'A man his horse and his dog'

A man his horse and his dog were walking along a street. After a long walk the man realized that the three had died in an accident. Sometimes it takes time for the dead to realize their new condition. The walk was very long , uphill, the sun was strong and the three were drenched in sweat and very thirsty . Desperate need of water.In a curve of the road , they saw a magnificent gate, all marble walkway leading to a square with gold blocks in the center was a fountain of clear water gushing . Walker spoke to a man from a checkpoint guarding the entrance. - Good morning - said the man - Morning - said the guard - What place is this , so cute - asked Walker - This is heaven - was the answer - I'm glad you 've come to heaven, I have very thirsty - You can enter drinking water ad libitum - - my horse and my dog are thirsty too - so sorry - said the guard - no entry here animals allowed the man said. The man was very disappointed because his thirst was great. But he would drink no leaving your friends with thirst. It followed its path. After long uphill, with thirst and fatigue multiplied , they reached a site whose entrance was marked by a semi old gate that opened onto a dirt road with trees on both sides that made him shade. In the shadow of one of the trees , a man was lying with his head covered by a hat. He seemed to be asleep. - Good morning - said the traveler - Good day - My horse , my dog and I have very thirsty - - There is a fountain in the stones - the man stating his said - said the man may drink at will man the horse and dog went to the spring and quenched their thirst - Thank you - said the traveler to leave. - Back when they want - the man replied - About - said the traveler - what is

the name of this place ? - Sky - said the man - Honey? ! But if the marble
gate keeper told me that there was heaven ? - That is not heaven , it's hell
Walker perplexed. - That false information must cause great confusion. - No
way - the man said - indeed we do them a great favor. There are those who
are able to leave their best friends.

35. THE PHOENIX GENERATION PT. 4: ECONOMICS AND POLITICS

Innovative change will emerge and provide creative solutions to current economic and political systems in the years, and decades, ahead. Such solutions are likely to emerge from the periphery; from what are known as 'disruptive technologies.' That is, creative alternatives are likely to appear as anomalies yet gradually develop to become serious new models. Such emerging alternative forms of finance and politics will gradually unfold over the coming years, yet may not appear overnight.

In terms of economics these new models may include the following:

- A mixture of both localized and global economic systems will emerge that operate together. The localized models will be based on alternative forms of exchange (city currencies; barter systems; digital payments) that support regional businesses and projects. Various forms of similar micro-currencies will pop up in communities around the world. The global systems are likely to be based upon fewer currencies (or credits) that are agreed upon by the international community – rather than being pegged to a particular currency favoring specific nations. Digital currencies are likely to become a major global player for local, global, and online transactions.

- Governments will learn that a new form of economics must take into account not perpetual growth but sustainable limits and domestic well-being. It will be abundantly clear that the perpetual growth paradigm of 20th century economics is no longer a viable option for maintaining a coherent and stable economic framework. The new economics will be more tangibly connected to value and worth, rather than to virtual hoarding and unsustainable speculating. Following the footsteps of Bhutan's Gross National Happiness index, different regions will consider their wealth based on the well-being of its peoples. Regional and international economics will value people and their unique contributions. The true wealth of a region will be measured by its local resources and services. Gross National Happiness will become more significant in a world where new minds are looking to create a sustainable, long term future for the planet.

- Debt will no longer be the principle economic driver. This will release people from debt bondage and other forms of forced social indenture. A new economics will once again be seen as a force for creativity, innovation, and development; rather than as a commodity that burdens and restricts people. A new economics will be seen as a medium and energy of circulation. This will include a new array of innovative funding options that will emerge to help small, local projects and needs across the globe.

- Individuals the world over will contribute in funding the projects they relate to and agree with. In a system that develops from the previous crowd-funding model, people everywhere will act as the shareholders, receiving a shared value in profits. Global economics will no longer need to rely on top-down funding, as it develops a strong and reliable decentralized model. This will not neglect the role of larger corporations as younger innovative minds will increasingly take on major roles in businesses of the future. Many corporations and businesses will have to undergo considerable re-structuring in order to survive the transition into the new era. This re-structuring will ensure that they are more responsive to peoples' needs, as well as the need to invest in the new thinking for a viable future.

- Off-shoring and tax havens will be monitored and, in most cases, dismantled. A newly formulated international financial-credit system will be created that is based on transparent transactions rather than opaque, offshore accounts run by private individuals/organizations. The corrupt international economic system of the early 21st century will be no more.

- The new economics will shrug off the old image of being a source of inequality and a major cause of injustice. Finance will re-brand itself as a means for implementing solid and positive change in the world. It will embrace the decentralized, connected culture and begin to circulate more freely between people in a way that is not restricted solely to financial exchange. An economics of welfare and well-being based on the exchange of services and assistance will also be prominent among the new generations: altruism will replace austerity.

By 2030 I foresee that new financial models will be based on a future that is increasingly decentralized and cooperative. Furthermore, new paradigm business plans will catalyze creative forms of leadership and inspiring role models. This will also impact current political systems.

Politics in the Age of the Phoenix Generation

Democracy has thus far shown itself to be open to corruption, manipulation, and inefficiency. In other words, it has not delivered on the goods it has always promised. Rather, democratic politics is a form of 'democracy' in name only, despite the relative progressive nature of western political systems. It has still not truly been a political process representative for the people – especially when the choices for voting are so limited. It has been similar to deciding between two varieties of product on the shop shelf (only to find out later that both products are owned by the same multi-national company!). Political processes the world over fall short in their offerings. They have yet to represent a truly inclusive and transparent political process. For this reason, the political process is set for change in the years ahead. I suggest the following:

- So-called 'political parties' will not be exclusively for politicians. The domain of politics will diversify and will consist of peoples from all areas of life to represent local, national, and international regions. Governments, and the political process, will not exclusively be the domain of career politicians: it will be comprised of representatives from all walks of life. These will include, but not be limited to, civil society; community representatives; trade representatives; scientists; well-known thinkers/intellectuals; architects/designers; and cultural creatives and artists. Furthermore, each person (voter) will be able to be included in the various stages of the political process through digital forms of participation.

- The new young voters of the Phoenix Generation will no longer accept the bickering and name-calling that has generally been called 'politics'. The new youth will not want the old divisive energies from the previous era. The new minds will wish for integrity, honesty, and transparency in the political process, irrespective of geography and culture. There will no longer be any space for the old debates – politics will have to drop the crude, often simplified and manufactured discussions of Left vs. Right; Capitalism vs. Anti-capitalism; Democratic vs. Republic, and the rest. The old paradigm mentality will wish to continue fighting over these ruptured and antiquated distinctions; yet those of the new model will no longer accept their rudimentary and divisive tactics. Increasing human awareness and instinctual intelligence will see through the theatrical two-dimensional charade that was once used to sway the masses. Those of the Phoenix Generation will instinctively know that the most destructive decision that an individual can make is to give away their own authority and decision-making power. This new era of change will herald the rise of participatory politics.

- Technologies for more inclusive and participatory democracy will emerge that will benefit the people. The political processes that will survive the transition years of the next two decades will be those that represent the participatory spirit of the people. The survival of politics as we know it will depend on the ability of personages and processes to re-calibrate and be in alignment with the increasing numbers of awakening individuals. Our digital technologies will ensure that participatory politics is a practical reality. The generation(s) to come will ensure that the practical reality becomes a genuine one.

- There will emerge a wave of conscious leaders who will not be out to sell themselves on superficial short-term promises. There will still be leaders in the field of politics, as there will be in other fields. However, the new leaders that will emerge from among the Phoenix Generation will be fully involved in participatory politics. They will know that they have a responsibility to listen to the feedback of others. The new wave of leaders will instinctively understand that theirs is a planetary society where a long-term future vision is required. This long-term political perspective will instinctively embrace a planetary perspective where peoples, nations, issues, and needs are all woven together into a penetrating and interlacing worldview. Participatory politics inherently recognizes that any regional problems and issues are global ones too and therefore shared. The young leaders of the Phoenix Generation will carry the new energy into the conflict regions, such as the Middle East and Africa. The new wave to emerge in politics will not be confined only to the so-called 'industrialized' nations but will, importantly, rise up and develop in those areas most in need.

- Political responsibility will be seen as critical. The goal of participatory politics that is set to emerge will have peace and transparent political responsibility as a priority. The prospect of peace and unity upon a diverse planet will be one of the radical shifts that signifies a change in direction for our planetary species. It will not happen overnight and will need time and effort.

The political process may be one of the harder institutionalized systems to adapt and change. Yet it will do so, in time, mainly because of a new wave of younger people entering its ranks with renewed vision and goals.

A Tale to Finish: 'To Teach'

A zealous disciple, who had a desire to teach others the truth, asked his Master for his blessing for him to begin teaching. However, the Master simply replied:
- Wait.

Year after year the disciple returned with the same question again and again – and each time the Master gave the same answer:
- Wait.

Finally, one day he said to the Master:
- When will I be able to teach?

And the Master replied:
- When your eagerness to teach has disappeared.

36. WELCOME TO THE 'NEW NORMAL'

We have entered a time which I refer to as the *New Normal,* and we need to understand that things are never going to be the same again. We have to get used to doing things differently – for these 'different things' will become our normal ways soon enough. This shift from older patterns and structures that once served us well, into a space where some things are no longer working for us can be unsettling and disturbing. Yet don't waste time with old energy patterns that are no longer working. We may feel frustrated in not knowing what to do – and yet this is only just the beginning. In terms of the longer time scale we still have a long way to go, for this change is going to be many years in the making.

Things may now change faster than they have ever done before – we are living in a reality that is on the move. It is likely that many of us have already experienced this – a sense of rapidity and uncertainty unlike previous years. There is no need for this feeling of 'shifting ground' to cause anxiety. Change does not mean something negative – people are only afraid of what they don't know. The easy part in all of this is accepting the need for a 'new normal' – the more difficult part is to actively engage in change, in a way that is balanced, stable, and not strange. Being a part of the 'new normal' also means normalizing ourselves: there is no more need to stand apart; that is, to use 'difference' as part of your personality or identity. You cannot express your full potential when imbalanced. The 'new normal' is not here to alienate oneself and others – it does not support divisive energies.

Sometimes change needs courage – courage to accept this change as the new normal. Some people are more used to and adaptive to change than others –

each person must find what is right and comfortable for them. However, we are not starting from scratch – arriving to where we find ourselves now is also part of the change.

In fact, it is stability which is the illusion as everything is in flux. Life is one complete flux-engine – if we can put it that way – and the human body is equipped for constant change. When there is imbalance in the body it naturally seeks to find balance: physically, emotionally, and energetically. We already instinctively know this, and how to practice it. By re-adapting to change and flux we propel ourselves forward – it is a force of momentum within our lives. The new re-balancing is not about going back to the old – it is about finding new positions and definitions. We have to re-define for ourselves what is the *new normal.*

We have to learn how to operate the new tools we have, and which we are expected to use. Religious belief and unquestioning faith were old tools, for example. Now we need to figure out what are the new tools we have, and how to use them. And within this period of new learning we may also need to do some personal 'clearing' – to get our own personal house in order.

So let's be clear: the *new normal* is consistent change – and this *normal* can change on a daily basis. Is this so difficult to accept and understand? It seems that many of the young people can work with this; it is not difficult for them to grasp the essentiality of change. For many young people, it seems obvious that change is an essential, and necessary, part of life. It is only us, entrenched in our years of conditioned stability that fear such flux and flow.

If anyone reading this is feeling a connection to this theme it is also because they sense the need for change within their own lives. They sense it is right – that there is some urge within them that is telling them that something needs to change – there is intent to know more. There's no better time than now for re-engagement – to reflect upon the question of 'what is "life" for me? – and how can I participate?'

The following are some of what I consider to be at the basis of change:

i)   Release the fear conditioning
ii)   Re-calibrate the definitions of what is 'normal'
iii) Observe emotions and emotional responses and needs
iv)   Get used to change – it is the *only* normal there is
v)   Be joyful with change and changing habits/patterns – learn to love it
vi)   Don't try to get back to the old 'normal' – adjustment is not a return, it's a moving forward
vii) Waiting for the 'old' is not an option
viii) Change works better when you are pro-active – so activate your engagement/participation. Get involved with your own changes!
ix)   Trust your intuition and intuitive feelings

It can be unsettling at first when trying to get used to something that is always moving! It is like a radio station that constantly shifts its broadcast frequencies – and every day you have to re-tune your radio to find the new frequency. Yet this constant shifting is also a way for us to find meaning and significance in our lives. We may find that many of the shifts that we choose to activate/act on will have a direct influence upon our need to find a renewed meaning in life. Another way to consider these changes is to view them as being part of the shift from survival mode to creation mode – creating a new way of living more suitable to how we wish to live life in creative and meaningful ways.

As we gradually (or even suddenly!) shift into the era of the new normal we may discover that we fall into one of the following categories:

i)   Manifestors

ii) Facilitators

iii) Nurturers

Each role is equal in importance – and yet each is different in how it relates and engages with others in life. The new normal is going to have a strong influence upon the values of connectivity, communication, consciousness, and compassion.

Our social, local, and global networks will be ever more important for us. Whether we manifest things in life, facilitate for others, or nurture others – each involves conscious participation. That is the core of the new normal – balanced, stable, conscious participation in finding meaning for ourselves and others; and to be creative and active in pursuing a positive future for all.

A Tale to Finish: 'The Shepherd'

At dusk a shepherd was preparing to lead his herd of sheep into the barn for the evening. Upon counting his flock he realized that one was missing and became very alarmed. Distraught, the shepherd began searching for hours until it was late at night. Eventually, realizing that he could not find the missing sheep he began to sob in despair. Then a man coming out of the tavern passed him, took two looks at him and said:

'Hey, why are you wearing a sheep on your shoulders?'

37. SPOTIFY YOUR MIND: CONSCIOUSNESS IN THE AGE OF STREAMING

What does it mean to say that we are 'plugged-in' to a source of creative streaming? And why is it that this phrase does not seem odd or out of place? Is it because modern lives, with its analogies of electrical 'plugging-in' and digital 'streaming,' have become the new vocabulary to understand our internal processes? Yet the concept of being plugged-in to creativity and insight has always been around – the Greeks knew it and every poet since - as being the work of the *muses*, those goddesses of inspiration. What is certainly changing is the language and *how* we understand these concepts. In today's world the following extract may not seem out of place:

> *Innovation doesn't emerge in a vacuum. It arises from a great collective ocean of thought into which we are all plugged-in. In this way, what is created from us is an expression of our streams of consciousness.*

And yet it is all modern – a modern myth, you might say. Our cultural experiences, our technologies, and our vocabulary, all develop in relation to one another to influence not only how we see the world, but also how we respond to it. What if all the above - our worldview, cultural experiences, languages, and technologies - are an expression of how we actually understand the nature of human consciousness? It seems to this writer that the world around us is an ongoing reflection of how we ourselves develop our understanding of human consciousness – and it seems like we're now being spotified! Let me try to explain what I mean by this.

Human technologies that are designed to enhance - or at least amplify - our relationship to the world have an essential, and often overlooked, connection with the state of human consciousness. Sometimes this innate relationship is out of balance, is lopsided and incongruous, and results in technologies of destruction. Other times the relationship is more aligned and results in creative innovation that aims toward the betterment of human life upon the planet. Our recent wave of technological progress can be traced back to the industrial revolution that emerged in the western world in the latter part of the 18th century. Yet it was the Second Industrial Revolution a century later that produced electrification and gave rise to the great technologies of communication (transport, radio, telephone, television, radar, etc). These industrial technologies embodied the mindset of progress and material betterment. Literature of the age abounded with metaphors of electricity as these technologies also sparked the creative imagination. The history of communications, with its increasing ability to establish connection and communication between peoples at further and further distances, called for a new reorientation of human perspective. A new perception of the dimensions of space and time began to birth a psychological consciousness – one that wanted to look beyond the borders and horizons of the physical frontier. The physical constriction of time and space mirrored the inner exploration that surged within the 20th century. The early part of the 20th century was a period when the 'collective unconscious' was becoming a conscious part of the collective mind. The theories of Freud, Jung, Reich, and other psychoanalysts were changing how people regarded human behaviour and parameters of human thinking. These developments coincided with the rise of the motion pictures - a way of projecting internal ideas onto the external screen - as a cultural phenomenon.

The 20th century thus became a time for asking and answering such questions as: What lies beyond life? What is behind matter? What lies behind our conscious thoughts? What lies behind all biological life? This thrust for seeking human meaning in both outer and inner realms reached a zeitgeist in the second half of the 20th century as the East came to meet the West. A Western counterculture emerged through the newfound popularity of Eastern teachings (Buddhism, Taoism, Sufism, etc.) and the experimental playfulness of mind-altering processes. People were increasingly exploring their own feelings, self-reflection, and the interior gaze. Timothy Leary was right to suggest that the new era had shifted to 'the politics of the nervous system.' By the 1990s the most popular poet in the United States was the Persian Sufi Jalalludin Rumi; holography and the holographic universe was a new popular paradigm; the left-right working of the brain hemispheres was a popular subject; the Internet was revolutionizing communications; and notions such as the noosphere, Global Brain, and collective consciousness were almost commonplace. The spectacular rise in global communication technologies (Internet-enabled devices, digital platforms, social networks, etc) reflected a new form of participatory consciousness, especially among younger people that did not exist previously.

The previous mindset – sometimes called the 'industrial mindset' – was one that viewed the materiality of life as the dominant consciousness. This was a consciousness of acquisition, possession, ownership, and ultimately control. It was all about who had the hardware, and the power to control the hardware over others. It was an age that flourished on patents and copyright, and restriction and centralization. It was all very tangible, and solid, and could be seen, felt, and known. It was about communications via cables (that could be cut), and everything was attached, and thus everything contained in the grid – in the physical matrix. Then technologies started to change: the cables began first to disappear beneath the ground (or sea), and then to disappear all together as wireless and satellite became main commercial and civilian channels. The leads between the keyboard, mouse, and monitor vanished too. Things started to connect in non-visible ways; and they got smaller too. Then instead of just the computer we had multiple devices to connect to the ethereal ('where-exactly-is-it') web. And then our technologies became increasingly distributed and decentralized as networking became the dominant paradigm and way of operations. All that was solid was now melting into air.

The visionary Buckminster Fuller noted this decades earlier when he wrote of 'ephemeralization,' in which he said there was a technological trend that was shifting from heavy cables and towers/masts to fibre optics, then to space satellites (he sadly wasn't around for wi-fi). This showed how a civilization was transforming from heavier materiality toward lighter, more subtle, forms of connectivity and functionality. Similarly, the British historian Arnold Toynbee coined his 'Law of Progressive Simplification' from his extensive meta-historical study on the rise and fall of civilizations. By this, Toynbee indicated that civilizational growth was not so much measured by material resources but rather by its ability to transfer increasing amounts of energy and attention towards non-material growth, such as culture, education, artistic pursuits, community, wellbeing, etc. Toynbee also coined the term 'etherealization' to describe the historical process whereby a society learns to accomplish the same, or more, using less time and energy. We could say that the current peak of this ephemeral/ethereal-ization is in digital streaming.

Human technologies are fast merging into our ambient environments - into the vast ocean – so becoming increasingly more ethereal and seamless. Technologies will progressively aim to stream into our environment and daily lives - to merge into and facilitate an age of access. This reinforces and facilitates our shift from a culture and mindset of acquisition toward one of participation, whereby the greater power is not in the control of ownership (the old mind/paradigm) but in the way of collaborative participation and in 'sharing the streaming.' The future is trending toward distributive and networked access rather than the ownership of things. We can see this in how technology is opening up new means of access in ride-sharing, crowd-sourcing, open-sourcing – from Netflix to Spotify (and the rest). We've moved from the ground (hardware/hard drive) to the clouds (software/cloud computing) – quite literally! And yet this also conveniently (or coincidentally) mirrors a new understanding of human consciousness.

Up until recently the mainstream theory on human consciousness was that consciousness is solely a by-product of localized brain activity. That is, it is the result of a sufficiently complex brain structure and activity. Just as a generator creates electricity, so does the brain produce consciousness – it's as simple as that, or so it was thought. And yet this theory has encountered too many anomalies of late to retain its validity[xii]. Another hypothesis is one which uses the computer terminology and metaphor of cloud computing, and views consciousness as something *stored* external to the brain. In this way, consciousness is conserved beyond the brain as a non-local phenomenon. To continue with the computer analogy, this is similar to how information would be conserved on digital platforms accessed by computer networks or other cloud-enabled devices. Likewise, using this analogy, the mainstream theory of consciousness would be akin to an old-fashioned computer without built-in-memory that would lose all its data once switched

---

[xii] It is not the aim, or scope, of this article to discuss all the anomalies or debates on human consciousness. There is already sufficient literature out there for the avid researcher.

off. In this regard, the cloud theory posits consciousness as non-local, rather than localized within the brain. Further, the cloud theory allows for not only individual consciousness to be stored, and be recalled, but multiple. This perspective of accessing multiple consciousnesses, beyond our individual one, is reminiscent of Jung's collective consciousness. This theory would appear to support the observations of psychiatrists and consciousness researchers who have induced altered states of consciousness in their clients. When in altered states a vast majority of people have the capacity to recall almost everything that has happened to them. Moreover, their recall is not limited solely to their own experience but can also include the experiences of other people as well.[xiii] This cloud theory therefore suggests something akin to a collective field of consciousness that makes complete information available relative to the mode of access. This perspective shares similarities with the scientific research on the Akashic Field[xiv] and Morphic Resonance[xv].

It is also the view of this author that consciousness is a non-local phenomenon that is accessed by the brain (and to some extent the human nervous system). In other words, consciousness is not a by-product of the brain, but rather the brain *receives* and *interprets* consciousness, which is infused throughout the cosmos, but does not *produce* it. We are not the *owner* of our thoughts; instead we are the *interpreters* of the streams of consciousness that we receive. Conscious thought is more about access than it is acquisition. Does this sound familiar?

[xiii] For example, see the work of Stanislav Grof - http://www.stanislavgrof.com/
[xiv] *Science and the Akashic Field: An Integral Theory of Everything* by Ervin Laszlo
[xv] *Morphic Resonance: The Nature of Formative Causation* by Rupert Sheldrake

We don't own our thoughts, any more than we own the songs we listen to on Spotify - we just have access to them, and we personalize their arrangement. We personalize conscious information and categorize it into our likes and dislikes according to our background (social conditioning). Just as we stream our music from the web and create our own individual, personalized playlists. The streaming of digital music - the Spotifying of music - is likely to be a permanent feature of the future precisely because it models how human consciousness operates. As discussed, our technologies are also shifting from 'possession' to 'access' - from owning a physical object (of music or thought), to receiving the stream of music or thought.

As the fruits of modernity we have enjoyed the embellishment of details - the record cover design, the fold-out cd sleeve, etc; and these have become a beloved part of our tactile experience. Similarly, we have taken great pride (and often ego) in treasuring the thoughts we assumed to be our own. We have been immersed for an incredibly long time within a tangibly solid, object-orientated environment. The music was the album in our hands; we felt the need - and we needed the feel - to celebrate the physical presence: art as object and object as art. We have been honouring the islands of the visible moored within the waters of the invisible without realizing that everything is 'in' and 'a part of' this single vast ocean. Industrial era technologies eroded the invisible realm in order to support the visible plane. In what now appears to be a reverse trend, the visible plane is increasingly stepping back from the front-line to support the expansion of the invisible amongst our lives. We're being spotified as our tangible technologies begin their march toward their embedded merging with our environment, out of sight, as if melting into the cloud. Our access is now progressively more through the *receiving* of information from the 'ethereal' digital cloud that is saturating the environment we live in. The environment, embedded with our technologies, is now streaming the information to us. While those of us from the pre-digital generations may find this some getting used to, those youngsters born into a fully-digital world understand this as completely natural. Why? Because this is how information/energy operates in the universe – it is already all around us, and yet each localized part *streams* the transmission from the nonlocal field.

Human consciousness is continually receiving the streaming transmissions from the music of the spheres (the cosmos). We take this thought-music and arrange it according to our personal affectations and tastes; and then we manifest it into the world. Consciousness is not a by-product we produce from what we carry around with us in our heads. The object (the piece of music) will become less about what we carry around with us in our hands and more about what we can *access*. Our technologies are shifting us toward a new form of tactile experience; one where we participate by customizing and adapting the streaming information to better fit our personal lives. This is a form of engagement with information to better manifest and in-form our lives. This participation with information flows and streaming is representative of the era we are moving into, as the tangible melts into the intangible; as the visible plane dissolves its technological objects into the realm of the invisible. Our digital identities, traces, networks, and lives become merged with our physical footprints. The world is made flesh through streaming; just as we self-actualize and awaken as we further open our reception to the streaming of consciousness. Let us spotify our minds by receiving the music of wisdom, and may we manifest these truths within our lived experiences.

In the end, no one owns anything permanently anyway - we cannot take anything with us when we go: 'Take only what you can save from the sinking ship,' yells the captain. In these crucial moments we know, and only wish, to save our selves. And yet our selves have always been safely stored in the great cloud all along...

A Tale to Finish: 'Dragons'

It is said that a man named Zhu Pingman went to see a famous teacher to learn to kill dragons. He spent three years working hard and devoted his fortune to acquire the art of killing dragons.

Unfortunately, when he returned to his life, he never found a dragon.

38. CONSCIOUSNESS, COSMOS, PURPOSE, PT. 1 - Implications of a non-local view of human consciousness

Philosophers, artists, and scientists have been debating for centuries the questions concerning human consciousness: what it is and how it emerges. The question of human consciousness has also been at the heart of many mystical teachings, although these have tended to be based on revelation rather than investigation and discussion. Over the course of these many and varied investigations, debates have been divided between materialistic and what may be rather loosely termed as spiritual-metaphysical worldviews. In recent decades, thanks largely to the advance of sophisticated scientific methods and technology, scientists have been able to map and study the human brain, including neuronal patterns, brain disorders, and pathways of human thinking. This has led to an increased certitude among many scientists of a material view of human consciousness. In other words, consciousness as a by-product of the physical brain and as such cannot exist without brain function. This is the dominant paradigm amongst materialist thinkers and scientists. In more recent years, with the further research into nonlocal phenomena and theories of a holographic universe, various investigators have been re-visiting our received understanding of human consciousness. From these renewed scientific insights into the nature of a nonlocal cosmos, new findings have appeared that throw light onto how consciousness may operate. Furthermore, a nonlocal understanding of consciousness can provide cutting-edge implications for an increasingly interconnected human society. The research and ideas that I am going to put forth in this series of essays will imply that the future of human evolution upon this planet is largely also a question of the evolution of consciousness – specifically, conscious evolution. And the implication of conscious evolution is that it provides purpose – meaning – for a life that participates in this developmental impulse. I begin by examining some of the new perspectives or 'concepts' regarding human consciousness.

In his *Consciousness in the Cosmos* trilogy[xvi] Ervin Laszlo put forth what he termed the 'Third Concept of Consciousness.' In brief, Dr. Laszlo outlined various anomalies in current orthodox scientific theories of consciousness. In his exposition Laszlo clarified how it was unlikely that consciousness could be generated by the brain as a form of by-product - what he referred to as the 'turbine theory.' In this theory, which is the current mainstream model, the set of experiences we define as consciousness is generated by the living brain. This is similar to how a stream of electrons would be generated by a working turbine (hence Laszlo's naming). Therefore, just as electricity is a by-product of the turbine, so too is human consciousness the by-product of a functioning human brain. This theory postulates human consciousness as being local; as being produced *from* something tangible. Also, when this producer stops functioning – i.e., the brain ceases to be alive – then consciousness, and related streams of experience likewise stop. Medical science has gone a long way to validate the 'turbine theory' of consciousness by repeated experiments on how impaired brain functioning results in distorted consciousness.

The basic premise of this understanding of consciousness is that neuronal networks in the human brain have evolved to such a height of complexity that they produce a level of self-consciousness above that of any other animal on the planet (except perhaps dolphins and porpoises). This 'turbine theory' is thus not limited solely to human beings but is applicable to the vast range of living beings on the planet. Yet the level of complexity

---

[xvi] As appeared in *Watkins Mind Body Spirit* magazine, vols. 39/40/41.

in biological evolution is, in this theory, related to the degree of consciousness produced by each specific living creature.

Even though in recent years there have been renewed calls for a neurological basis for consciousness such pioneering theories still maintain an orthodox position. For example, neuroscientist Christof Koch, chief scientific officer at the Allen Institute for Brain Science, has publicly stated that 'consciousness arises within any sufficiently complex, information-processing system. All animals, from humans on down to earthworms, are conscious... That's just the way the universe works.'[xvii] For Koch, consciousness is a by-product of complexity; thus, complex systems produce varying levels of consciousness, and 'how much consciousness they have depends on how many connections they have and how they're wired up.'[xviii] Another so-called 'cutting-edge' theory from science is "orchestrated objective reduction" ('Orch OR'), which was first put forward in the mid-1990s by eminent mathematical physicist Sir Roger Penrose, and prominent anesthesiologist Stuart Hameroff.[xix] This theory claims that consciousness derives from deeper level, finer scale activities inside brain neurons. Although controversial at the time it has now gained greater credibility since the recent discovery of quantum vibrations in "microtubules" inside brain neurons now appears to corroborate this theory. Yet despite such recent examples of radical new scientific theories of consciousness, they still cling to the basis of an old paradigm 'turbine theory.' In other words, that consciousness is a secondary phenomenon resulting from primary activity located in the human brain.

[xvii] See http://www.wired.com/2013/11/christof-koch-panpsychism-consciousness/all/
[xviii] See http://www.wired.com/2013/11/christof-koch-panpsychism-consciousness/all/

[xix] See http://www.sciencedaily.com/releases/2014/01/140116085105.htm

Despite the apparent strengthening of the mainstream outlook on consciousness such a perspective has come under increasing critical doubt, owing to a range of experiences that appear to throw doubt upon its validity. Challenges to the turbine theory of consciousness have come from increasing evidence of 'after death' conscious experiences. According to the orthodox view, consciousness ceases when the brain dies – i.e., no generator, no current. For most of us this may seem like an obvious deduction. However, evidence to the contrary is now contradicting this theory. Many cases are now proving that human consciousness is maintained even though a person is technically declared brain dead. The near-death experience (known as the NDE) has been reported by sufficiently large numbers of people who were declared brain-dead. Conscious experience in brain dead people has been reported in almost 25 percent of tracked cases. The NDE phenomenon has now been widely researched and discussed by many credible sources.[xx] Furthermore, this phenomenon is not new and there are accounts of NDEs occurring in medieval times.[xxi] The existence of consciousness – a by-product of brain activity – in the absence of brain function cannot be accounted for by the mainstream turbine theory. There are also numerous indications that human consciousness exists in cases of permanent death. That is, many years after a person has died their consciousness remains available for contact and communication; whether through channelling or forms of ESP. However, in

---

[xx] Notable examples include *Science and the Near-Death Experience; How Consciousness Survives Death* by Chris Carter; *Dying to Be Me: My Journey from Cancer, to Near Death, to True Healing* by Anita Moorjani; *Proof of Heaven: A Neurosurgeon's Journey into the Afterlife* by Eben Alexander; *The Immortal Mind: Science and the Continuity of Consciousness Beyond the Brain* by Ervin Laszlo & Anthony Peake; *Return from Death: An Exploration of the Near-death Experience* by Margot Grey; and *Whole in One: The near-death experience and the ethic of interconnectedness* by David Lorimer.

[xxi] *Otherworld Journeys: Accounts of Near-Death Experience in Medieval and Modern Times* by Carol G. Zaleski

these cases the actual person is unable to return to life to corroborate the experience personally. Yet there is now enough credible evidence to put doubt into the mainstream theory that consciousness is solely a by-product of localized brain activity.

From this position of critical uncertainty Laszlo took the next step to suggest that a way to account for such anomalies is to assume that consciousness is in some way conserved beyond the brain; that is, as a nonlocal phenomenon. Laszlo posited the 'cloud theory,' to use computer terminology. In this hypothesis, consciousness is something *stored* external to the brain. In terms of Laszlo's 'computer theory' of consciousness, this is similar to how information would be conserved on digital platforms accessed by computer networks or other cloud-enabled devices. Likewise, using this analogy, the mainstream theory of consciousness would be akin to an old-fashioned computer without built-in-memory that would lose all its data once switched off. In this regard, the cloud theory posits consciousness as non-local, rather than localized within the brain. Further, the cloud theory allows for not only individual consciousness to be stored, and be recalled, but multiple. This perspective of accessing multiple consciousnesses, beyond our individual one, is reminiscent of Jung's collective consciousness. This theory would appear to support the observations of psychiatrists and consciousness researchers who have induced altered states of consciousness in their clients. When in altered states a vast majority of people have the capacity to recall almost everything that has happened to them. Moreover, their recall is not limited solely to their own experience but can also include the experiences of other people as well.[xxii] This cloud theory therefore suggests something akin to a collective field of consciousness that makes complete information available relative to the mode of access. This

---

[xxii] For example, see the work of Stanislav Grof - http://www.stanislavgrof.com/

perspective shares similarities with the scientific research on the Akashic Field[xxiii] and Morphic Resonance[xxiv]. Yet it also appears that despite the appropriateness of the cloud theory of consciousness, it too does not account for all observations.

In various recorded accounts of altered state consciousness it appears that contact/access is not only made with traces of one's nonlocal consciousness but also with distinctive separate conscious intelligence. That is, with an active consciousness that is not the consciousness of a living person. Such experiences, once the realm of shamanic or indigenous traditions, has increasingly entered into mainstream cultures. Previously, such 'encounters' were labelled as *mystical* or simply conveniently ignored as a quirky anomaly. However, as western science has developed its exploration of the inner realms (such as in transpersonal psychology and similar practices), such experiences have become more widespread and thus need to be accounted for. From this evidence a remarkable conclusion arises: that human consciousness can connect, and often communicate, with conscious entities that not only manifest a sense of self, but also carry distinct memories and information. This experience can neither be accounted for in the mainstream turbine theory nor the more radical cloud theory of consciousness. According to Ervin Laszlo, the most likely explanation is a 'third concept' – that consciousness is a cosmic phenomenon with holographic qualities (the 'hologram theory').

For Laszlo, the hologram theory posits that consciousness may manifest 'in' spacetime yet is a source that exists in a realm beyond spacetime. In other words, consciousness has its origins in a deeper dimension (in a 'unitary cosmic matrix'), and yet is manifested as a

---

[xxiii] *Science and the Akashic Field: An Integral Theory of Everything* by Ervin Laszlo
[xxiv] *Morphic Resonance: The Nature of Formative Causation* by Rupert Sheldrake

holographic projection within our quantifiable reality. This, Laszlo tells us, posits that all forms of localized consciousness are manifestations of an integral consciousness that is beyond spacetime. The implications of this understanding are that consciousness is not 'in' the brain, 'produced' by the brain, nor 'stored' beyond the brain, but is a localized aspect of a conscious intelligence that infuses the cosmos with its source beyond spacetime. Such understanding takes us beyond linear thinking, where consciousness is seen as a by-product of the brain, to integral thinking that says the brain *receives* and *interprets* consciousness, which is infused in the cosmos, but does not *produce* it. This realization, aided by the very latest scientific findings, points toward a unified cosmic matrix (also previously referred to as zero-point, cosmic plenum, or vacuum) as generating what we perceive as spacetime. The materiality of spacetime is thus a holographic projection, coded from an underlying cosmic matrix, which is the source of conscious intelligence. All things which emerge into our reality are holographic projections from a deeper dimension.

The understanding that consciousness belongs to a deeper dimension of reality has been the domain of a long perennial tradition that has been embraced by many well-known spiritual figures, artists, and even a handful of intuitive scientists. Now it is emerging as the new scientific paradigm for our era. And the evidence for this, it appears, lies in the incredible coherence of the cosmos.

A Tale to Finish: 'The Fox and The Rabbit'

Once upon a time a fox met a young rabbit in the woods. The rabbit asked:
'What are you?'
The fox replied:
'I'm a fox and I could eat you if I wanted.'

'How can you prove you're a fox?' asked the rabbit.

The fox did not know what to say, because in the past the rabbits always ran away and never asked such things. The rabbit said:

'If you can show me a written proof that you are a fox, then I will believe you.

So the fox went to the lion, who gave him a certificate stating that he was really a fox. When he returned, the fox gave the rabbit the paper. After glancing at the certificate, and while the fox was waiting, the rabbit quickly ran into his hole and was never seen again. The fox returned to the lions den, where he saw a deer conversing with him. The deer was saying: 'I want to see a written proof that you are a lion...'

The lion immediately killed and ate the deer. The lion turned to the fox and said:
'When I am hungry I do not need to give anything in writing.

The fox said to the lion:
'Why did you not tell me this before when I asked you for a certificate for the rabbit?'

'My dear fox' said the lion; 'you should have told me it was for a rabbit. I thought it was for a stupid human being, rather than an animal which has learned of this stupid hobby.'

39. CONSCIOUSNESS, COSMOS, PURPOSE, PT. 2 - Living in a Coherent Cosmos

If our observed universe is indeed a projection – of 'in-formed' – from an underlying conscious matrix (as suggested by the hologram theory), then we would expect the universe to manifest a marked degree of order. That is, there would be evidence that the universe we inhabit is not the end result of a random assembly of forces. In fact, cutting edge science has now shown that our universe is remarkably coherent. This coherence, which statistically is far beyond randomness[xxv], reveals that coherence is the dominant driver ("attractor") in the universe. From quantum behaviour – the smallest observable entities – to atoms, complex molecules, and living organisms, coherence appears to be an underlying purpose. There are, it seems, coherent relationships between events from one end of the universe to the other. The universe may not be a fully coherent system, yet coherence appears to be an innate universal orientation. This non-random nature of the universe suggests order above chance. Such order has now been scientifically measured in two principle forms: the numerical parameters of the universe, and the alignment (or fine-tuning) of its physical constants.

In terms of the universe's numerical parameters there are a number of 'coincidences.' One of the earliest to be discovered (by Arthur Eddington and Paul Dirac in the 1930s) was the ratio of the electric force to the gravitational force, which is approximately 10^{40}. Similarly, the ratio of the observable size of the universe to the size of elementary particles is likewise about 10^{40}. There are also other numerical alignments, such as the ratio of

---

[xxv] See 'Consciousness in the Cosmos: Part II – The Evidence of Consciousness in the Cosmos', *Watkins Mind Body Spirit* magazine, vol. 40

elementary particles to the Planck-length (which is 10^{20}) and the number of nucleons in the universe[xxvi].

Likewise, the physical processes that underlie our universe appear to be incredibly fine-tuned. It is not possible within the scope of this article to list all the staggeringly precise universal constants that 'just happened' to occur in order for life as we know it to arise in the universe. One example concerns the expansion rate of the early universe. If the expansion rate had been one-billionth less than it was, then the universe would have re-collapsed almost immediately. Similarly, if the expansion rate had been one-billionth more, it would have flown apart so fast that matter would not have been able to form. Another precise fine-tuning exists between the strength of the electromagnetic field relative to the gravitational field. If the difference had been other than it is, stable stars like our own sun would not have formed. Thus, the evolution of life on planets would not have been possible according to known laws. Yet another example is the difference between the mass of the neutron and the proton. If the mass of the neutron were not precisely twice the mass of the electron then no substantial chemical reactions could take place. Our universe has a stable configuration, in terms of matter, precisely because the electric charges of electrons and protons have an accurate balance. In other words, our universe is incredibly fine-tuned beyond any possibility of chance. It could be said that we exist in a 'just-right' universe. According to the calculations of mathematical physicist Roger Penrose, the probability of coming across such a universe, fine-tuned to life, by random selection is 1 in $10^{10^{123}}$. Physicist Bernard Haisch has wryly noted that there is a greater probability than this that our universe is teeming with intelligent life! There are no other words for it –

[xxvi] For further numerical alignments see 'Consciousness in the Cosmos: Part II – The Evidence of Consciousness in the Cosmos', *Watkins Mind Body Spirit* magazine, vol. 40

our universe is spectacularly coherent beyond our comprehension. And this drive toward emergent coherence also pervades our biological evolution. According to Laszlo, this trend is reflected throughout life on planet Earth.

The intricate elements and processes that make up what we call life all exhibit forms of entanglement that, according to quantum science, show remarkable coherence. Physicists Eric Cornell, Wolfgang Ketterle, and Carl E. Wieman demonstrated that complex molecules, cells, and even living organisms exhibit quantum-type processes (and received the 1995 Nobel Prize for their discovery). What this tells us is that complex organisms could not have evolved on this planet without some form of quantum coherence. The human body is one example, where each cell produces 10,000 bio-electro-chemical reactions every second, and there exists a constant flux of inter-reactions and processes connecting molecules, cells, organs, and fluids, throughout the brain, body and nervous system. Recent findings in biophysics have demonstrated that a form of quantum coherence operates within living biological systems through what is known as biological excitations and biophoton emission. What this means is that metabolic energy is stored as a form of electromechanical and electromagnetic excitations. Further, a quantum-level correlation in organisms is neither limited to the organisms themselves but also operates among organisms. That is, a complex ecology of organisms exists on this planet that is 'fine-tuned' via coherent fields establishing a biosphere that is interactive and participatory. Life on this planet is a *dance of coherence* between organisms and their environment.

Physical, chemical, and biological coherence leads ultimately to a degree of perception/comprehension regarding types of relations and interconnectivity (Laszlo uses the term 'prehension,' which he borrows from Alfred North Whitehead). What this implies is an element of conscious interconnectivity between the various sub-parts of any system. That is, as parts of a given system become more complex and interdependent, there arises a greater degree of 'emergent perception' regarding the relations of interconnectivity. In other words, coherence becomes a conscious purpose. As coherence is the dominant driver/attractor in physical, chemical, and biological (species) development, so may it be an expression of social development. Hence, a society may display chaotic, random, and disruptive behaviour, and yet be governed at an innate and essential level by remarkable coherence. This may, in fact, be a necessity and fundamental prerequisite for not only sustaining life, but for its future development. The implications here are that social and cultural disequilibrium (including disruptions, chaotic events, and anomalies) may function as 'tuning adjustments' required for developmental potentials in the social environment. This perspective positions social disruptors ('chaotic disruptors') as mechanisms for adjusting to potentials that allow for greater degrees of coherence. Stated plainly, social disruption and chaotic events could be viewed as physical occurrences that assist in the drive toward greater coherence in the social realm.

The universal trend toward coherence exists in the physical universe – in its laws and processes (chemical and physical) – as well as in and amongst living organisms (the biological realm). This trend, it appears, is toward more sensitive and stable coherence, as well as a drive toward emergent conscious interconnectivity. Behind this phenomenon, it has been hypothesized, exists a cosmic matrix of conscious intelligence. Upon this planet the ultimate physical manifestation of coherence may very well be social order at a planetary scale – a planetary civilization. Could this be the arena where immanent universal order meets with a transcendent emergent consciousness?

Social Coherence on a Planetary Scale

A grand sweep of history will show the rise and fall of countless civilizations, empires, and cultural manifestations. From another viewpoint it will also show a marked shift in the perceptive traits of human consciousness. How we *see* the world, and our place in it, has influenced how we participate in the world around us. And until very recently the consensus has been to view the world as exterior to us – separate and fragmented. Previous empires sought to conquer and control; and to create, as far as was possible, their idea of a uni-polar world. Yet no empire ever truly succeeded in this endeavour. Previous city-states, societies, civilizations, and empires have represented the emergence of groupings ('systems') seeking greater stability and out-reach – in a word, coherence. This fundamental need for coherence and stability that came with complex groupings was often critically centred on resources. The overshoot of a society/social system in the face of dwindling resources often resulted in sudden collapse[xxvii]. As in the physical, chemical, and biological examples mentioned previously, the dominant attractor is coherence. The drive toward achieving greater levels of coherence – especially amongst increasingly complex systems – appears to be a universal trend. According to this hypothesis, by applying the coherent attractor to social systems then the ultimate scale-up on this planet would be a planetary civilization. Are we currently on the cusp of a developmental impulse toward a planetary civilization? Is this the purpose/drive behind the coherent order underlying existence in our spacetime?

[xxvii] See *The Collapse of Complex Societies* by Joespeh Tainter

We have entered a period where a uni-polar world is no longer possible – the age of empires is at an end. Our present multi-polar world reflects a level of deep interconnectivity between the dominant, and also not-so-dominant, nations, states, and regional blocks. Paradoxically, however, this early stage of global interconnectivity and interdependence is creating conflict amongst the major players – the very opposite of what we would expect to see in a drive toward coherence. So, where is the underlying coherence behind this display of social disruption?

In recent years we have witnessed the rise of an empathic consciousness amongst the diverse peoples of the world[xxviii]. A major catalyst behind this emergence has been our global technologies of communication. As was previously noted, a developing degree of 'perception' of the interconnection between parts of a whole serves as both an expression of coherence as well as a driver toward further coherence. The World Wide Web – our global Internet – represents an exterior form of this underlying need for manifesting interconnectivity. Earlier commentary on the rise of global interconnectivity discussed this in terms of a 'Global Brain.'[xxix] We know from recent neuroscience that the mind operates throughout the human body, and is largely centred in the human heart. The concept of the human brain and its functioning is increasingly referred to as an *extended mind*. Our technologies of connection and communication serve as the tangible expression of our species extended mind, and as such function as channels for our conscious communication. The post-industrial world is establishing a global environment where unprecedented information flows, through distributed (and wireless) networks, are allowing for new levels of connection, collaboration, consciousness, and compassion.

[xxviii] See http://www.kingsleydennis.com/awakening-to-our-empathic-mind-pt-1/
[xxix] Most notably *Awakening Earth - The Global Brain* by Peter Russell

We have become increasingly conscious of our inherent interconnectivity upon a social/physical level, as well as upon a virtual/digital and nonlocal one. Moreover, as the older borders and boundaries (both real and invented) separating us on this planet further dissolve, we find that there is greater unity within our diversity than we realized – and our social fears dissolve too. And how we *see* the world also influences how we interpret our *received* consciousness. It is likely that the current drive toward social coherence on planet Earth will first emerge through the individual consciousnesses of us, the people. From the Internet to smart phones, from social media and video-sharing, from blogging to vlogging – we are connected, passionate (and with compassion), and striving to collaborate like never before in our history as a species. And much of this shift is taking place under the radar of the mainstream status quo. The fundamental universal drive toward greater coherence may very well be manifesting through a marked shift in human consciousness that is increasingly being played out on a global field.

A Tale to Finish: 'Angst'

Once upon a time in a faraway country two princes fought a duel. As was customary at that place, the winner could refrain from killing his losing opponent immediately, thus granting a stay of execution. Yet execution would be inevitable.

The prince who finally lost the duel was taken to the winner's palace and instead of being locked in a dungeon was installed in one of the best rooms in the palace. Everyday he was attended with great solemnity, as befitted his lineage, and they had great parties and exquisite meals. But the prince knew that sooner or later he was going to be executed and each passing day his anguish grew. On a day of his choosing he could send a message to the winning prince asking for charity, to end his suffering and to take his life.

The imprisoned prince sent this plea, and the winning prince agreed to his plea and arranged to have the execution take place the next day.

The morning of the execution the court summoned everyone to the biggest party you can imagine. There was music and dancing, the best food and drinks were served on huge tables, and a great event organized. It was magnificent – yet the prince could not forget that the time for his execution was always at hand and his anguish was growing by the minute. The party continued, and a group of dancers danced in the centre of the large room with huge curved swords in their hands - to the amazement of the audience their dance and their turning gave the impression of flying.

Finally the prince could stand the anguish no more and cried out to his generous host:

'Please, perform my execution now – I cannot stand this anxiety!'

'Dude, you've already been executed! Move your shoulders, and see as your head hits the ground' replied the winning prince.

40. CONSCIOUSNESS, COSMOS, PURPOSE, PT. 3 - Emerging Planetary Consciousness & What it Means for Us

Emerging Planetary Consciousness

The philosopher Karl Jaspers referred to the period from 800-200 BC as the Axial Age. It was a time that, according to Jaspers, new yet similar ways of thinking appeared in Persia, India, China and the Western world. He indicated also that the Axial Age represented an in-between period, where old certainties had lost their validity and new ones were yet to emerge. The new religions that arose in this time – Hinduism, Buddhism, Confucianism, Taoism, and monotheism – influenced new thinking in terms of individuality, identity, and the human condition. These new emerging religions[xxx] helped to catalyze new forms of thinking and expressions of human consciousness. And yet, over time, we have seen how they were not wholly successful in developing coherence in a social context. Author and educator Duane Elgin has recently referred to our present time as the 2nd Axial Age[xxxi] in that religions of separation are being replaced by a new spirit of communion. In other words, says Elgin, the world is moving into a spiritual communion and empathic connection with a living universe. There is nowhere else to go, Elgin tells us, when the universe already exists within us. A major feature of this emerging empathic consciousness is that it actively seeks for conscious participation. Furthermore, it exhibits a direct-intuitive perception, rather than a linear-rational one. The more individual consciousnesses that connect across the planet the greater will be the

---

[xxx] The etymology of religion is most likely from the Latin *re-ligare*, to re-bind, to reconnect

[xxxi] 'The Buddha Awakening, Integral Expanding, and a Second Axial Age for Humanity', Journal of Integral Theory and Practice, 2014, 9(1), 145-154.

perception ('prehension') of this interconnectivity, which in turn catalyzes the innate fundamental drive toward seeking further coherence. This realization of our communion *in* consciousness further initiates the *receiving* of a consciousness seeking to manifest coherence as a universal natural order.

This is speculation, yet the purpose of sentient human life upon this planet may well be the drive toward manifesting a coherent planetary consciousness. In other words, the 'bringing in' of the consciousness field (outside of spacetime) into greater spacetime manifestation – in our case, upon the Earth. There is a correlation here with Aurobindo's concept of the Supermind, in that a form of higher consciousness can be made immanent upon the material plane. This would require the preparation of human consciousness in order to actualize this –a form of *transcendence* in consciousness. That is, raising localized aspects of consciousness (individual perceptions and awareness) in order to increase the coherence of consciousness amongst the whole. And this can be made tangible by local conscious actors – each one of us – becoming aware and participating through our everyday acts of right thinking, right behaviour, and right being.

We are no longer either isolated individuals or an inarticulate mass – we are localized consciousness acting through aware individuals who seek to consciously connect, collaborate, and care about the future. Each one of us – as localized consciousness – is a reflection of non-local consciousness; and in this way we are also a reflection against each other. This analogy was beautifully expressed in the concept of Indra's Net[xxxii] where each jewel in the net reflects all the other jewels – it is a simple metaphor for the interconnectedness of our reality. This energetic reality, validated by quantum science, is now increasingly manifesting in our localized spacetime

---

[xxxii] http://en.wikipedia.org/wiki/Indra%27s_net

environment. We now have the means to interconnect non-locally –
through our technologies – as well as through our physical networks (made
easier through increased social mobility). These are the signs of an emerging
planetary civilization that respects diversity as well as unitary coherence.
And as we connect and share our consciousness – our thoughts, ideas,
visions, etc – we will be helping to strengthen the signal – the *reception* – of
consciousness and thus the *bringing in* of a coherent cosmic consciousness. A
planetary consciousness upon Earth, as expressed through a sentient,
individualized humanity may not only be a real possibility – it may very well
be a fundamental cosmic purpose.

Human Consciousness and Purpose

It has been suggested in this paper that an underlying cosmic matrix that is
beyond spacetime codes our known universe, which behaves in a way
consistent with what we know as a holographic projection. In other words,
the universe is *in-formed* from a deep consciousness beyond it. The universe
thus acts as a whole non-local consciousness field, of which sentient life acts
as localized manifestations. It has been inferred through various religious
and sacred texts and traditions that the universe (material reality) came into
being as a way for its Source 'to know itself' – "*I was a hidden treasure and
wanted to be known.*" This is reminiscent of *Know Thyself*, the famous maxim
from the Delphi oracle. Self-consciousness is ascribed to those creatures at
the peak, or greater actualization, of consciousness. Self-reflection is one of
the prized attributes of self-consciousness – yet how can the whole reflect
upon itself? Self-realization is something we credit to each attained
individual consciousness. As speculation, I wonder what self-realization
upon a greater scale would be like? Self-realization as a planetary
consciousness?...as a galactic consciousness?... and finally as a cosmic

consciousness fully realized and self-conscious through all of its localized manifestations? Astounding initiation.

Human consciousness is a part of the greater whole. As sentient beings we receive part of the consciousness that pervades spacetime, and thus we are affected by it – *animated by it* – as well as feeding back into the whole. Our individual expression of consciousness in manifested spacetime also reflects back into the greater non-local consciousness field. The greater our individual perceptions and conscious realization, the greater the total reflection of the consciousness hologram in its entirety – just like the further polishing of each jewel in Indra's Net will influence the overall radiance of the whole net. The cosmic matrix of consciousness is thus in-formed through emerging conscious awareness of its sub-parts. As each one of us wakes up, the cosmic net shines that little bit brighter. If enough localized consciousness awake upon this planet we may catalyze a localized planetary field into conscious awareness – a planetary net is sufficiently prepared (polished) to 'bring in' the greater consciousness pervasive in the cosmos: the immanence of the Supermind, to use Aurobindo's terminology. In this case, we are each a conscious agent of cosmic realization and immanence. We each have an obligation in our existence on this planet to raise our individual, localized expressions of consciousness. In doing so, we both infect and inspire others in our lives to raise theirs, as well as reflecting back our conscious contribution into the source THAT IS. The hidden treasure that is at the very core of our existence wishes to be known - for **us** to be known – by our individual journeys of self-realization, and to bring it all back home (to paraphrase Bob Dylan).

After individual self-consciousness comes collective and planetary consciousness. The emerging technologies and social movements upon this planet may well be part of this process, in-forming an extended mind and empathic embrace across the face of the earth. And one day we may witness a grand awakening, unprecedented upon this planet – and this may very well be the purpose for sentient life, as conscious agents of evolutionary unfolding. This is likely to be more reality than fantasy. We are not alone – a great planetary future awaits us: as a great treasure that wished to be known.

In summary

The views of investigators such as Ervin Laszlo and this author represent a recent emergence of thinkers who are attempting to broaden the discussion on the nature of human consciousness. Principally, by taking a spiritual-material worldview based on cutting edge research in quantum physics and investigations into the nature – and construct – of material reality, we are able to propose new insights into one of the most important questions of our time: what is human consciousness? We are now on the cusp of great advances in understanding, particularly concerning the nature of human cognition and perception.

Today the age-old divide between science and spirituality is finding ever increasing areas of convergence and commonality. At the same time, a spiritual-material worldview is gradually becoming more acceptable by mainstream investigators. By revising our constructs of knowledge on this subject it is also possible to re-engage with questions over the potential future of human evolution on this planet. As our species moves ever closer to the reality of a planetary civilization, there has never been a more opportune time than the present.

References

Alexander, Eben (2012) *Proof of Heaven: A Neurosurgeon's Journey into the Afterlife*. Oxford: Piatkus

Carter, Chris (2010) *Science and the Near-Death Experience; How Consciousness Survives Death*. Rochester: Inner Traditions

Elgin, Duane (2014) 'The Buddha Awakening, Integral Expanding, and a Second Axial Age for Humanity', Journal of Integral Theory and Practice, 2014, 9(1), 145-154.

Grey, Margot (1986) *Return from Death: An Exploration of the Near-death Experience*. London: Arkana

Laszlo, Ervin (2004) *Science and the Akashic Field: An Integral Theory of Everything*. Rochester: Inner Traditions

Laszlo, Ervin; Peake, Anthony (2014) *Immortal Mind: Science and the Continuity of Consciousness Beyond the Brain*. Rochester: Inner Traditions

Lorimer, David (1990) *Whole in One: The near-death experience and the ethic of interconnectedness*. London: Arkana

Moorjani, Anita (2012) *Dying to Be Me: My Journey from Cancer, to Near Death, to True Healing*. New York: Hay House

Russell, Peter (1988) *Awakening Earth - The Global Brain*. London: Arkana

Sheldrake, Rupert (2009) *Morphic Resonance: The Nature of Formative Causation*. Rochester: Park Street Press

Tainter, Joseph (1990) *The Collapse of Complex Societies*. Cambridge: Cambridge University Press

Zaleski, Carol G. (1988) *Otherworld Journeys: Accounts of Near-Death Experience in Medieval and Modern Times*. Oxford: Oxford University Press

A Tale to Finish: 'Indigent'

A monkey once said to a man: 'Do you not notice how I'm homeless? I have no home, no clothes, no excellent food as you, no savings, no furniture, no land, no ornaments - nothing at all! You however, possess all these things and more. Also, you are rich.

The embarrassed man gave the monkey everything he had, becoming himself a beggar. Once the monkey had taken legal possession of all the goods, the man asked:
'And now, what are you going to do with all that? The monkey answered:

'Why should I talk with a homeless fool like you?'

41. ACCESSING THE LIVING INTELLIGENCE, PT. 1 - The Rise of an Intuitive Humanity

Social and cultural change is occurring fast right now across this planet and it looks as if it will accelerate further. Many people are experiencing a wide range of personal impacts, disruptions, and rearrangements in their lives. At the same time we are also seeing how our social infrastructures and modes of communication and connectivity are adjusting and shifting to these changes. Within the last 150 years alone we have witnessed an amazingly rapid process of transition in human civilization, perhaps even without being consciously aware of it. In terms of the bigger picture, this is an incredibly swift rate of change.

The ebb and flow of human history has cradled the gradual unfolding of the individual, and the growing responsibility that this implies. This emerging 'blooming of the individual' has occurred alongside the story of the slow decline in aristocracy, elite rule, and the demise of tyranny. This human story has accelerated in recent centuries, with the fall of feudalism; the birth of democracy; and the growth of an increasingly connected global humanity. Alongside this we have also seen the increasing acceptance and sharing of planetary values. We could say that human society is in the early contractions of the birth of a planetary civilization.

Conscious development is a psycho-spiritual process; aided by socio-cultural impulses and influences that have woven throughout our history. Most recently, the strong impulses in the 1960s, and the end of the 1980s, have helped to catalyze the conscious awareness of many people the world over. Many seeds were planted that would actualize over time. The psychic states experimented with in the 1960s showed that there were alternative dimensions of consciousness, and gave a taste of these to a hungry young audience. The fall of the Berlin Wall in 1989, and the end of several archaic political institutions, gave a taste of the power for change when many thought it almost impossible.

Impulses of renewal and regeneration have long been part of the ongoing processes of human, cultural, and psycho-spiritual development. True revolutions are not those of physical violence but of radical shifts in perceptions, knowledge, and ultimately the individual self. The increasing presence of human consciousness has been evident over the years through the expansion of intelligence, psychological awareness, humanitarianism, empathy, and creative innovation. The emergence of the intuitive human has been seen out on the playing fields of the world - in stadiums, fields, and in streets the world over. The collaborative nature of sport, with its team work, its shared rules and game-play, is one example that has arisen to help shift the human spirit.

What I am suggesting is that as this trend unfolds we are likely to see new generations of individuals coming into the world who will *be the change*, rather than being *born into change*. And these new arrivals will challenge even further our social systems and 'big institutions' from the very fact that they will be acting more from instinct and intuition. The age of Guru-hood, spiritual elitism, and the throng of commercial 'Teaching' methods is going to be replaced by a greater gnosis within humanity. External belief systems that we often depend upon will be challenged, and gradually replaced, by the recognition of a living intelligence – an intelligence that has always existed within the human race. When the truth is known instinctively, it no longer requires cultural preservation: domes, spires, institutions, or Teachings. The living intelligence is more fluid and exists everywhere, for everyone, all of the time. We only need the means to *access it*. This means of access is a process that will increasingly manifest as developmental impulses between human-planet-cosmos continue to unfold.

Over the coming years of this century humanity will increasingly gain greater access to heightened inner awareness (gnosis) as the connection to a pervasive living intelligence strengthens. The old roles of central hierarchy are diminishing; human societies around the globe are forming decentralized networks of connection and communication, much the same as our ancestral bacterial networks. Our social milieu is increasingly mirroring how biology has long since organized itself. This new arrangement facilitates a different *form* of energy to be active upon the planet. An energy that supports a different way of doing things and of making things happen. The days of a singular Messiah speaking to the multitudes are over. We are now moving into a time upon this planet where it will be the multitudes that will amplify and spread the new understanding.

Our young children are being born into a world where on a daily basis – 24/7 – human thought patterns and consciousness flows through millions upon millions of computers, networks, and connected devices, forming a nonlocal realm of information and living intelligence. Yet this is not only occurring in the digital spaces but also through the cultural sphere of artifacts such as movies, books, articles, songs, videos, etc, forming a field of connectivity that transcends our old temporal and spatial boundaries. Our external information technologies are now increasingly mirroring, or being superimposed upon, the living field of intelligence that underlies our reality. Such a physical matrix/construct is the external reflection of our inherent, non-visible connectivity. These impacts (or overlays) are also likely to catalyze a release of some form of transformative energy. There is no external model of communication and connectivity that does not have its corresponding reality in consciousness.

The children and young adults of today are beginning to break the old patterns and become the early wave of pioneers and system-change agents. They are showing a remarkable intuitive grasp of our modern technologies. They are reaching out and connecting, forming networks, supporting ecological practices and alternative health practices, forming community projects, seeking out healthy food, prioritizing well-being over career roles, re-invigorating a sense of the sacred, and pushing out the boundaries for new thinking. It is not occurring everywhere, or with everyone. There is still much confusion and emotional angst in our younger generations. However, a more intuitive human *is* coming through.

The Emperor Finally Has No Clothes

New thinking patterns and expressions of consciousness are now emerging in communities and societies throughout the world that are no longer tolerant of the old paradigm structures of separatism, egoism, and conflict. Rather than being a full-frontal revolt against incumbent systems, a more subtle wave of reformist change is arising that contributes to constructive social transition. Part of this reformist change will be the increase in transparency in our social systems. It is already happening now – we are seeing increased instances of corruption (political, financial, personal, etc) coming to the surface and being exposed. As the sun rises, they say, the shadows will at first become sharper and more visible. As the patterns of a different consciousness begin to be expressed through people, the inadequacies of many of our systems will increasingly be exposed. Those institutions, practices, and societies built upon fear and disingenuous values will falter as a new awareness within people demands a change in values and integrity. Old patterns of thinking – especially the disruptive patterns – will become increasingly obsolete over time as an intuitive intelligence is expressed through human consciousness. Soon, even our youngest babes will be pointing at the old idols and declaring, open-mouthed: 'But look, they are not wearing any clothes!' At that point, edifices and traditions will be forced to either disintegrate or re-calibrate themselves according to the new patterns.

The protective veneer of social appearance and status that once held sanctuary for certain people will no longer operate. Celebrities, politicians, wealthy elites, religious figures, once-respected public figures, and the rest - the façade will drop for many such people and the wave of transparency will make visible their misdemeanors. So much dirty laundry will be washed in public as a generation of intuitively-driven young minds and hearts will wish to heal a planet in order to bring in reform. The early tremors of youth insecurity (witnessed in violent outbursts and psychological instability) will come to be replaced by greater expressions of human intuition and inner confidence and balance. Many of us are already becoming students to our children and to the young adults in the world. We are seeing how our once unquestioning faith in external sources of information, opinions, and authority are now questioned by these young minds. Young people the world over are stepping away from dogmatic belief structures that they find limiting to the self and that take away the responsibility for an individual's own self-empowerment.

A new form of common sense will emerge – one that is neither 'common' nor makes 'sense' to us now – and it will originate from a different state of awareness. Human behavior that made sense for when we imagined we lived as islands of individuality will no longer 'make sense' – nor be functional – for a species that consciously experiences the interconnectivity of all life. The more the human species transforms internally, the greater the change we will see occurring in our physical world – in our societies, technologies, culture, etc. The next generation can not be the same as the present, or the previous. In this moment of human history, to give birth to a duplicate generation – with the same ideals and values – would result not in a perpetuation of human societies but in their demise. That is why we need transformational change at the psycho-spiritual level both within and between generations. For those of us in the world now it has taken consistent exertion and energy to challenge our conditioning structures. In the past also we have struggled greatly against socio-cultural systems that were opposed, or unsupportive, to individual inner development. Now, however, change will come easier and at a more rapid pace.

The changes that we are likely to see in the coming years will be more profound than the changes that took place during our previous industrial revolutions. The period of our western industrialization transpired over several centuries. Now we are going to witness great changes set to occur within the span of just one single human lifetime. We will observe that communication, transparency, and honesty are much more powerful tools than secrecy, fear, and confrontation. The emperor's false suit of body armor will disintegrate in the face of transparent, honest eyes. The sham elements within our political, financial, corporate, and media structures will scramble to maintain their façade. Yet their desperate actions will be viewed for what they truly are in the eyes of a more aware, informed, and awakened generation of young minds and hearts.

With or without us, the new young minds will create their own freedom to inspire and renew their world into being. They will have access not only to a vast intuitive inner world, but they will simultaneously be connected to a planetary network of information, contacts, and friends. Fearful incumbent structures of authority will attempt to control such networks of connection and communication[xxxiii], yet they will ultimately fail against the inevitable tide of great human awakening.

The younger generation(s) will likely be the ones to free humanity from the dominance of erroneous ideas - ideas that forged war, created poverty and hunger, and sustained dis-ease. We are seeing a generation that will be successful in removing these illusions from old thinking patterns. The new intuitive human has been in the making for some time now. Our world is far more peaceful today than it has been at any time in recent past epochs – despite what the mainstream media may be saying. This signals to us that the way energy patterns flow over the Earth is changing, encouraging people to seek peaceful solutions wherever possible. The living intelligence that is a part of the intuitive human is also a spiritual, empathic, and nurturing intelligence, which has been lacking in much of modern civilization.

Those of the new generation(s) will usher in a period where the feminine and masculine energies of the world will be re-configured and placed into greater balance and harmony. Human values of love, compassion, understanding, patience, tolerance, and empathy will be more openly expressed and part of an informed world – and not erroneously seen as being only predominantly 'female' values. The division that separates the masculine and feminine energies will continue to dissolve, and be replaced

---

[xxxiii] See my earlier book '*The Struggle for Your Mind: Conscious Evolution & The Battle to Control How We Think*'

by a newer energy of unity – of coming together. Similarly, the artificial stigma around 'male' and 'female' roles in the world will be challenged and forced into change through the younger men and women actively re-modelling role expectations. Women's participation will be more keenly appreciated, sought after, and brought into collaboration in such major areas as global politics, economy, and business. An intuitive energy will be more present in the world in the upcoming decades, and will find expression as younger women increasingly hold key influential positions in society. We are more open to recognize now that notions of duality - of one side having dominance over the other, whether male or female - is an old energy. The newer energies will be focused more on balance, and on bringing everything together into an integral whole that respects diversity within unity.

Humanity is now poised upon the cusp of a transition for which developmental potentials have long been preparing for. It seems that the rate of our preparedness grows exponentially with each passing year. A new form of energy has now entered upon this planet, and which facilitates an altogether different mode of operation. It is an energy that supports a networked and decentralized way of connectivity. It is now working through our human societies to engage with change from within. Its aim may be to help form a membrane of conscious human-planet intelligence across the Earth.

These energies are also spreading more rapidly from human to human through our integrated digital and biological fields of energetic connectivity. Soon there will not be an area isolated from such influence, as each village and town will have amongst its midst a new intuitive human –

more so when the younger generations enter upon the Earth and begin to take up their roles and responsibilities.

There is something immensely exciting happening here on this planet. Something is rising within us, amongst us, through us, and penetrating the very fabric of our reality. It is a transformation without words, passing through each and every individual. It appears that some latent human capacities are now set to become activated, in alignment with evolutionary requirements.

A Tale to Finish: 'Without End'

There was once a wise man so old that no one in the town knew his age. He himself had forgotten, among other reasons because he had transcended any attachment to human greed. One day as he was sitting under a huge tree staring at the horizon, the mind still as a cloudless sky, he suddenly notice a young man approach a nearby tree and throw a rope over one of its main branches and tie the other end around his neck. The wise man, realizing the intentions of the boy, ran quickly to him and asked him to desist from his purpose if only a few minutes to listen. The young man agreed, and they sat together under the tree. The old man said softly:

'I will make a bargain with you, dear friend. Listen to me for just one minute of your time, and then I will interfere no more. Now', continued the old man, 'imagine a single turtle living within a huge ocean and which only comes to the surface once every million years. Further, imagine a small rubber ring floating on the waters of this vast ocean. Now imagine the chances of the turtle raising its head above the water and entering its head within this ring. Imagine the difficulty to achieve this and yet this is so much harder than to obtain the human form. Now, friend, proceed as you see fit.'

The locals still tell of how that young man became old and wise himself.

42. ACCESSING THE LIVING INTELLIGENCE, PT. 2 - Life in Valis

VALIS is a 1981 science fiction novel by Philip K. Dick and stands for *Vast Active Living Intelligence System*, which in some respects is very close to the living intelligence I discuss in this series of essays.[xxxiv] A living intelligence also suggests a non-local field view of reality. The latest findings in the quantum sciences (notably quantum mechanics and biophysics) posit a field-view understanding that is said to underpin the construct of our universe, and hence the nature of our reality. In the past, various people – mystics, psychologists, and consciousness researchers - have alluded to this intelligence field by a variety of names: cosmic consciousness, superconsciousness, transpersonal consciousness, integral consciousness, etc. All these descriptions share common themes; namely, a heightened sense of intuition and empathy, a feeling of greater connectivity to the world and to people, a sense of 'inner knowing' (gnosis), and the realization that humanity exists and evolves within a universe of intelligence and meaning. Forms and intimations of these new consciousness patterns are already emerging in the world, but as yet they have not become a part of our accepted paradigm.

As Dr Richard Bucke stated in his work *Cosmic Consciousness* the early signs of this new evolutionary development have been appearing within humankind for some time:

> The simple truth is, that there has lived on the earth, 'appearing at intervals', for thousands of years among ordinary men, the first faint beginnings of another race ... This new race is in the act of being born from us, and in the near future it will occupy and possess the earth.[1]

[xxxiv] See the first part - *The Rise of an Intuitive Humanity*

Such signs – or evolutionary mutations – have included, for example, visionaries, mystics, artists, psychics, and a splattering of young gifted children. I would posit that social and cultural events have occurred throughout world history that have served to seed higher functioning into human consciousness. Such events would have taken the form of artistic movements; scientific innovations; faith movements; cultural/social revolutions; architecture; fraternities; myths and legends; sporting fixtures, and more. All such socio-cultural impacts affect human consciousness in a way that prepares the human mind for periods of development and change. Within these seemingly random occurrences lay the components that act as the 'technologies' for developing human consciousness. In recent years we have seen the rapid expansion of our informational flows, and thus human awareness in general.

The increasing manifestation of a collective human consciousness – or rather a collective of minds accessing the living intelligence - is most likely to be in line with certain evolutionary necessities. Preparation has been necessary through a succession of events that overall form a pattern of mutually reinforcing stimuli aimed at raising humanity's psychic awareness. This includes the expansion of intellect, psychological awareness, social development, humanitarianism, empathy, and creativity. These developments have also served to stimulate human intuition. In other words, there have been moments throughout recent human history that helped prepare the 'mental soil' for new patterns of consciousness to slowly seed and grow. According to one well placed commentator on this subject:

> The human being's organism is producing a new complex of
> organs in response to such a need. In this age of the transcending
> of time and space, the complex of organs is concerned with the
> transcending of time and space. What ordinary people regard as

sporadic and occasional bursts of telepathic or prophetic power are…nothing less than the first stirrings of these same organs.[2]

Similarly, the revered Persian poet Jalalludin Rumi stated, '*New organs of perception come into being as a result of necessity/ Therefore, O man, increase your necessity, so that you may increase your perception.*'[xxxv]

On the whole, socio-cultural and material forces are slow to react to changes in expressions of human consciousness. Yet this is nothing new as throughout history there have been individuals, who feeling the need for transformational change, have been caught up in social-cultural upheavals. These events and human efforts, according to Gopi Krishna, indicate a stirring of the human evolutionary impulse:

> I can safely assert that the progress made by mankind in any direction, from the subhuman level to the present, has been far less due to man's own efforts than to the activity of the evolutionary forces at work within him. Every incentive to invention, discovery, aesthetics, and the development of improved social and political organizations invariably comes from within, from the depths of his consciousness by the grace of … the superintelligent Evolutionary Force in human beings.[3]

I would further add that in order for continued human development to occur there are particular periods of human history wherein humanity becomes ready, or in need of, the activation of particular faculties – our evolutionary potentials. During such transitional periods humanity will acquire – or be coerced into developing - new capacities for accessing consciousness (a.k.a. the living intelligence). As in all paradigm shifts, old energies must inevitably give way to the new.

In these years ahead a new wave of young people will be manifesting a consciousness that is simultaneously open to spiritual impulses as well as

---

xxxv Taken from Rumi's *Masnavi*

to the latest in scientific research. A new generation will be growing up with the desire to develop a collective sense of wellbeing, connectedness, empathy and creative vision. What we refer to as the 'nonlocal' will to them be the same as integral interconnectedness, and will feel natural and normal. New patterns of thinking and a stronger sense of intuition will also be a sign that greater access to the field of living intelligence is occurring. This access is the same as, in our older language, direct interaction with nonlocal and non-ordinary states of consciousness. The experience of direct nonlocal consciousness used to be the domain of experienced practitioners (shamans, mystics, psychics) who would have undergone rigorous and lengthy training. Our 'everyday consciousness' of the local view of the universe has been until now largely unprepared for the realms of non-ordinary reality. In Western civilization especially, the nonlocal mode of perception (subjective experience) has not been encouraged, or even recognized. As such it has lain dormant, atrophied, and largely left to the province of the esoteric sciences. The myopic, linear, and rational view of reality has resulted in the dominating values of competition, power, ego, and greed. A nonlocal, intuitive sense of reality, however, will be one that embraces the values of **Connection ~ Communication ~ Collaboration ~ Consciousness ~ Compassion**. It is my view that the new generation(s) of young people in the world will be the first to embody these values in a widespread manner – thus ushering in a new epoch for the development of human consciousness.

Connected to Living Information

It appears that the Earth is now receiving different forms of energetic impacts – especially electromagnetically – which will alter the Earth's resonant energy signature. As the Earth's magnetic field is not a static shield, but rather like an oscillating wave, fluctuations in the field are known to affect living systems upon the Earth. Biological bodies, being electrical energy units, are sensitive to external energetic and atmospheric variations, though usually these reactions operate at a subconscious level. Likewise, magnetic variations can have unusual effects on human consciousness. Our sciences are now understanding more and more how human life – our thoughts, emotions, and behavior - are affected directly by fluctuations in Earth's magnetic field.[xxxvi] As the energetic resonance of the Earth alters over time this will undoubtedly affect how human DNA calibrates itself as a newborn enters into the world.

The knowledge that human DNA can be influenced and modulated by frequencies (sound, light, language, and thought) has been utilized by various spiritual traditions over the ages. This can be seen in the variety of exercises that utilize thought focus (prayer), sounds (music, chanting, singing), light (both natural light and produced light, such as in stained glass), and language (specific recitations such as a mantra and zikr). Similarly, various shamanic practices have alluded to the notion that DNA can be accessed through deliberate, conscious intention.[4] DNA appears to function, therefore, not only as a protein builder (the minority function) but also as a medium for the storage, receiving, and communication of information.

If we understand that information is processed by us on a neurobiological level then we can accept that our nervous systems are channels for information. Since we know that DNA is present throughout our cellular structure, we can be sure that our complete physiology is involved and related to external energy fields – electromagnetic, gamma bursts, solar rays, as well as consciousness fields. It appears that part of our human DNA 'energetic signature' can be re-calibrated in our lifetime through exercising various techniques, such as in a range of meditative

---

[xxxvi] See research material at HeartMath Institute - https://www.heartmath.org/research/research-library/

practices and associated stimuli (as described above). For many people, these are the exact practices which have guided them through their lives; and indeed the lives of many thousands of people. It may be that in past epochs direct intervention – such as wisdom teachings, mystery schools, and the like – were required in preparing individuals to access the living intelligence as the current environment was not sufficient alone to provide the sole catalytic trigger. This situation, I speculate, may now be changing. The young children being born today appear to be already more connected with a form of intuitive intelligence. Contact with one's own intuitive intelligence is another way of saying a person manifests a degree of gnosis. And true gnosis is a form of *transceiving* of information; that is, the receiving as well as transmitting of nonlocal information. Such gnosis is likely to be in the form of informational exchange between the human nervous system and living intelligence, which together in-form the body consciousness field. A more coherent connection between a person and the living intelligence field suggests greater potential/capacity for a self-initiated awakening, without the need for external teaching environments. It may be the case that humanity has just been waiting for the establishment of an energetically conducive environment. And that time may now be at hand.

Fields of Resonance

In preceding years the human socio-cultural environment was not conducive to individual development upon a large scale. For this reason many wisdom teachings or streams of perennial wisdom had to operate quietly, or even as clandestine operations. And yet the human capacity to access consciously the living intelligence field is without doubt an in-born natural ability. Only that for most people this capacity has lain dormant as, like an under-exercised muscle, it was never properly used. As one source recently pointed out – 'The information you need is encoded in the structural makeup of every single cell in your body. Contact is there.'[5] The same source also noted that:

> When you are aware of your totality, the Life-impulse will transmit to you everything that you need to know in any given situation. Its message will always come as your first spontaneous impulse. Be attentive.[6]

We now know that the entire genetic information for a human body is contained in each of the body's many trillion cells. It may be the case – only speculative at this stage – that accessing the living intelligence also operates through connection/communication with the information that is en-folded in these communicating fields of energy. That is, our human physiology – DNA, cellular structure, nervous system, etc – acts as a whole, coherent, transceiving apparatus that filters our consciousness from the nonlocal intelligence field. The bodily 'transceiving apparatus' resonates with the various energy fields that originate literally under our feet as well as above our heads.

Geologists are developing their understanding of how Earth energies are transmitted, both along the surface of the crust as well as within the core of the Earth. Latest research indicates that the Earth's core behaves more along the lines of a crystalline structure, rather than as a molten mass that many of us have as images in our heads. In 1936 it was discovered (by the seismologist Inge Lehmann) that the Earth is separated into having a solid inner core distinct from its liquid outer core. This solid inner core was deduced by observing how earthquake-generated seismic waves were being reflected off the boundary of the inner core. Likewise, the outer core was found to be liquid, as earlier suspected. However, more recent observations have shown that the inner core is not completely uniform. Rather, it contains large-scale structures indicated by seismic waves that pass more rapidly through some parts of the inner core than through others. It has even been suggested that the inner solid core is formed from iron crystals. What is known by science is that the inner core, through its dynamo action, plays a significant role in the generation of Earth's magnetic field. Similarly, the crust of the Earth is known to support a network of energized, or 'magnetized' paths – variously called ley lines, Earth grid, pilgrimage routes, etc. In some form it appears that the Earth manifests particular tracks, or routes, of increased energy upon which it is said many ancient temples, ceremonial sites, gatherings, and the like, have been based upon. Indeed, many gatherings and buildings today continue to be based upon certain accepted energized 'hot spots.' Quite literally, the energy fields of the Earth pulsate under our very feet. In addition to this, above our heads the Earth's magnetic field, interacting with solar and cosmic rays, envelopes humanity in a bubble of fluctuating energy.

The latest findings in science tell us that the Earth's electromagnetic field is a sensitive membrane that responds to solar activity such as sun spot cycles, solar flares, coronal mass ejections, and solar winds. We also know from neuroscience that human brain activity creates small electrical charges. Further, the human heart is now understood to act as a vibrant generator of electromagnetic energy. Collate this with a human nervous system and cellular structure that communicates as a coherent quantum field then we have intrinsic resonance between human biology and our terrestrial, solar, and cosmic environments. We are literally living amidst a *VALIS - Vast Active Living Intelligence System.*

This understanding connects us with notions of a nonlocal field of consciousness that has been referred to over the years as the *noosphere* (Teilhard de Chardin; Vladimir Vernadsky); *Overmind* (Sri Aurobindo); and the *world sensorium* (Oliver Reiser). We can also consider this 'noosphere/overmind' – a.k.a. living intelligence field - as emerging as a form of planetary consciousness. If this is the case, then humanity may be instrumental in facilitating the emergence of a single planetary organism with a shared living intelligence (ie., consciousness). A collectively aligned conscious and aware human civilization could become a physical channel for this living intelligence. This suggests that, as a species, we would have arrived at the point where we now needed to *interiorize* the evolutionary process for further development to occur.

The manifestation of consciousness through humanity appears to be undergoing an increased psychic compression that may serve to synchronize life on this planet. This process, in fact, is nothing 'esoteric' as it has been part of human civilization from the first day our ancestors began to worship an external presence. The convergence of human consciousness/thought patterns takes place in ceremonial worship, and is central to human prayer. If we look at the *salah* practice of formal worship in Islam (it constituting one of the Five Pillars of Sunni Islam), we see that this ritual prayer obliges the worshipper to pray five times a day facing Mecca. These specifically designated times of concentrated states of consciousness create an intense convergence and focused stream of energy across the globe directed toward the geographical location of Mecca. We have many other forms of consciousness convergence (or mental synchronization) upon this planet, throughout a myriad of socio-cultural-religious-spiritual ceremonies, events, gatherings, etc. For example, the 'Global Consciousness Project'[xxxvii], established by Roger Nelson at Princeton University, has demonstrated how human consciousness becomes collectively coherent and synchronized at moments of global emotional release. In the past, however, heightened

---

[xxxvii] See http://noosphere.princeton.edu/

synchronization in the human collective consciousness field was induced by external triggers[xxxviii]. It is to be speculated whether a change is underway upon this planet that will result in supporting greater coherence in the human consciousness field. If this is the case, we may suspect that this will facilitate a clearer contact between the human transceiving apparatus (the human body) and the nonlocal living intelligence field.

It is my own sense that the coming generation(s) will be among the first of those to awaken *en masse* to an era of instinctual gnosis. That is, a generation of instinctively aware young children who inherently feel an *intentional* connection and communion between their 'self' and the living intelligence. This contact will be a young person's primary contact in their life, providing trustful feelings and instinctual guidance. This, we can hope, will assist in making our epochal and monumental planetary transition less turbulent and more coherent. The 13th century Persian poet Jalāl ad-Dīn Rūmī – known in the West simply as Rumi – suggested this *intentional coherence* when he accurately wrote about the distinction between acquired and instinctual intelligence:

Two Kinds of Intelligence

There are two kinds of intelligence: One acquired,
as a child in school memorizes facts and concepts
from books and from what the teacher says,
collecting information from the traditional sciences
as well as from the new sciences.

With such intelligence you rise in the world.
You get ranked ahead or behind others
in regard to your competence in retaining
information. You stroll with this intelligence

[xxxviii] Examples include the death of Princess Diana in the UK, and the World Trade Center collapse in the US.

in and out of fields of knowledge, getting always more
marks on your preserving tablets.

There is another kind of tablet, one
already completed and preserved inside you.
A spring overflowing its springbox. A freshness
in the center of the chest. This other intelligence
does not turn yellow or stagnate. It's fluid,
and it doesn't move from outside to inside
through the conduits of plumbing-learning.

This second knowing is a fountainhead
from within you, moving out. [7]

This 'second knowing' which is the 'fountainhead' within us corresponds to
the source of living intelligence – present within our very cells. Through
accessing this contact/communication we are likely to find ourselves
actively engaging with a developmental impulse unfolding upon this planet.

[1] Bucke, R. (1972/1901) *Cosmic Consciousness: A Study in the Evolution of the Human Mind.* London: The Olympia Press.

[2] Shah, I. (1982) *The Sufis.* London: Octagon, p.54

[3] Krishna, G. (1993) *Higher Consciousness and Kundalini.* Ontario, CA: F.I.N.D. Research Trust, p.166

[4] Narby, J. (1999) *Cosmic Serpent: DNA and the Origins of Knowledge.* London: Phoenix.

[5] Carey, K. (1995/1982) *The Starseed Transmissions.* New York: HarperCollins, p.47

[6] Carey, K. (1995/1982) *The Starseed Transmissions.* New York: HarperCollins, p.41

[7] Jalāl ad-Dīn Rūmī, 'Two Kinds of Intelligence', *Mathnawi* IV:1960-1968 (Trans. Coleman Barks)

A Tale to Finish: 'Prosperity'

A wealthy man once asked Sengai to write some verses for him for the prosperity of his family; as a symbol that could be passed from generation to generation. Sengai took a large sheet of paper and wrote:
- "Father dies, son dies, grandson dies."

The rich man was very angry:
- "I asked you to write something for the happiness of my family! Why are you laughing at me?"
- "I did not mean to laugh at you" - explained Sengai. "If you die before your son does, this will cause great pain. If your grandson should die before you and your child then you will both be heartbroken. If your family, generation after generation, die in the order I've written, it will follow the natural course of life. I call it I prosperity."

43. ACCESSING THE LIVING INTELLIGENCE, PT. 3 - Normalizing the Multi-Verse

Human awareness is the real game changer. Human awareness not only alters our perceptions of our self but also transforms how we understand the world. The awareness we have about our place in the world and our part in the 'bigger picture' is ultimately a question of how we transceive (transmit-receive) consciousness. When how we receive and express human consciousness changes, then *everything* changes. Consciousness is that which connects – it is the nonlocal information field that binds us all. We can also refer to it as being the living intelligence that underlies the matrix, the construct, of our known reality. The living intelligence is the underlying consciousness from which all materiality arises.

As discussed in the previous essay in this series[xxxix], there is a different form of energy now being supported upon this planet. Further, that there is an interaction/immersion – leading to a state of greater resonance – between the energy fields of human physiology and those from our environment. The coherence between information fields (biological-environmental-cosmic) is increasing, resulting in what I speculate as being a stronger access to living intelligence. This stronger contact-communication is manifesting in the younger generation(s) who appear to exhibit increased intuitive intelligence as opposed to acquired information (conditioning). One way to visualize this is by seeing the new energy calibration as being like a different sound/vibration pattern entering, and altering the older patterns. Consider how sound/vibration waves can alter matter: particles

---

[xxxix] See 'Part II - Living in Valis'

scattered on a surface are reformed into new orderly geometric shapes in response to changing sound vibrations (this is known as cymatics).[xl]

A new energetic signature - 'sound vibration' – entering our collective nonlocal field will re-calibrate the transceiving of consciousness into a new modality. The change in the 'pattern recognition' of the consciousness field could likely affect how we filter and interpret, and thus perceive, the constructs of our reality. It may also open up the human transceiving of consciousness to other dimensional perspectives. In other words, humanity is possibly on course to re-calibrate its potential to transceive other modalities of nonlocal information. By altering our capacity to receive other wavelengths of information, humanity will be broadening its awareness, understanding, and connection with a greater range of dimensional realities. We may then come to realize that our perception of reality, and our understanding of the cosmos, is in accordance with our capacity to access the living information. Once this state of access is altered, new perceptions emerge. One of these new perceptive states would likely be the recognition that *intelligent life* exists in a wondrous profusion of multi-verses. At this point we will be forced to officially change our antiquated mythology of 'what is life?'

For a long time the dominant scientific consensus has been that we were lucky enough to have found ourselves in a 'just-right' universe – a universe that happened to have been accidentally created by chance. And now we are struggling for survival on a dead chunk of rock hurtling through 'empty' space in a so-far lifeless universe. However, according to the calculations of mathematical physicist Roger Penrose, the probability of randomly coming across such a universe as we find ourselves in - fine-tuned to life - is 1 in $10^{10^{123}}$.[1] With these incredible odds there would, somewhat

---

[xl] *Cymatics – see:* http://en.wikipedia.org/wiki/Cymatics

ironically, be more statistical chance of living in an intelligent universe. In this case it appears that a biased human thinking pattern cannot accept that we exist in a universe that is itself biased toward life. After all, life has been returning again and again on planet Earth after each major extinction event.[xli] One would assume that such persistence does not occur in a random universe not biased toward life? However, the mythology of living in a dead universe has been compatible - dare we say it 'useful' - for the dominant ideology of consumerism that has saturated modern life. If we are living a life of blind chance within a world of lifeless, materialistic forces, then it makes more sense that humanity should exploit its surroundings to make the best of it for itself. In this scenario, human life – our existence – has no greater purpose or meaning. However, there is a shift underway in how we are beginning to understand what we mean by the question 'what is life?'

Nobel Prize scientist Francis Crick, co-discoverer of the DNA sequence, could not understand how even a single assembled protein could have emerged by chance. Crick calculated the odds of this happening as just 1 chance in 10^{260}: this is an incredible (and immeasurable) sum when we consider that all the atoms in the entire visible universe have been calculated to amount to 'only' 10^{80}. Both Francis Crick and astronomer Fred Hoyle believed that life was already too complex when it first appeared on Earth and thus must have originated from elsewhere; that is, off-planet. Hoyle is now infamous for stating, somewhat controversially, that for complex life to have originated by chance is statistically the same odds as a hurricane blowing through a scrap yard and producing a Boeing 747. Hoyle also

---

[xli] Estimates of the number of major mass extinctions in the last 540 million years range from as few as five to more than twenty (Wikipedia) - https://en.wikipedia.org/wiki/Extinction_event

supported the general Panspermia hypothesis[xlii] which states that life exists throughout the universe and is distributed by bacteria being present on passing/crashing meteoroids, asteroids and planetoids. Similarly, Crick famously stated that since it was highly unlikely that complex bacteria on Earth arose by random chance it was therefore more likely to have arrived at Earth by what is known as 'Directed Panspermia'[xliii]. That is, the seeds of life (perhaps early bacterial forms of DNA) may have been purposely spread by an advanced extraterrestrial civilization(s). The reasons for this could be many, such as an advanced civilization facing extinction; as a means for terraforming planets, perhaps for later colonization; or as a design to spread the spiritual seeds of life within a particular universe/dimension. Crick concluded his hypothesis by stating that DNA is 'not of this Earth.'[2]

Another latest finding that is inexplicable to the current paradigm is the recent discovery that organic molecules are produced in stars. What this means is that the basic substances on which life is based (as we know it) are already produced in the evolution of stars. Organic molecules necessary for life are created in the deep furnaces of stellar evolution and then ejected into surrounding space. These molecules may then coat clumps of interstellar matter that then subsequently condense into stars and planets. This understanding could offer us another picture of how organic matter arises in the universe. This picture shows us a universe that is a veritable factory for life, with stars pumping and spewing out the molecules for creation like huge generators all dotted across the universe. The idea that we live on a lifeless rock is now becoming itself a dead idea!

Once we accept that we exist within an immense universe teeming with the potentials for life, it is a natural next step to question whether other

---

[xlii] See http://en.wikipedia.org/wiki/Panspermia
[xliii] See https://en.wikipedia.org/wiki/Directed_panspermia

conscious intelligences exist in the cosmos. A follow-on question might be whether transpersonal states of consciousness can form a connection, or bridge, with other intelligences and/or dimensional realms? That is, whether a stronger access to the living intelligence also facilitates a broader scope of communion, connecting us with other sentient beings whom are also in communion with the nonlocal living intelligence field. In fact, this very question and subject is not new – it has been at the heart of the human experience for millennia. The transpersonal access of consciousness has been known for millennia amongst various traditions, regardless of the fact that it has been largely denied and dismissed by our rational scientific paradigm. Historically, those persons more able to access this capacity - such as shamans, mystics, prophets, etc - have often done so for the benefit of their communities. For those people who are accustomed to connecting-communicating with such realms, the notion of intelligent life, multi-dimensions, and multi-verses is second nature. Furthermore, virtually all human beings have the capacity to access these alternate realities. In fact, many people are already doing so without actually realizing it - casting it off as coincidence, fluke, good luck, or weird anomaly. In recent years, however, there has been a significant increase in the number of people either experimenting or experiencing what are termed as 'extra-sensory' states. These occurrences, rather than being anomalies, may well be the first wave of experiences that are part of the new incoming *normalization* of human perception. In other words, the 'actual experience that extra-sensory states exist may be the foundation for a future which contains extra-sensory experience as a widespread attribute.'[3] These initial experiences by the few earlier on is part of a natural process of acclimatizing the human being to a reality/state so that these realities can become *actualized* and *normalized* later.

New Dimensional Perspectives

Consciousness researcher Dr Strassman believes that communication with transpersonal realms may help humanity along its own evolution, as well as with the problems we are currently facing here on Earth:

> Establishing – with a sober, altruistic intent – reliable and generally available means of contact with these different levels of existence may help us alleviate some of the pressing issues we are facing on this planet in this time-space continuum. It even may be that the information and resources we gather in these noncorporeal realms are more important to our survival – and ultimately our evolution – than that which we obtain via strictly physical means.[4]

The idea of contact with 'non-corporeal' realms having a function in our evolution offers a new, and potentially significant, dimensional perspective for human life. The existence of non-corporeal realms of reality has been known for millennia amongst various traditions. Likewise, the practice of communication/interaction with other non-human intelligences has been widely known across human cultures for centuries.

What I sense may be happening through a variety of socio-cultural phenomena and anomalies – drug experimentation, transpersonal states, wisdom traditions, out-of-body practices, alien abduction, and more – is the preparation of humanity for its next phase of evolutionary development. These earlier stages utilized individuals as channels – or transceivers – by which to affect the collective energetic/vibratory state of our species for purposes of transformation. Furthermore, part of this transformation involves the creation of new organs of perception with which to perceive aspects of a newly emerging reality that is multi-dimensional. In other words, we have been working towards normalizing the multi-verse, and thus assisting to bring it into being through the perceptual faculties of the human species. In modern vocabulary, we are beginning to download the bigger picture.

As mentioned previously, the idea that we live in a multidimensional universe populated by other intelligences and life-forms is not new to many non-western, non-orthodox traditions and to many indigenous peoples of the world. Yet the means of access - the discipline to *train the body and mind* to be able to sustain this communion - has been available in past times to the relative few. Now all that is likely to be changing. The next step, it seems to me, is a major planetary roll-out – a *massification* of the evolutionary process. It may well be that the new generation of children arriving upon the planet will be amongst the first wave to engage more fully with this developmental impulse, in a natural and organic way.

Re-Calibrating Reality

The capacity to access non-ordinary states of consciousness is the natural heritage of humankind. Yet, on a physiological level, we may need preparation so that we are able to sustain the energetic state related to heightened perceptions. This was the intention of the Integral Yoga work of Sri Aurobindo, in preparation to receive the immanence of the *Overmind.* According to consciousness researcher Gopi Krishna, humanity 'will be brought in touch with another level of creation, other intelligences and states of being pervading the universe, a universe now completely shut out from our sight because of the limited capacity of our brains.'[5] The human species may thus be on the verge of breaking free from its perceptual quarantine.

The younger generations, with their inherent intuitive intelligence, will be the initial wave in this transformation occurring through the received consciousness of the human species. They will come to recognize – as if second nature – that humanity shares a cosmic neighborhood with a radiant profusion of other intelligences. We were never alone – and we will look back at our antiquated thinking and laugh at our short-sightedness and lack of vision. Just as we look back to the early days of black and white television and silent movies, where we knew the real images existed in color yet we didn't have the transceivers capable of receiving the 'bigger picture.' Through the new generations coming into the world we will be introducing the re-calibrated consciousness patterns into the collective blueprint of the human species.

Our latest scientific discoveries are finally catching up with a body of knowledge that has been known for centuries amongst certain wisdom traditions. Quantum biology, for example, now reveals that a multidimensional energy exists within the innermost core of the human body. A state of quantum coherence is achieved as each of the 100 trillion molecules in the human body emits its own magnetic field, each one overlapping with the next. This then creates a nonlocal energy field that allows for instant communication throughout the body. With trillions of overlapping DNA fields - each with a mini electromagnetic field - a unified quantum state is created that has been suggested could have multi-dimensional properties. It is known that there are magnetic fields at the centre of atomic structure that physicists refer to as inter-dimensional fields. Physicists are also debating whether inter-dimensional energy exists at the centre of galaxies, and whether galactic centers exist in a quantum state. This relates to the information Ken Carey received:

> 'the fully activated human sensory system is more than just an interdimensional communication device. In miniature it replicates in the structural pattern of its biogravitational field the same pattern found in planetary, solar, galactic, and universal fields.'[6]

The old consciousness patterns were not sufficiently conducive to transceiving the multi-dimensional aspects of the living intelligence field. However, the new generation(s) of humans to arrive on the planet will encounter an environment with a different energetic signature and their DNA will re-calibrate accordingly. This shift will, I speculate, facilitate a greater access to the living intelligence, leading to expanded patterns of received/expressed consciousness. This greater resonance with the living intelligence field will also grant partial access to the reality of multi-dimensional existence.

This new understanding of being a part of multi-dimensional existence will be humanity's shared inheritance; and not the preserve of a few. We will undergo the transition from a time when we thought we were alone in a 'dead universe' to the understanding that we are part of a vast, inconceivably rich living universe – one amongst many multi-verses teeming with intelligent life. We will have begun our journey to join the neighborhood of cosmic **L.I.F.E.** – in Living a more Integrated and Fulfilling Existence. This will mark the beginning of living in resonance with a new sacred reality:

> '...all creatures inhabit and live within a single field of shared
> consciousness, that all are projections of a single Being, and that
> all of us - angels, humans, animals, vegetables, microbes and
> minerals - are differentiated aspects of one conscious and
> coherent whole. This recognition is the cornerstone of the new
> Sacred Reality....'[7]

When this new perception of life – planetary, cosmic, and dimensional – is integrated and normalized in the psyche of humanity, far-reaching and revolutionary change will occur in every sphere of human life. Humanity will form a sacred connection with all forms of life and with a living cosmos. We will collectively recognize the evolutionary impulse in humankind, and seek to nurture self-development and well-being. Human values will no longer be based upon a paradigm of materialism - *matter realism* – but will foster human dignity, compassion, tolerance, unity, and the actualization of our higher morality. Eventually, through this new awareness and understanding, we shall work as a collective species toward the formation of a genuine planetary society upon the Earth. It will not happen overnight, nor within a single generation – yet it will eventually come to pass over extended time. This is the expression of the developmental impulse within the creative consciousness of living intelligence. In time, profound transformation will occur on planet Earth as the impulse of love will nurture our collective spirit and creative intention to make a future for humanity within the cosmos.

[1] Cited in Pfeiffer, T & Mack, J E (eds) (2007) *Mind Before Matter: Visions of a New Science of Consciousness.* Winchester: O Books, p96

[2] Crick, Francis (1981) *Life Itself: Its Origin and Nature.* New York: Simon & Schuster

[3] Scott, Ernest (1985) *The People of the Secret.* London: Octagon Press, p237

[4] Strassman, R., Wojtowicz, S., Eduardo Luna, L., Frecska, E. (2008) *Inner Paths to Outer Space: Journeys to Alien Worlds through Psychedelics and Other Spiritual Technologies.* Rochester, VT: Park Street Press, p80

[5] Krishna, Gopi (1993) *Higher Consciousness and Kundalini.* Ontario, CA: F.I.N.D. Research Trust, p197

[6] Carey, Ken (1996) *The Third Millennium: Living in the Posthistoric World,* New York, HarperCollins, p94

[7] Carey, Ken (1988) *Return of the Bird Tribes.* New York: HarperCollins, p169

A Tale to Finish: 'The Lighthouse'

There was once a man who began building a lighthouse in the middle of the desert. Everyone started to make fun of him and called him crazy.

'Why a lighthouse in the desert?' everybody wondered.

Yet the man would not listen and kept on quietly doing his work. One day he finally finished building his lighthouse. At night, without moon or stars in the sky, the magnificent lightning started spinning its light in the darkness of the air, as if the Milky Way had become a carousel.

And it happened that as soon as the lighthouse began to give her light there suddenly appeared in the desert a sea lit by a river of light, with beautiful ocean going ships, sail boats, submarines, whales, dancing dolphins, merchants of Venice, the pirate Barbarossa, mermaids, sirens, and many more ...

Everyone was amazed, except the builder of the lighthouse: for he knew that if someone turns on a light in the darkness, from the brightness of that light will spring up many wonders.

APPENDIX

i) QUANTUM CONSCIOUSNESS: The way to reconcile science & spirituality

It is vain to be always looking toward the future and never acting toward it.

John Frederick Boyes, English essayist (1811 - 1879)

The human being has to become what he thinks himself to be

Rudolf Steiner

Human thinking is in need of a new model that constructs the human being and consciousness within an energetic universe that is compatible with both modern science and spiritual teachings. However, this need not demand of us that we throw away the knowledge that we have learned up to this point. On the contrary, we are required to not only work with our current knowledge-base but also to expand these resources to help us move forward into new paradigms of thought concerning human consciousness and the processes operating within the human being. In this time of our developing sciences and new technologies we have the assistance of ever-greater analysis and emerging discoveries that are evolving the parameters of our thinking. It is likely that the next stage in our human sciences will be centred on our understanding of consciousness; and how we are intimately connected to each other and our wider energetic environment.

We have discovered from recent science that each of us carries around with us a 100 billion-cell bioelectric computer that filters and ultimately interprets what we come to see as our 'reality'. Almost all of its 100 billion neurons were established the day we were born, with around 250,000 neurons created every minute whilst our bodies were forming in the womb. Still, this phenomenal 'reality shaper' has undergone monumental perceptual change over our evolutionary history. However, when compared to the skeletal remains of prehistoric human beings there appears to have been no observable change in human anatomy for at least 100,000 years. In comparison, our human mind has taken leaps from its earliest cave-art beginnings. This suggests that we have shifted from biological to cultural to a neuro evolutionary path and that further advance involves the development of the human nervous system and our consciousness. What is required, at this significant juncture, is again another catalyst of consciousness change. The next step that is required is likely to be a neuro-genetic evolutionary shift, and will be a necessary step in order to move beyond the limitations of our current developmental impasse. Civilizations in our historical past (and perhaps also in our unknown past) have collapsed as they evolved to the limits of their material resources without there being a parallel development in human consciousness. At such vital transition periods it is essential that a conscious 'energy force' be introduced into the stream of human life in order to catalyze the next spurt in evolutionary growth. Without such conscious energy the material systems are in danger of either running out of control (as is the case now) and/or breaking down – which may also be the case in the near future. Such a conscious 'energy force' needs to serve as an impulse to help catalyze human civilization towards new modes of self-knowledge and understanding, often referred to under Maslow as self-directed actualization. Such a catalyst may appear, as this paper hopes to show, through discoveries in the field of quantum biology, quantum physics, and neuroscience.

It is my contention that emerging research in the 'quantum sciences' throws new light upon the workings of the human mind/brain and consciousness, as well as the human nervous system and our genetic blueprint - DNA. This research, as this paper discusses, creates a bigger picture whereby emerges a coherency between our biology, our human physiology, and an energetic field of consciousness. Because of this, we could say that we are at the edge of a possible *quantum evolution* of the human species. It may also be reasonable to say that there are already new generations of people who, as evolutionary agents of change, are manifesting symptoms of such transformational changes. As in any evolutionary *shift* there appear amongst the species the initial beginnings of such transformation before the change becomes more widespread. These speculations will be returned to later in the paper.

It is fair to say that our global civilization now finds itself at a critical crossroads of development, both in terms of physical resources as well as modes of thinking. It thus becomes imperative that we orientate our perceptive faculties in favour of the potential evolutionary transformation of human consciousness. In recent years our western societies, at least, have developed in detriment to conscious evolution. This is one of the major reasons behind the cultural failings of our critical times. There has been little preparation, discussion, and research into how humanity, both physically and mentally, can deal with great change when it disrupts both scientific and religious belief systems. In our material age there is a tendency to dismiss spiritual concerns as realms of fantasy; likewise, those people of spiritual leaning often dismiss science as being inadequate to guide us into the future. Thus, a great amount of our energies have been channelled into creating an unstable and radically polarised world. What is required, however, is a reconciliation of the scientists with the humanists (C.P. Snow's 'Two Cultures') and a combination of research and energy into stimulating a progressive understanding of the evolutionary trajectory of our species. In the worst case scenario we could face a process of devolution; it is my contention, however, that this will not be the case. Part of our dilemma though rests in our blindness over how our mental and perceptual faculties operate.

The human brain as a collection of nerve cells operates as a multi-layered frequency receptor. Due to initial conditionings early on in life each receptor becomes wired to perceive a particular wave frequency. As the brain's receptors tune-in to a particular pattern of frequency waves a 'pattern recognition' response is received by the brain and interpreted according to the perceptions allotted to the frequency. In other words, the act of *tuning in* involves picking-up familiar frequency patterns out of the ocean of frequencies that surround us constantly. By tuning into the same patterns again and again we are reinforcing a particular reality-set. We are thus tuning into a consensus reality pattern unconsciously and forming our perceptions continually from this. Unfamiliar patterns often get ignored since they do not fall within our receptor remit. Perception is thus dynamically created moment by moment as the brain constantly scans the bands of frequencies that surround us. However, if this pattern-recognition behaviour does not evolve over time our perceptual development is in danger of becoming stalled. The result is that we become fixed – or trapped – within a particular reality. This is why human development requires that we move through various paradigm shifts[xliv] in order to evolve our collective thinking/perceptual patterns. In other words, our development rests upon simultaneous biological processes as well as psychical. According to noted consciousness researcher Gopi Krishna, the 'maturing of the nervous system and the brain is a biological process, depending on a host of psychic and material factors' (Krishna 1999: 56).

The vulnerability of this process is that we become too accustomed to particular perceptual patterns and ignore other sensory inputs or influences. Also, as a species we have been collectively un-informed about methods obtainable to shift among various frequency bands and patterns. This knowledge has been available within various wisdom traditions (such as shamanism and occult and mystery schools) yet kept out of the public domain. The end result is that we become fixed and dogmatic in our sensory 'beliefs' and cling desperately to the small section of reality we perceive as the whole. Yet the human brain, and nervous system, is flexible enough to shift between frequency patterns and to interpret 'realities' beyond the consensual pattern. In past generations many mystery schools considered humankind too immature to undertake such training – hence the need for rigorous and strict initiation rituals and testing. This embargo on such knowledge and techniques has helped foster the domination of materialistic science to the point whereby we are taught to dismiss subjective and intuitive impulses and experiences. However, it has now become an evolutionary necessity that our dominant reliance upon material pursuits be balanced with an increase in consciousness research that supports the significant role of a 'shared mind'. The next stage of human development, I posit, will be of a neuro-genetic nature which using present terminology aligns with a form of quantum consciousness.

Quantum Coherence, Quantum Consciousness

The human body is a constant flux of thousands of chemical/biological inter-reactions and processes connecting molecules, cells, organs, fluids, throughout the brain, body and nervous system. Up until recently it was thought that all these countless interactions operated in a linear sequence, passing on information much like a runner passing the baton to the next runner. However, the latest findings in quantum biology and biophysics have discovered that there is in fact a tremendous degree of coherence within all living systems. It has been found through extensive scientific investigation that a form of *quantum coherence* operates within living biological systems through what is known as biological excitations and biophoton emission. What this means is that metabolic energy is stored as a form of electromechanical and electromagnetic excitations. It is these coherent excitations that are considered responsible for generating and maintaining long-range order via the transformation of energy and very weak electromagnetic signals. After nearly twenty years of experimental research, Fritz-Albert Popp put forward the hypothesis that biophotons are emitted from a coherent electrodynamical field within the living system (Popp, et al 1988). What this effectively means is that each living cell is giving off, or resonating, a biophoton field of coherent energy. If each cell is emitting this field then the whole living system is, in effect, a resonating field – a ubiquitous non-local field. And since it is by the means of biophotons that the living system communicates, then there is near instantaneous intercommunication throughout. And this, claims Popp, is the basis for coherent biological organization – referred to as quantum coherence. This discovery led Popp to state that the capacity for evolution rests not on aggressive struggle and rivalry but on the capacity for communication and cooperation. In this sense the in-built capacity for species evolution is not based on the individual but rather living systems that are interlinked within a coherent whole:

> Living systems are thus neither the subjects alone, nor objects isolated, but both subjects and objects in a mutually communicating universe of meaning…Just as the cells in an organism take on different tasks for the whole, different populations enfold information not only for themselves, but for all other organisms, expanding the consciousness of the whole, while at the same time becoming more and more aware of this collective consciousness (Popp, Ho 1989).

Biophysicist Mae Wan Ho describes how the living organism, including the human body, is coordinated throughout and is 'coherent beyond our wildest dreams'. It appears that every part of our body is 'in communication with every other part through a dynamic, tuneable, responsive, liquid crystalline medium that pervades the whole body, from organs and tissues to the interior of every cell' (Ho 1998: 82).

What this means is that the 'medium' of our bodies is a form of liquid crystal, thus an ideal transmitter of communication, resonance, and coherence. These relatively new developments in biophysics have discovered that all biological organisms are constituted by a liquid crystalline medium. Further, that DNA is a liquid crystal lattice-type structure (which some refer to as a liquid crystal gel) whereby body cells are involved in a *holographic* instantaneous communication via the emitting of bio-photons (a source based on light). This implies that all living biological organisms continuously emit radiations of light that form a field of coherence and communication. Moreover, biophysics has discovered that living organisms are permeated by quantum wave forms. Ho informs us that

> ...the visible body just happens to be where the wave
> function of the organism is most dense. Invisible
> quantum waves are spreading out from each of us and
> permeating into all other organisms. At the same time,
> each of us has the waves of every other organism
> entangled within our own make-up...We are participants
> in the creation drama that is constantly unfolding. We are
> constantly co-creating and re-creating ourselves and other
> organisms in the universe...(Ho 1998: 116).

This incredible new information actually positions each living being within a non-local quantum field consisting of wave interferences (where bodies meet). The liquid crystalline structure within living systems is also responsible for the direct current (DC) electro-dynamical field that permeates the entire body of all animals. It has also been noted that the DC field has a mode of semi-conduction that is much faster than the nervous system (Becker 1998). If biological living systems are operating within a non-local interwoven field of resonating energy, then perhaps it is possible to see this manifesting in physical behaviour?

Mae-Wan Ho describes how coherent excitations in living systems operate in much the same way as a boat race, where the oars-people must row in step so as to create a 'phase transition'. This indicates that there is an inherent tendency in Nature, and in living systems, to resonate together 'in sync' as a way of maintaining order and coherency. This type of behaviour serves to reinforce the relationship between the individual and the collective that before had been thought random. This discovery is important in that it lends validity to the emerging paradigm of the 'global brain' and of the growth of a planetary empathy. Systems philosopher Ervin Laszlo defines the global brain as 'the quasi-neural energy - and information - processing network created by six and a half billion humans on the planet, interacting in many ways, private as well as public, and on many levels, local as well as global' (Laszlo 2008: *intro*). On this physical level there is already a great deal of information-exchange occurring at ever-increasing speed. Emerging social networks (such as Facebook and MySpace) are also developing empathy-at-a-distance between worldwide users. In this context there is already underway a transformation in the relations between a significant number of people in the world. Yet now hard-science is taking these developments further by positing that people are increasing not only their empathic relationships with each other but also their *entanglement*. This view has recently been corroborated by neuroscience with its finding of 'mirror neurons'.

A 'mirror neuron' is a brain neuron that is activated ('fires') when a living being (such as humans and other animals such as primates and mammals) observes the action of another. In other words, if an individual watches another person eat an apple, then the exact same brain neurons will fire in the person observing the action as if they themselves were performing the act. Such neuron behaviour has been found in humans to operate in the premotor and inferior parietal cortex. This phenomenon of 'mirror neurons' was first discovered by a research team in Italy in the 1990s when studying the neuronal activity of macaque monkeys. This discovery has led to many notable neuroscientists to declare that mirror neurons are important for learning processes (imitation) as well as language acquisition. In more modern general terms we might also say that this capacity is what ties a person in sympathy and empathy to another's situation. It may also explain why people become so emotionally attached to events on television, and even cry in response to watching someone crying on the screen. In this way we are emotionally *entangled* through a mirroring of brain neuronal firing. When we also consider that our bodies are *entangled* through a quantum field of electrical bio-photon resonance, it explains how we are affected by and from others – via wave/field interference. This information is significant when considering a shift towards heightened empathy between people both near and at-a-distance (via digital communications) as well as the potential for catalyzing future abilities for telepathic communication between individuals.

Neuroscience, quantum biology, and quantum physics are all now beginning to converge to reveal that our bodies are not only biochemical systems but also a sophisticated resonating quantum system. This helps us to understand how the body can be efficiently coherent, as well as explaining how we feel 'drawn' to others, especially when we use such terms as 'good vibes'; 'good energies'; and 'we just seem to click'. Our bodies then, as well as our brains, appear to function like receivers/de-coders within a constantly in-flux information energy field. This explains how the human brain is able to store a lifetime of memories and experiences[xlv] as a wealth of data may well be stored within the informational field that encompasses the brain, and indeed the whole body. This new understanding of the quantum human informational field also gives credibility to the existence of extra-sensory perceptions (ESP) and related abilities. Human consciousness is not only empathic, in a 'wave-interference' relationship with other mind-fields, but also is constantly transmitting and receiving information. However, modern materialistic science has, up until recently, focused largely upon 'hard' physical evidence and is still grappling with the complexities of quantum mechanics. As Niels Bohr famously remarked – 'If quantum mechanics hasn't profoundly shocked you, you haven't understood it yet.' The abstract, or 'soft', realm of imaginative insights and visions are usually left to the eccentric artists, mystics, and fringe creative innovators. Much of our modern minds have been denied their left-right brain full working and pulled into a tight left-brain rational functioning that operates as mechanical, linear, competitive, and narrow. The abstract right-brain, with its magical world of creative visionary thinking, has been mostly sidelined and laid latent (McGilchrist 2009). Much of this right-brain activity was the source for indigenous wisdom, shamanic practices, and similar traditions that western materialistic thought has sought to ignore over the years. Often our own intellectual training conditions us to think of such 'magical practices' as primitive, barbaric, and worthy of little more than western colonialism and/or re-education. Yet those of us in the 'civilized' West, with our left-hemisphere dominated brain, live in the everyday world of material things and external attractions. We are shown to exist as separate forces, as islands in a chaotic sea of physical and natural impacts, and at the whim of random neutral influences. Yet we now know that this is not the case.

To recap, quantum biology has shown that the body displays an incredible degree of *quantum coherence*, and that a quantum consciousness field exists throughout the human DNA and thus the human nervous system. Our biochemical structure is composed of a confluence of energies in complete entanglement and which operate as a non-local field within and without the human body. Further, that DNA is a liquid crystal lattice-type structure that emits bio-photons, which are light-based. What this leads to is a new understanding that human DNA operates also as a quantum field.

Hyper-Communication and the Quantum Field

In light of these recent findings we can begin referring to DNA as *Quantum DNA*. This suggests that the 97% of human DNA which is not involved in protein building is active within a quantum state. It may well be that a future manifestation of quantum consciousness will come from part-activation of the 97% quantum DNA that so far has baffled our scientists with its function. This quantum DNA activation may likely be related to the state of human consciousness and has remained dormant in response to human consciousness not being sufficiently prepared, or made ready, for its manifestation. This field 'life-force' may be similar to the pervasive 'pranic energy' which, as Gopi Krishna states, forms the impulse for evolutionary growth in the human nervous system:

> an ever-present possibility, existing in all human beings by
> virtue of the evolutionary process still at work in the race,
> tending to create a condition of the brain and nervous
> system that can enable one to transcend the existing
> boundaries of the mind and acquire a state of
> consciousness far above that which is the normal heritage
> of mankind at present (Krishna 1997: 226)

This transcendental stage of consciousness that is depicted above as being a part of our natural evolutionary heritage is connected with the human brain and nervous system. We now know that we have a DNA quantum field activated within our bodies. Some biophysicists are already discussing whether quantum processes may not be a common denominator for all living processes. As such a quantum informational field throughout the human body will determine the coherence of our light (biophoton) resonance as a vibratory rate. If human consciousness begins to shift its vibratory rate, as a reaction to various external impacts (cosmic, environmental, cultural), then there is every likelihood that DNA – as a quantum field – will likewise show a resonance shift. This may result in parts of its 97% hitherto 'inactive' capacities being brought online (i.e. re-activated). This may or may not be linked to the increase in electromagnetic frequencies now impacting our solar system from the precession of the equinoxes.[xlvi] It also now appears that this 'inactive' part of our DNA may manifest a form of hyper-communication.

The Russian biophysicist and molecular biologist Pjotr Garjajev, who has studied human DNA with his research team in Moscow, has found that the 97% 'inactive' DNA actually has complex properties. Garjajev discovered that the DNA which is not used for protein synthesis is instead actually used for communication, more exactly - for *hyper-communication*. In their terms, hyper-communication refers to a data exchange on DNA level using genetic code. Garjajev and his group analyzed the vibration response of the DNA and concluded that it can function much like networked intelligence, and that it allows for hyper-communication of information amongst all sentient beings. For example, the Moscow research group proved that damaged chromosomes (such as damaged by x-rays) can be repaired. Their method was to 'capture' the information patterns of particular DNA and then to transmit these patterns, using focused light frequencies, onto another genome as a way of reprogramming the cells. In this way they successfully transformed frog embryos to salamander embryos simply by transmitting the DNA information patterns. Garjajev's research shows that certain frequency patterns can be 'beamed' (such as with a laser) to transfer genetic information. This shows how DNA operates through resonance and vibratory frequencies. It also shows that human DNA can be modified – or altered – through the impact of external frequencies. These research results go some way towards validating the existence of such phenomena as remote acts of healing, and other psychic attributes. It also suggests that DNA is a living, fluid, and dynamic 'language' that as a quantum informational field is responsive not only to laser waves (as in the above experiment) but also EM waves and sound – given that the correct frequencies are applied.

The knowledge that human DNA can be influenced and modulated by frequencies (sound, light, language, and thought) is likely to have been known to various spiritual traditions, mystics and teachers, over the ages. This is perhaps why a variety of exercises have existed that utilize thought focus (prayer); sounds (music; chanting; singing); light (specific locations both natural light and produced light such as in stained glass); and language (specific recitations as in mantras and zikrs). DNA appears to function not only as a protein builder (the minority function) but also as a medium for the storage, receiving, and communicating of information. Somewhat more controversial is the report that Garjajev and his Russian colleagues also found examples where DNA could cause disturbing patterns in a vacuum, resulting in the production of what seemed to be magnetized wormholes.[xlvii] These wormholes appeared to function as connections outside of our normal fields of time and space (which hints at inter-dimensional communication). This phenomenon is indeed worthy of further analysis and experimentation. Yet it does seem probable that DNA is involved with various forms of hyper-communication of which, at present, we know very little about.

To support Garjajev's claims of hyper-communication we can see how similar principles are operating within Nature. For example, the organization of ant colonies appears to make use of a distributed form of communication. When a queen ant is separated from her colony, the worker ants continue to build and construct the colony as if following some form of blueprint. Yet if the queen ant is killed then all work in the colony ceases, as if the blueprint had suddenly been taken off-line. This suggests that the queen ant not need to be in physical contact to continue to transmit the blueprint, yet upon death the group consciousness ceases to operate within a hyper-communicative informational field. We can thus refer to these forms of hyper-communication as quantum field consciousness, or simply as *quantum consciousness* (since quantum implies non-local field effect).

In a similar manner, such at-a-distance human phenomenon as remote healing, remote sensing, and telepathy may work along comparable lines. On a more basic level we could say that many of us experience this as the sense of intuition and moments of inspiration. We may even be receiving these forms of hyper-communication when we are asleep. There are countless examples of people, artists, and designers etc, who gained inspiration for their work in their dreams. One example here is that of the Italian composer Giuseppe Tartini who one night dreamt that a devil sat beside his bed playing the violin. The next morning Tartini wrote down the piece from memory and called it the Devil's Trill Sonata. These experiences seem to be on the increase; or perhaps it is because people now feel more open to speak of such experiences. Also, there are indications that the newer generations of children being born are manifesting a higher level of clairvoyance and other extra-sensory capacities.[xlviii] These developments may indicate that a higher form of group consciousness is emerging within humanity and that these abilities are now finding greater expression. In this respect we would do well to return to those practices recommended for centuries by spiritual traditions and teachers: that is, mediation, reflection, watchfulness, and mindfulness, etc. Einstein was famous as a daydreamer throughout his life and he often claimed that greatest inspiration came to him when in such states. Enhanced connectivity between humanity may thus be served by each of us paying more attention to our inner states and to strive for harmony and balance in our lives.

Quantum States and the Akashic Field

Materials exist to help in enhancing these inner (or 'quantum') states, and can be found within many traditions, whether from the major religions (Christian, Islamic, Judaism, Sikh); or from other streams of wisdom such as Buddhist, Tao, and meditative practices. There are also many written materials (books, tales, and poems) that have the function to stimulate right-hemisphere activity. This is the case with many Sufic stories (such as the Mulla Nasrudin tales)[xlix], as well as famous stories such as the Thousand and One Nights; and poems from Jalalludin Rumi (which are now best sellers in the West). Many of these traditions also encourage group meditation as a way of stimulating group consciousness and quantum connection. It has been shown that practiced meditators can achieve an extremely high level of cross-hemispheric synchronization. Similarly, people who mediate together have been discovered to synchronize their brain activity. Through the use of EEG brain scanning it has been found that brainwave activity is synchronized amongst the participants of the group. We can now speculate that this is a result of resonance occurring between the various quantum fields, as shown by the latest research in biophysics. To some extent this has been replicated by the vast array of hemispheric audio material that is now available on the mass market (at various quality levels). These stimulants act to induce an altered state of consciousness; what some practitioners have referred to as transpersonal consciousness. In these states people have experienced very profound connections with what has generally been termed the collective consciousness. Philosopher Ervin Laszlo refers to this collective information field as the *Akashic Field* (Laszlo 2004).

There is now reason to speculate that this so-called non-local *Akashic Field* is in fact a part of our shared (and over-lapping) quantum fields of consciousness. If this is so, then this leads us to further question whether DNA, which emits biophotons and exhibits inter-dimensional properties, may not itself be the seat of quantum consciousness. Modern science has for a long time considered the human brain as the centre of consciousness; yet this belongs to the materialistic and linear thinking that consciousness is a product of complex matter. The brain is indeed our most complex neurological arrangement consisting of the most intricate network of synapses. Yet it is more likely that the brain functions as a receiver and transcriber of electrical signals that are emitted from the quantum DNA. In this way the trillions of parts of our human DNA acts as a coherent quantum field to regulate every part of our body in each simultaneous moment. The human body is thus a resonating quantum field which, exhibiting potentially inter-dimensional properties, may also be a repository of consciousness. Our reality is thus provided by the work of the brain that transcribes signals into perceptions, yet it is the DNA which is a living intelligence. This idea of DNA being a living intelligence is not new to many indigenous wisdom traditions. For example, as anthropologist Jeremy Narby pointed out, shamans who undergo trance states often seem to be communicating with DNA as a means of acquiring knowledge about plants, healing, and spirit worlds (Narby 1999). Subsequently, Narby explored how Nature is also imbued with this form of living intelligence which acts as survival patterns to enable evolutionary growth (Narby 2006). Shamans, intuitives, and others who are able to tap into this living intelligence find a 'design' or blueprint behind all physical structures, which points to a quantum field of living intelligence that acts as an evolutionary impulse within all living systems.

We can thus speculate that human DNA, which acts as a quantum energy field, is also likely to be the seat of human consciousness. Further, it is possible to say that this *quantum consciousness field* is the very same as what has been referred to as the 'Akashic Field'. Also, recent research suggests that DNA is receptive to particular external influences such as can be manifested through prayer, meditation, and specific sounds/vibrations. This offers startling possibilities for our well-being and human evolution if we are capable of some form of communication with our own living Intelligence (our own 'Higher Selves'?). We may even have the potential to interact with our own physical cellular structure through focused minds and directed intentions. The implications of this are profound and even infer that humanity may have a future opportunity to be in a relationship, through quantum consciousness, with its own DNA and living design. Further, if resonance/vibratory patterns of quantum consciousness can be passed between generations then it may be that the new generations now being born will exhibit different consciousness patterns. This may be the initial signs in the neuro-genetic evolution of humanity. These new generations will be the 'evolutionary agents' that will lead the way through a social-cultural-human renaissance and renewal.

Evolutionary Agents – Our Next Quantum Leap?

Quantum consciousness – living field intelligence – could well represent the next stage in human evolution; that is, evolution of the global mind of humanity. Various mystics and consciousness researchers have alluded to this by a variety of names; they range from cosmic consciousness, superconsciousness, transpersonal consciousness, integral consciousness, and more. All these descriptions share a common theme; namely, the rise of intuition, empathy, greater connectivity to the world and to people, and a sense of 'knowing' about what each given situation demands. Further, such a form of quantum consciousness would likely instil within each person a sense of the greater cosmic whole: the realization that humanity exists and evolves within a universe of intelligence and meaning (perhaps even inter-dimensional). This would serve to impart within humanity a more profound, and acknowledged, spiritual impulse.

We can speculate that a variety of forces that include a shifting of the Earth's geomagnetic forces (as is already occurring); varying solar radiations from each sun cycle; galactic pulses from the centre of the galaxy; our solar system moving through a more 'energized' portion of interstellar space; could all in some way result in increased wave patterns (vibrations) entering into the quantum DNA field and catalyzing a shift in the consciousness of humanity. The bridge that divides us at present from another level of living intelligence is in essence a vibratory shift. If such a vibratory shift is a potential means of catalyzing quantum consciousness, this could then lead to increased intuitive faculties and extra-sensory phenomena not only becoming an implicate part of our lives but also to opening up access to greater creativity and inventive capacities for participating in our own human futures. The rise of these attributes in a critical mass could be the key to our next 'evolutionary leap'. Forms and intimations of these new consciousness patterns are already emerging in the world, but as yet they have not become a part of mainstream research. Such evolutionary 'mutational' agents include visionaries, mystics, artists, psychics, intuitives, spiritual Teachers, and what have been termed as the new 'Indigo Children'. These children (labelled 'Indigo' because of their purported coloured auras) are described as possessing increased empathy, creativity, curiosity, and self-will. They are also reported to be spiritually inclined from a young age, and to exhibit strong intuitive capacities. Because of their natural and inherent resistance to authority they are seen as being distracted, rebellious, or alienated in the conventional school system. Yet this is nothing new as throughout recorded history social revolutionaries have felt impelled, and inspired, to resist authority and instigate change (Billington 1998). Many individuals who have felt an awareness of the need to seed an evolutionary impulse into social life have been caught up in revolutionary events and/or been involved in social-cultural upheavals. These human efforts, Krishna notes, come from evolutionary impulses:

> I can safely assert that the progress made by mankind in any direction, from the subhuman level to the present, has been far less due to man's own efforts than to the activity of the evolutionary forces at work within him. Every incentive to invention, discovery, aesthetics, and the development of improved social and political organizations invariably comes from within, from the depths of his consciousness by the grace of…the superintelligent Evolutionary Force in human beings (Krishna 1993: 166).

These indicate efforts, attempts, or social movements to help prepare the 'mental soil' for a new consciousness to slowly seed and grow. On the whole social/cultural/material forces are slow to react to the need for an evolving paradigm of human consciousness.

We can say that in order for continued cultural and species growth there are particular periods of human history whereby humanity becomes ready, or in need of, the activation of particular faculties and/or evolutionary traits. It may be that during this critical phase of human culture that humanity will adapt, or be forced to develop, new creative and inspired aspects of consciousness. This transition period – a stage of what I term neuro-genetic evolution – will challenge many of the now-outmoded social structures that have polarized much of human thinking. However, as in all paradigm shifts, old energies inevitably must give way to the new, and it may only be a matter of time before new generations move into evolving consciousness and its physical expressions. It is thus critical that an understanding of spiritual matters begins to permeate through our everyday lives as a counter-balance to our social materialism. It is important in these years ahead that we try to develop a consciousness that is both open to spiritual impulses whilst simultaneously aware and attentive to the latest in scientific research. It is imperative that we revitalize our collective sense of well-being and connectedness – our *entanglement* – as part of our shared evolutionary development. It is possible that a new state of quantum consciousness will allow humanity access to an unimaginable *energetic field of information.* This would then open up new vistas of creative intelligence that could be the forerunner to the next stage of along our ascending evolutionary path.

Conclusion

To summarize, humanity as a global species may be in the throes of passing through a transition towards a different state of consciousness. This new state may likely be characterized by quantum properties such as coherence and non-local field information. Because of this I have termed this new state as that of a *quantum consciousness field*. This consciousness field will transform how we relate to other people, the world around us, and expand our perceptual realities. It may also catalyze into being other hitherto dormant human faculties such as increased intuition, telepathy, and visionary thinking. Some of these features are already appearing within younger generations being born into the world today and which have been referred to as 'Indigo children'. This evolutionary development manifests a transition from biological and socio-cultural forms of evolution to incorporating a new level: that of neuro-genetic evolution. This neuro-genetic phase is essential, I argue, to allow humanity to evolve to the next stage upon the evolutionary ladder. As one thinker recently stated:

> We live in changing times whereby humanity is undergoing a transformation. Our consciousness, which has a vast potential for further development, must undergo a release from old, binding structures, and break out towards a rapid expansion...We need to understand phenomena at deeper levels, and not just accept what we are told, or what is fed to us through well-structured social institutions and channels. We must learn to accept that our thinking is a great tangible spiritual force for change (Gulbekian 2004: 251).

If a person is not sufficiently prepared for these changing impacts then it may cause unbalance and confusion. Personal responsibility means each person must seek to balance the energies of both their inner and outer lives;

and to strengthen their sense of connectedness, empathy, and creative vision.

The new discoveries in neuroscience, quantum biology, and quantum physics have shown that a form of nonlocal connected consciousness has a physical-scientific foundation. What this demonstrates is that certain spiritual or transcendental states of collective Oneness have a valid basis within the new scientific paradigm. Our evolutionary future(s) need not be polarized between the sciences and the humanities but can be – *should be* – a creative fusion and collaborative partnership.

Notes

[i] See Thomas Kuhn's *The Structure of Scientific Revolutions* for information on paradigm shifts.

[ii] Eminent mathematician John von Neumann calculated that during an average lifetime of seventy years we accumulate some 280 trillion bits of information.

[iii] The precession of the equinoxes (or the Great Year) refers to the gradual shift in the orientation of Earth's axis of rotation, which traces out a cone in a cycle of approximately 26,000 years.

[iv] For more information see the work of Grazyna Fosar and Franz Bludorf.

[v] See the numerous reports that talk of the 'Indigo Children' or 'New Children'.

[vi] See the corpus of tales from Idries Shah

References

Becker, R. O. (1998) *The Body Electric.* New York: William Morrow

Billington, J. H. (1998) *Fire in the Minds of Men.* New Jersey: Transaction Publishers.

Gulbekian, S. E. (2004) *In the Belly of the Beast: Holding Your Own in Mass Culture.* Charlottesville, VA: Hampton Roads.

Ho, M.-W. (1998) *The Rainbow and the Worm: The Physics of Organisms.* Singapore: World Scientific.

Ho, M.-W. and Popp, F. A. (1989) 'Gaia and the Evolution of Coherence'. In *3rd Camelford Conference on The Implications of The Gaia Thesis: Symbiosis, Cooperativity and Coherence.* The Wadebridge Ecological Centre, Camelford, Cornwall

Krishna, G. (1993) *Higher Consciousness and Kundalini.* Ontario, CA: F.I.N.D. Research Trust.

Krishna, G. (1997) *Kundalini: The Evolutionary Energy in Man.* Boston, MA: Shambhala.

Krishna, G. (1999) *The Dawn of a New Science.* Markdale, ON: Institute for Consciousness Research.

Laszlo, E. (2004) *Science and the Akashic Field: An Integral Theory of Everything* Rochester, VT: Inner Traditions.

Laszlo, E. (2008) *Quantum Shift in the Global Brain.* Rochester, VM: Inner Traditions.

McGilchrist, I. (2009) *The Master and His Emissary: The Divided Brain and the Making of the Western World.* New Haven, CT: Yale University Press.

Narby, J. (1999) *Cosmic Serpent: DNA and the Origins of Knowledge.* London: Phoenix.

Narby, J. (2006) *Intelligence in Nature.* London: Jeremy P. Tarcher.

Popp, F.-A., Li, K.H., Mei, W.P., Galle, M. and Neurohr, R. (1988) Physical Aspects of Biophotons. *Experientia,* **44**576-585.

ii) FIGHTING FOR OUR CONSCIOUS EVOLUTION IN A CHAOTIC & CHANGING WORLD – AN INTERVIEW[1]

Interview with Kingsley Dennis

Author: Jaime Leal Anaya (SuperConsciousness Magazine)

SuperConsciousness had the opportunity to have a conversation with sociologist expert, writer, and cofounder of WorldShift International, Kingsley Dennis, PhD. His latest new book, *The Struggle for Your Mind, Conscious evolution and the Battle to Control How We Think*, is a thorough and well-researched contribution to the current global effort from many groups and movements in the world seeking real change to build a new society and become a more evolved humanity. Enjoy!

SC: Would you be able to tell us a little bit about yourself, about your background, and what led you to write your new book, *The Struggle for Your Mind*?

Kingsley Dennis: For many years I worked as a sociologist at university and so I've been very aware of social systems, group consciousness, individual consciousness, and also throughout my life I've been following conscious evolution and more spiritual subjects and concerns. I lived and worked for five years in Turkey, in Istanbul, where I had contact with spiritual traditions. I came to a point in my life where I wished to combine both elements, my professional sociological background and my very deep personal interest in consciousness studies and conscious evolution. I wanted to bring them both together because this is a perfect time where we have the readiness to understand how these concepts are working together rather

---

[1] This interview was first posted on the SuperConsciousness webpage - http://www.superconsciousness.com/topics/society/fighting-our-conscious-evolution-chaotic-and-changing-world

than apart. I was part of a Sufi Mevlevi group in Istanbul and spent a number of years being exposed to their traditions and teachings.

For five years I was based in Lancaster University, which is in the Northwest of England. I was a coordinator of the Complexity Network Group and so I was looking at how online community networks were coming together in a form of collective consciousness but were using social media to share their experiences and to connect. From that I had a very strong sociological interest in the human experience and also on how human consciousness was becoming more shared, more global. Obviously, that triggered in me to want to have further research in the ethereal or non material aspects of consciousness and how that was filtering out through our technologies and our social systems. I view technologies and social systems as being an exterior manifestation of what is already happening at the inner or non-material level.

SC: The main title in your book, *The Struggle for Your Mind,* seems more of a personal conquest at first. But the subtitle — *Conscious Evolution and the Battle to Control How We Think* — definitely broadens the personal struggle to possible external influences of control. Can you comment on this?

KD: This is the core question, the individual interior self and how that relates, corresponds, or resonates to our external environment. This has been an ongoing situation throughout our civilization. We are susceptible or vulnerable to external impacts. There are social impacts and there are technological impacts and we are developing, especially this century, a level of awareness and consciousness which is manifesting more and more. But in order to have social civil society, nation states, and governments, they have been maintaining a collective control or management of individuality. There are certain social structures which have always been used to manage and influence thinking patterns throughout the collective society. Sometimes these are called ideologies. What I see happening is that there's an increased interior and individual awareness, which is manifesting more and more. This is manifesting in our social lives with social protests happening around the world, people trying to develop alternative lifestyles. They are less and less manipulated by what the government says, what media says, and they're developing their own awareness. This is a potential threat to authority and governing structures in play now. I call this the clash of mythologies. You have the old mind, which is trying to control the mass consciousness, behavior, and thinking patterns, and is a vertical, top-down hierarchical system. Then we have a lateral, horizontally distributed understanding: global connectivity, people sharing information, coming together throughout the world through virtual networks and an increasing awareness. This is clashing or conflicting with the control mechanisms and is what's happening now.

SC: There are many fundamentalist religions that actually believe in Satan and hell and demonic influences in our evolution, correlating to the opening metaphor story of Satan and his minions in your book. Yet it is very interesting how the fundamentalist religions themselves have played a big role in preventing our conscious evolution and preventing people from thinking freely or exploring different options, sometimes even new scientific discoveries. What's your view of religion in relation to the concept of conscious evolution?

KD: Religion is just another social institution. The original element of religion would have been an energetic evolutionary impulse, such as the impulse behind Christianity, Judaism, Islam. The original impulse would have been very beneficial but what happens is that evolutionary impulse over time in our physical environment becomes crystallized, becomes set like stone and it loses its kinetic power. Over that, you have a hierarchical system, so Christianity and the Catholic Church, for example, became a hierarchical social system. Then those systems operate by a form of polarization between good, evil, light and dark. Humanity is in a sense socially conditioned into a polarized world but in the original teachings there is no polarization, and good and evil are an aspect of the same divine energy. What we're dealing with now is something which has been corrupted. I see orthodox social religious institutions as being a decayed form of an original impulse. When you have polarization, division, that's a sign that something has lost its original power. This polarization causes discomfort, causes warfare, causes a lot of death and chaos. What we need to do is go beyond polarization back into unification. Consciousness is unification. Social structures are polarization. They're two different things.

SC: You use all three enigmatic words in the title of your book: mind, consciousness — conscious evolution — and also thinking. Can you tell us how are mind, consciousness, and thought different or the same?

KD: Consciousness and mind and thought are different things. I would say that consciousness and the consciousness of humanity exists external to our physical bodies. That's why we can talk about collective consciousness or quantum consciousness or the akashic field. This is an energetic field of intelligence, which exists beyond the physical. The mind is what we can refer to as the physical apparatus or organ within the body, which picks up on the external consciousness and thoughts are what we produce from that. For example, when you turn on the television, the TV program is not inside the television, it exists outside of it in terms of the broadcast. The TV is an antenna that picks it up, and the technology inside is what translates it into pictures. In this analogy, consciousness is the broadcast, the mind is a television's antenna, and the thought is the picture which gets interpreted.

SC: In reference to the external forces that influence us, you say in your book that "these forces are aware of our true power of human consciousness." What is so powerful about human consciousness?

KD: Human consciousness has such a powerful capacity to interact with the material environment. Science is actually verifying that we live in an energetic environment and, therefore, matter is a secondary manifestation. Our old mind would say that matter is first and consciousness second. But this now is no longer a valid paradigm. Hermetic sciences always said for centuries, all the way back to Egypt, that the universe is mental. The universe, or what we know as the universe, exists as mental conscious energy. If you understand that, matter is formed from the power of intentional consciousness and focused thought.

If we could develop the power of consciousness we would have a much greater participation of how reality and matter manifest around us. That is very dangerous if people are not aware of how to use that. Obviously, to have a governing society, you don't want people trying to manifest their own reality and participate in their own sense of the world around them, because they're much more difficult to manage then. So there are forces which are trying to keep this knowledge away from us. Centuries ago this knowledge was maintained only in mystery schools. The initiates had to go through long training to gain this knowledge because it's very powerful. Today this knowledge is now being distributed a lot more freely because people are more prepared to understand this reality and understand the true capacity of focused thought. Meditation practices, visualizations, are a way of concentrating our thought. Let's use a metaphor or the analogy of the laser. If you enter a room and switch on the light, the room is illuminated by light but the light is not powerful. But if you take that light and concentrate it into a laser beam then you can cut through a wall of a room. Thought is like this. If it is dispersed, it's not concentrated and has lesser power. If you can focus it, then it has great power to manifest. The difference of consciousness is we are moving more from a dispersed consciousness towards a concentrated form and it has greater capacity to interact with our material environment.

Enlightenment is access to the consciousness field. By going through certain exercises and focused intention — the prime keyword is to focus how we think and our thought processes — allows us to access the consciousness which exists outside of us. The mystery schools knew that this was a very powerful access to that consciousness, so the initiates had to go through deep training. The capacity of consciousness within people is very powerful when concentrated. That's why it doesn't come overnight. People have to work on themselves. I'm disconcerted about certain New Age teachings that say illumination comes easily, you should just sit down and meditate for half hour every day and you have higher consciousness. No, higher consciousness takes real work on one's self, real inner change, because it's a powerful tool of focused intentional thought. More people are becoming aware of this and taking it very seriously in a lot of inner work. We are going to see a rise of a lot of increased conscious people upon the earth, especially the younger generation.

I see orthodox social religious institutions as being a decayed form of an original impulse. When you have polarization, division, that's a sign that something has lost its original power. This polarization causes discomfort, causes warfare, causes a lot of death and chaos. What we need to do is go beyond polarization back into unification. Consciousness is unification. Social structures are polarization. They're two different things.

SC: You speak about the various forces that prevent or slow down our conscious evolution. You say that they target the remaining spaces left of free choice and free will? Can you comment on how we are doing at this point in our evolution, in this battle for free choice and free will?

KD: There are governing ruling structures which want to control all our thought patterns. So we don't have space and time to put into conscious awareness. What I see happening is that we're going through a transition period where not only our social structures are falling down or collapsing, such as the economy and similar social structures, but there is increased energy entering into the earth at this time. These are evolutionary moments.

My personal understanding is that our DNA is being responsive to these increased energies coming into the earth. What happens is that the DNA gives off an electromagnetic field of energy. According to biophysics the DNA is a liquid crystal which emits bio-photons so it's very susceptible to an external energy environment. Because of this increased energy environment, it's impacting our DNA. So we are having change agents, people who are becoming more aware of the outside environment and the changes which are happening. But these are only sporadic people and is not a mass movement. Many of the younger people are being born and are growing up within a different energy environment. If you're born into a different energy environment, your DNA will react and respond differently. So many of the younger people are hard-wired to a different energy environment and they understand that something is not right. If they go to school, they lack attention because the education we give them is not fulfilling them. Unfortunately our educational institutions are giving them drugs like Prozac or for Attention Deficit Disorder. This is totally incorrect because our younger generation doesn't need drugs, what they need is a different social nutrition, a different spiritual nutrition to feed them. These people will be the beginning wave of a new generation to rise up which won't accept the old structures, the old mind. They'll be thinking differently. If we don't change our educational structures we won't be able to deal with these new generations of children. I think in 20 years' time and by 2030 we are going to see a youth generation between 20 years old who are going to react and respond very differently to the world today and they will be bringing in change.

If we could develop the power of consciousness we would have a much greater participation of how reality and matter manifest around us. Obviously, to have a governing society, you don't want people trying to manifest their own reality and participate in their own sense of the world around them, because they're much more difficult to manage then.

SC: Are you referring to movements like the Arab Spring last year and the Egyptian revolution, which got going through Facebook and social media and the youth? Was that part of this conscious evolution that you are speaking about?

KD: I think these are the first wave and technology is very interesting because a lot of the younger generation understand technology immediately. A lot of us, especially, the older generation, are worried that technology is being used for controlling people, which it is. We are saying that technology makes the younger generation illiterate, etcetera, but on the other hand, the younger generation is using technology in a very different way, such as the social protest movements and Arab Spring. They are using technology to come together and form these protest groups. They are hard-wired differently. They look at technology and say, "Wait. I'm not going to use this for it to control me. I'm going to use it to connect with my fellow brothers and sisters." So this is a different way of thinking. It is the old mind versus the new mind. Young people are really doing it for themselves and using technology to empower themselves and that's very interesting. According to neuroscience, we have neuroplasticity. Our brainwaves, our brain patterns, can be changed according to how we use them. If we use technology in a different way, we can actually rewire our neuropathways to understand technology differently.

SC: This is a fascinating part of your book, where you speak about cultural evolution, neuro-genetic evolution, and then conscious evolution. Can you describe what these three forms of evolution are?

KD: Our general conception of evolution is biological evolution, the old Darwinian evolution. This is a very slow process over many, many, generations. We do have biological change in this way. Then we have social/cultural evolution whereby our artifacts, our literature, our thinking gets passed on through books and through ideology and through religion. Every generation can learn the previous patterns of knowledge. That's social/cultural evolution, what we pass on. We can read a book today that someone wrote a hundred years ago and we learn from that. That's a quicker form of evolving than Darwinian evolution.

The third stage is neuro-genetic evolution. Our DNA is being changed by our shifting energetic environment upon the earth. Ten percent of the DNA is used for protein building, that's what we know as DNA. The other 90 percent is often referred to, misleadingly, as junk DNA. But this DNA responds to the environment and is part of our energetic field around the body. If we are born to a world that has a different energetic signature, the DNA will respond differently and pass on information on to the child differently. The child responds to the environment immediately. Bruce

Lipton has talked about this in terms of epigenetic process in evolution. So the cells of our body, our DNA can actually change within a generation itself.

Biological evolution can take place in many, many generations. Social/cultural evolution can take place over one generation to the next by passing on our information through literature, films, religion, etcetera. But neuro-genetic evolution can be shifted within a generation and that is a "gnosis." Gnosis is interior knowledge, which we pick up and is going to be very effective for a few generations of human evolution.

SC: What is neuro-censorship about that you mention in your book?

KD: This goes back to programming using neuro-signifiers, and propaganda advertising being very effective. Neuro marketing is an area of advertising which is very popular these days. If you advertise a film which has won an Oscar, the film has this big golden Oscar and this is a very visual signifier because the brain responds to these images. If you have advertising which shows little puppies wagging their tails, or little cats purring, that's an emotional response. When you have politicians, likewise, talking about "hope", "change", "Yes We Can", these are strong signifiers which the brain picks up. Advertisers and PR people are very clever and what they do is that they experiment first on how the brain reacts to the signifiers. They use EEG scans, they pick up the electromagnetic impulses from the brain. They put a person in front of a television and they scan how the brain reacts to these signals and they know that emotional responses, linguist responses, bypass the brain and give a subliminal response in the individual. When we watch TV we know that we are being targeted to have a certain reaction which is often unconscious. Politicians use that a lot. It's also been used in

NLP, Neuro-Linguistic Programming. We react to language, to emotional stimulus, to visuals, but this is all very highly programmed. It's not an accident they use these visuals, that politicians use these words. They've been tested before to make sure that they have a very strong response. If you want to read more about this, Google neuro-marketing. It is happening now and is a very sophisticated technology.

It is the old mind versus the new mind. Young people are really doing it for themselves and using technology to empower themselves and that's very interesting.

SC: You also mentioned about the esoteric and spiritual traditions using conscious intention as a tool for DNA mutation and evolution, that spiritual practices can actually have an effect on our physicality. Tell us more about this.

KD: The spiritual traditions always knew about the influence of the mind upon one's cellular structure or DNA but centuries ago they didn't have the vocabulary that we have today. DNA was not discovered officially, so they couldn't talk about that. What spiritual esoteric traditions teachings did is they introduced such things as prayer, mantras, visualizations. They used certain colors such as meditating within a room of certain colors or certain sounds or certain smells. This would impact one's interior state. Think about it in terms of modern science. If we have a mantra or a Dhikr, if we repeat certain sounds, certain words over and over, everything is a vibration structure. Words are vibration, sounds, colors are vibration and DNA is an electromagnetic energy field. Therefore, it is influenced by vibration. By being in this meditative state we are giving certain impulses into our interior cellular structure and that can have an effect on our development, understanding, and consciousness. Ancient traditions actually understood the science of our cellular structure very, very well. It's just that they did not have the vocabulary to explain it.

SC: There's a great line in your book that says that the human being is really an unfinished project. In connection to this idea, you describe psychic ability in a very different way from the traditional understanding. You consider being open to new ideas, creative thinking and visionary concepts, and a drive for self-actualization as physic development. Can you tell us why?

KD: I refer to the human being more in terms of the human becoming, because the human body is a physical structure which is incredibly well formulated but yet consciousness is an element which operates throughout the body. Our access to consciousness is not a finished project. We can open up and develop our access to greater consciousness. That is the unfinished project also. I feel is part of why we are here on planet earth, to develop our access to the greater consciousness and filter that into the planet and also develop our physical structures and societies by being energy filters and energy processors.

We are "becoming" in terms of our increased access to that. When we have increased access, we start to have what we may call anomalies. For example, 100 years ago the great work Cosmic Consciousness by Richard Bucke. This work talked about these initial people who had transcendental experiences and didn't know how to interpret them. These transcendental experiences are the beginning signs that we are opening up our conscious awareness and maintaining contact. I call this "polishing the bridge". Polishing the bridge between our own sense of self towards the greater higher self, and the more we polish that bridge the more we have inflow of physic experiences.

Many people find that they have an inspiration between waking and sleeping. These are the states where we can ease the mind, as the mind is constantly talking to itself, chatting away. This is a disruption between the consciousness or higher consciousness and what we filter in our bodies, our minds. There are certain states where we have greater psychic access to these states of consciousness.

I feel that these states are developing more and more. Many young children today have been called indigo children or similar names because they are already having greater access and greater awareness of these psychic states. I don't want to talk about these psychic states as being esoteric; I want to say they are the new normal. Initially they may be anomalies, but all paradigm changes begin with anomalies and over the next years more of us, yourself, myself, general people are going to have flashes of inspiration, flashes of transcendental moments. These are the new consciousness coming into awareness, coming into manifestation, and this is going to become the new normal. We shouldn't talk about it as being New Age or weird or strange. Our role is to try to normalize the new "human becoming".

SC: Why is it that we haven't been able, collectively as a civilization, to rise out of the sedative state, the amnesia state you mention, in spite of all the good will on earth?

KD: It's not just a case of turning on a light switch and everyone wakes up. If everyone woke up, society would collapse. Its sounds strange but it's true, because we have to shift or transition to a new society in more of a gradual move. There will be people waking up at different times and participating in this move. Some people in this generation won't wake up perhaps in this lifetime. It is partly outside influences and partly inside work. It is not just a gift to us. We have to work on it, be aware of it. The first question is we have to be aware that we are a conscious being and we are a human becoming in this physical 3-D world.

More and more people are going to be aware of this and waking up but not all at once. It doesn't work like that. If everybody woke up all at once the systems would collapse. People would not go to work, not accept the economic system. It would not benefit society. We must change in a way which is beneficial to our external world in harmony with our inner world. It's not about having an electric shock. It's about having a gradual understanding and awareness that we can work with. Spiritual realization must be applicable to our external world.

SC: You said that humanity is in a threshold, a transition period, but it hasn't reached the tipping point. Are we going to reach this tipping point soon? How are we looking?

KD: What I say is only my own intuition and my feeling is that we will reach the tipping point. We don't need a majority of people for the tipping point. In fact, we need only a minority but we need a minority of consciously aware people who are focused and can project their awareness into our external environment. I feel the next ten years, especially, are going to be a kind of disruptive time whereby there will be many people waking up but being shocked by the reality of the situation. When you are aware of what's really going on, how the world really works, how we are programmed, how we are so conditioned, how our social matrix tried to manipulate us and brainwash us, it is very unsettling. At first it may be a shock and then we need to work with that to bring in a new understanding, to bring in new thinking, to talk to our family, our friends, our communities and do our work. I feel that although this initial shock may come about, a tipping point will come. Imagine 10 years ago having this conversation. It would have been very difficult. I can't speak with my grandparents about these subjects because they look at me strangely. Even my parents look at me a little strangely, but if I talk to people like you or people in our generation or younger, they understand it. That's a sign that we are moving towards a tipping point.

SC: You touch on some of the Mayan culture and their teachings in your book. How do you see the various prophecies and traditions of drastic changes happening in 2012 in relation to what you're talking about?

KD: The 2012 movement is very hard to ignore and I feel it's a case of polarization and that on the one hand the ancient indigenous traditions such as the Mayan prophecy, but not only the Mayas, the Aztecs and the Hopis have talked about the different cycles, the different ages and 2012 is astronomically and astrologically significant. What is important is that it represents a very definite positive time whereby we need to start changing our paradigms of thought. This is the time to catalyze a new consciousness.

2012 will pass. It will pass, it won't be the end of the world. For me that is an important marker because when it passes people will say, "Okay, we're still here. The world is still a bit chaotic, so what do we do?" Okay, now it's time to work, time to work in the world, to work on yourself, to work on consciousness. Because the end hasn't arrived, we have the future to look forward to.

On the other hand, I talk in the book about what I call the Armageddon Meme. There are many elements in society which have used the Mayan 2012 calendar to instill fear in people: that we are going to have this polar shift, we are going to lose continents, and are going to have many deaths. When you have fear you have disempowerment. People then give away their responsibility and say, "Okay, I'm afraid. I give my responsibility to the governments. You sort it out." This is dangerous. I feel there has been a deliberate manipulation of 2012 to create insecurity and fear. I feel it's our responsibility to use 2012 as a positive marker by saying when we pass it we are still here, it's time to get to work and use consciousness for the betterment of our societies, which is the original intention of the Mayan prophecy. A new world is coming into being and it is human becoming, not human end.

SC: You say that humanity will be forced into change and how we deal with it will be a measure of our maturity as a species. If it is really up to us, then, how we will fare in this moment of change and transition in our evolution?

KD: It is totally so. We are a collective family. It doesn't matter so much about our physical circumstances or status. We are a collective species called humanity and earth is our responsibility as collective custodians. Why do we want to give away our power? Why do we want to say, "Oh, there's an elite minority who control the governments and financial institutions and corporations. They will sort it out." No, that's totally upside down. We need now to understand that humanity has a collective responsibility to act, both collectively and individually, to take power back into ourselves and work with the earth, work in harmony with environmental structures, and understand how evolution works.

I feel there has been a deliberate manipulation of 2012 to create insecurity and fear. I feel it's our responsibility to use 2012 as a positive marker by saying when we pass it we are still here, it's time to get to work and use consciousness for the betterment of our societies, which is the original intention of the Mayan prophecy. A new world is coming into being and it is human becoming, not human end.

Evolution works through participation. Human "becoming" is human becoming responsible. We may not have a choice in what happens upon the earth. The earth is shifting, there will be physical changes, water cycle changes, geographic, geophysical changes, such as earthquakes, which is the earth realigning itself. We can't control that nor should we but we can respond to it. The sign of our integrity, the sign of our maturity as a species is not by trying to control things but responding to events with consideration, compassion, equilibrium, harmony with our environment and fellow humanity.

iii) TALES OF CONSCIOUS AWAKENING – A RECENT INTERVIEW

MY TALE

Was there a particular event or experience that was a turning point in your life and somehow changed your view of the nature of reality?

I'd like to think that I now have a conventional view of reality, and perhaps the consensus is the unconventional view. I'm not sure it was a rational journey at all. I think if I listened to rationality I probably wouldn't have arrived at where I am. But, saying that, my understanding of reality is that we only perceive a very thin sliver or slice of reality. So what we agree to be the consensus is an interpretation based on a minimum of senses. To give an example, my understanding and experience is that we don't originate thoughts within our head or brain. We actually receive thoughts externally and that the human brain acts as an antenna. So what this means is that reality is part of a whole field, a quantum field of intelligence, which exists in a nonlocal environment throughout our physical universe. Our physical universe is a secondary manifestation from a primary source of energy/consciousness.

So for me, consciousness is primary. All matter and physical manifestation is secondary, and therefore the human apparatus is a kind of deciphering mechanism that receives and interprets. What we receive is an aftereffect of primary reality. To gain access to reality is what I and others would call, "work on oneself." By working on oneself we can develop our perceptual faculties to receive and therefore interpret primary reality to a greater degree. So the journey throughout my life is one of working on myself to polish my perceptive apparatus, to receive more or larger slice of reality and of the bigger picture.

The beginning is what I call the internal alarm clock. From earliest memories as a child of around 8 or 9 years, I always had a different take on the world. I used my imagination a lot. I had a sense that I was in contact with the world but also a nagging sense of "this isn't it," which took me on a personal quest and investigation. I call myself a traditional seeker, in that I've never had a one–moment, wow!, epiphany. But I had this internal alarm clock, which drove me incessantly to try and find out the answers to this nagging internal feeling. That took me through more than 30 years of experiences and encounters, traveling and working on myself to arrive where I am. So that feeling has been with me from earliest memories, and that's what has driven me to travel and to seek.

MY INSIGHT

What insight did you have as a result and how did that affect what you do now?

I learned to trust my instinct, and that has driven me in different directions in different parts of my life. Examples of these are trigger moments when an instinct comes to me that I can no longer continue where I am. This has happened in several times in several countries, such as Prague in the Czech Republic and Istanbul, Turkey. And just when I thought I was going to continue in that position my instinctual sense told me that I would not learn anything more, that I was treading water. So that instinct drove me to take decisions that may have seemed irrational, like changing countries and ending career paths, but it has always worked.

I refer to my present path as the perennial philosophy. What I've been seeking is the kinetic knowledge which has been at the heart of all the wisdom traditions. What I mean by kinetic is that it is no longer static or crystallized into an orthodoxy or human institution, that then no longer is able to transmit the living and modern contemporary version of that wisdom tradition. So I came to that in my early 20s through the Gurdjieff schools. I then made contact with what you might call a modern, contemporary version of Sufism; I studied under a Mevlevi master in Istanbul. What I found was that the living streams of these traditions don't tend to stay with these names or categories, and so I have tried to follow the living essence. I have said to people that we are in a time where we have to make the new age the new normal.

I don't call myself a mystic, but I work to try to normalize what people may call mysticism or spiritual themes. I would call myself a spiritual person. I have met many way-showers or guides along the way but perhaps only two people whom I would call completed teachers.

MY MESSAGE

What message would you like to leave with the reader?

My understanding is that the human species is an unfinished species. That alarm clock that I spoke of earlier is within each person, and it is up to each of us to pay attention and to begin the first step on that journey to completion. Not only do we have the alarm clock within each one of us, but we have the capacity. It is therefore the responsibility of each person to decide consciously if they wish to make that journey of self evolution and self-development, which would open up perceptual faculties to have a completely different perspective on the world—a perspective which I would argue is the natural, organic understanding of humanity's place in the cosmos and its relationship to Truth and Primary reality. That's an evolutionary journey for each one of us. You don't have to be special to have those stirrings.

Many people are having the sense that something's not quite right, that there's more to it, to life. It's just, perhaps, that they either dismiss it or they don't follow it up. I think I'm very normal, and I try to put that across in all my work that I'm not anything special or different from anyone else that I'm speaking to. It's just that I took it up, and I went with it.